D1224971

Sunrise Europe

Sunrise Europe

The Dynamics of Information Technology

IAN MACKINTOSH

Basil Blackwell

© Ian Mackintosh 1986

First published 1986

Basil Blackwell Ltd
108 Cowley Road, Oxford OX4 1JF, UK

Basil Blackwell Inc.
432 Park Avenue South, Suite 1503,
New York, NY 10016, USA

British Library Cataloguing in Publication Data

Mackintosh, Ian, 1927–
    Sunrise Europe: the dynamics of
    information technology.
    1. Electronic data processing — Europe
    2. Information storage and retrieval
    systems — Europe   3. Technological
    innovations — Europe
    I. Title
    001.5   QA76

    ISBN 0–631–14406–4

Library of Congress Cataloging in Publication Data
Mackintosh, Ian, 1927–
    Sunrise Europe.

    Includes index.
    1. Computer industry—Europe. 2. Market surveys—
Europe. I. Title.
HD9696.C63E8547   338.4'7004'094   86–6077
ISBN 0–631–14406–4

Typeset by Photo·graphics, Honiton, Devon

Printed in Great Britain by Butler and Tanner, Frome, Somerset

Contents

List of Tables

List of Figures

Foreword

The Information Revolution has already arrived and the time is long overdue for Europe to wake up fully to all of its threats and promises.

I have long been convinced that the European Community needs to act cohesively in tackling this problem. Recent initiatives of the European Commission – for example, the ESPRIT and RACE programmes for collaborative R&D with which I was closely involved during my time as Vice President responsible for industrial affairs – have focussed specifically on encouraging trans-frontier co-operation in high technology. But it is difficult to resist the impression that in some of Europe's capital cities and its boardrooms neither the scale of the problem nor the pressing need for co-operation is recognized with equal clarity.

It therefore gives me great pleasure to contribute the Foreword to this important book by Ian Mackintosh. He has been known to me for several years as one of the most perceptive and knowledgeable of consultants grappling with the strategic complexities of the international electronics industry, and he and his colleagues have contributed significantly to the work of the Commission's Information Technology and Tele-communications Task Force, headed by Director-General Michel Carpentier.

Sunrise Europe makes a powerful and well-documented case for the nations of Europe to join together in mounting a massive campaign to effect a lasting European IT renaissance. I wish Ian Mackintosh, his book and his ideas the greatest possible success.

Viscount Etienne Davignon
Brussels

To Fiona and Andrew – the best progeny a man might hope for.

Preface

Technology has become too big to be left to the technologists, nor should information be the sole preserve of the already enlightened. Information technology now concerns us all, and the days are past when the many could rely on the expertise of the few. The 'high-tech' revolution is pervasively encroaching on the ordinary man, and the invisible barriers of incomprehension which have separated him from the cognoscenti must now be dismantled. One of my aims, therefore, is to contribute to a wider understanding of the massive implications of the Information Society.

In fact, the advent of information technology represents the single most revolutionary economic development of the twentieth century. Based on the relentless advances in electronics technology which began in mid-century, the manufacture and use of the tools of information technology are already beginning to cause fundamental changes in social patterns of behaviour and in the economic well-being of nations. Moreover, these technology-based changes will accelerate during the next 50 years or so, to the point where developed countries which fail to build a competitive capability in information technology will suffer an irreversible decline in economic activity to a degree which will seriously erode many of their long-established political and social foundations.

This sort of apocalyptic declamation is not new, of course. Similar words, usually rather more equivocal in tone, have been used before. This has been especially evident in those nations of Europe (and of some other parts of the world) which have relied historically on the manufacturing sector to contribute substantially to the Gross Domestic Product. Even in the United States and Japan, currently far outstripping all other nations in the creation of wealth and jobs through the intelligent and vigorous application of electronics technology, similar statements can sometimes be heard above the quiet bustle of 'high-tech' production. In those countries the purpose is to provide a stimulus to even faster technological advance, and to even greater efforts to compete against their trans-Pacific rivals.

But in Europe and similar regions, such warnings are usually voiced by observers who have come to recognize the rapid advances in information technology (IT) in the US and Japan and whose objectives are to spur greater catch-up efforts in their own countries – usually by government.

Indeed, this sort of persistent pressure, coupled with more tangible evidence (such as a worsening trade balance in electronic goods and services), has already stimulated many governments to act in ways which they believe would be remedial. In several member states of the European Economic Community, for example, governmental actions have generally taken the form of financial aid for industrial research and development and/or the encouragement of inward investment by high-tech multinational companies – usually, by definition, of American or Japanese origin. And in South America (e.g. Brazil), some governments have responded by setting up various mechanisms to protect their infant, indigenous high-tech companies.

It is now clear, however, that such remedies simply do not work. In the first place, there is recent, strong evidence (presented in this book) that despite growing support over many years by several European governments for their information technology and electronics industries, their overall national capability is falling further and further behind that of Japan and the US. It is impossible to resist the conclusion, therefore, that past policies, having manifestly failed, will need to be changed – perhaps radically.

The analyses presented in later pages also show that, such has been the rate of divergence between the Japanese/US IT (and related) capabilities and those of the 'second-division' countries, coupled with the massive economies of scale which now prevail in most segments of the electronics industry, the costs of catching up are becoming huge. In fact, the evidence has become exceedingly strong that no single nation – not even such powerful countries as France, the UK and West Germany – can realistically afford to finance the establishment of a wholly national competitive capability in all of the key, interdependent product segments of the electronics sector.

Another justification for this book, therefore, is an attempt to broaden the base of understanding of these dynamics of the international IT industry. Although the case must obviously be argued in economic terms, the discussion is fully explicable in outline to any businessman, and is conducted almost exclusively in streetwise economics. Moreover, apart from an intelligent layman's appreciation of the basic differences between the major products of the electronics sector (computers *versus* industrial controls *versus* word processors *versus* video cassette recorders, for example), such an understanding is not predicated on a knowledge of electronics technology *per se*.

As will already be clear, I believe that these analyses of the macro-dynamics of information technology imply some radically new perceptions of what the laggard nations must do to have a realistic chance of catching up. And this, coupled with the latest evidence of the rate at which the nations of Europe, for example, are falling behind suggests that a renewed call for action is timely. This, I hope, is further justification for my book.

But it clearly shouldn't stop there. It is hardly enough merely to prove that the process of restoring technological parity of Europe with the US and Japan is immensely more difficult and expensive than we have previously understood. If the promise of these sunrise industries is to be believed (and in light of the very high growth rates achieved in the past 20 years or so, who could seriously challenge that promise?), and if the overwhelming evidence of America's and Japan's domination of the 'sunrise sector' is accepted, the fundamental challenge for Europe is to devise a realistic strategy for overcoming these difficulties. In other words, what is urgently needed is a feasible set of policies to get us from where we are now – facing a techno-economic catastrophe – to where we know we would like to be. Namely, to commanding our fair share of the rapidly growing worldwide high-tech markets, based on the secure foundations of technological competence, financial investment, production strength and large domestic markets.

A fourth justification for this book, therefore, is that I believe it does point to a way of solving this important and difficult problem. It clearly will not be easy, given the enormous lead currently enjoyed by the US and Japan. But the strategy which is proposed (based on the European model, but generally applicable to other regions) is certainly feasible in technological terms and, with the right degree of political commitment, is also feasible in economic terms.

So the book is primarily addressed to those who, collectively, represent political will. This, of course, does not mean simply the politicians – because although they, poor souls, must make many of the final decisions, the time and ability they have available to become fully informed about these apparently abstruse matters is strictly limited.

It is the opinion formers in general whose attention must be engaged, and agreement obtained. Men of finance, economists, journalists, broadcasters, trades union leaders, professors, civil servants, and the men and women in the street are all part of the target. And also the electronics industry itself. In Europe, at least, it has largely been the fault of past generations of management that many electronics companies (with a few honourable exceptions) have performed so dismally. Therefore, an understanding of the principles outlined briefly in the following pages could be of some significance in orientating new management generations in the direction of a lasting economic renaissance based on the increasing importance and power of the information revolution.

Two final points, by way of introduction. The evidence, arguments and proposals outlined in this book also need to be absorbed and understood, I believe, by those who advocate low-tech, no-growth industrial strategies. While their approach has the apparent attractions of appealing to man's atavistic yearnings for a simpler, somehow more wholesome lifestyle, it needs to be appreciated what such policies would cost in terms of jobs, wealth and a nation's economic ability to provide such basics as decent standards of education and health care.

If the views of those who want to opt out of high-tech competition are allowed to prevail then, my arguments suggest, the present rate of high-tech slippage will accelerate to the point where the sometime-powerful nations of Europe, among others, will be reduced to the status of once-industrialized countries – or OICs.

And finally, the critics of my book, and of the immense projects it advocates to secure a European technological revitalization, will no doubt focus on what they see as exaggeration, compounded by purple prose. But there *is* no exaggeration: the salient facts are available and any objective analyst is bound to draw the same dispiriting conclusions as I have done.

As to the style, what is a chap to do? As mentioned earlier, several of us in or associated with the international electronics industry have been trying, for many years, quietly and persistently to force-feed politicians and other decision-makers with these unpalatable facts and with a sense of the urgent need to take drastic actions, but the results so far have usually been a case of too little, too late. Now, as I believe this book conclusively shows, many European nations are facing a major industrial and economic crisis based on their waning competitiveness in information technology, and this is exacerbated by concomitant high levels of chronic unemployment.

The time therefore seems ripe to lay out the facts as clearly as possible, to present the consequences of failure without equivocation, and to plead for a realistic, coherent renaissance strategy with some degree of passion. These are my aims.

Ian Mackintosh
London, December 1985

Acknowledgements

All of the analysis, advocacy and opinions expressed in this book are entirely my own. In particular, they should not be construed to reflect the views of the Commission of the European Communities (CEC) or of my ex-colleagues in Mackintosh International Limited (MIL) and its parent company, Business Intelligence Services Limited (BIS).

Nevertheless, considerable work obviously goes into a treatise of this scope and detail, and I am beholden to a considerable number of individuals and organizations for their support and assistance in my attempts to make a coherent whole out of a mass of research, observations and statistics.

Principal among these are the CEC, its recent Executive Vice-President, Viscount E. Davignon, and its Director General, Information Technology and Telecommunications, M. Michel Carpentier. The original support from the CEC gave some of my ex-colleagues and myself the privileged opportunity to build on some of our previous work in this area, to analyse the real nature of the European deficiencies in information technology and to seek ways by which this weakness might be overcome.

My gratitude is also due to the directors of MIL and BIS for agreeing, however reluctantly, to an interruption in my past responsibilities as Chairman of MIL in order to write this book.

In trying to consolidate my own experiences of the international electronics industry over the past 30 years or so, and to address the European high-tech malady in a way which I hope is comprehensible to the numerate layman, I have received the advice and assistance of a large number of individuals, to whom it is a pleasure to express my thanks. *Primus inter pares*, Peter A. Walker has worked with me for many years, including two major CEC studies. His knowledge and creative ideas have always been of great value to me in trying to grapple with some of the complex strategic issues which pervade the electronics industry worldwide.

I also want to make a special point of recording my thanks to Robin S. (Bob) Whiskin, a trusted and valued colleague for more than 20 years. He is a remarkable amalgam of detailed knowledge of many segments of the electronics business and impressive vision about where the industry is going. I have relied on him in various chapters to provide the book with a secure foundation of knowledge and fact.

Beyond these, I have received so much help from personnel in MIL – from Research Assistants to Principal Consultants to Directors – that it is impossible to acknowledge them all but individious to mention only some. Nevertheless, justice and friendship require that I record my thanks to Gerry Clare, Deborah Gee, Ian Galbraith, John Godfrey, Janice Haigh, Martin Lam, Gary Price, Tony Pyne and Alan Walden – all associated with Mackintosh International Limited at the time of writing.

Lastly, gratitude should be expressed to my secretary, Mrs Diana Harris, for the patience and care with which she has cheerfully coped with my innumerable drafts.

Introduction

This is not a technical treatise on information technology (IT), nor a history of the evolution and impact of the micro-chip. Rather, it is an attempt to provide a measure of Europe's growing deficiencies in the IT sector, and to propose a strategy whereby Europe could re-establish parity of high-tech performance with the United States and Japan.

Nevertheless, no discussion of the dynamics of this industry can be conducted sensibly without an overview, at least, of the scale and scope of the information revolution. Nor can the pivotal role of the micro-chip be ignored if the lessons of history are to be used constructively in building a renaissance strategy. The purpose of this introduction, then, is to fill these two needs and to set the scene for what follows.

The Information Society

There are few areas of work or leisure which will not be affected profoundly by the widespread availability of low-cost, easy-to-use information. If this seems in any way surprising, it may be because society in general has not yet fully cottoned on to the concept of information as a resource which is often as valuable as money or manpower. In the same way, it took a very long time for society to come to grips with previous waves of industrial change based on revolutionary new concepts such as the steam engine, electricity and the jet engine.

In this case, the problem has been that, until recently, much information was simply too difficult to obtain, sift, convey, display and analyse – so a range of techniques had to be developed for making do without it. These tend to be called instinct, or experience, or gut feeling, or flair. But considering what most people are already capable of, despite the dearth of information and a limited memory, man's intellectual horizons will be expanded enormously through the colossal capabilities of electronics technology to process and deliver information at very high speeds and very low costs.

In education, inter alia, the eventual ability to access essentially any database of information on any subject will lead to a radical change in teaching methods, with almost all the emphasis being on interpretation of the easily available facts and the creative use thereof, rather than the old-fashioned memorizing of data. In health care, diagnostic skills are already being honed through the use of computerized information banks, and this process will accelerate significantly as the information revolution gathers pace. Information technology (IT) products will add a new dimension to the use of leisure time, just as personal computers are already doing in many homes. And straightforward entertainment will be enhanced by the availability of a wide choice of speciality, high-fidelity radio and video programmes delivered primarily by some form of 'cable'.

Communications will be revolutionized by low-cost IT products. Although the printed word – in the form of books, newspapers and magazines – will retain a vital (and highly convenient) role in education, entertainment and the provision of general information, the display screen will become pervasive. This will encourage banking, working and shopping from home (with major implications for the High Street, urban traffic patterns and local authority finances), and the ultimate universal ownership of videophones may adversely affect the growth of business travel.

In manufacturing, the production processes and the quality of the end-products will be improved through the extended use of electronics-based techniques of measurement and control. Most important, however, will be the exponential increase in industrial automation generally and small, special-purpose robots in particular, for carrying out precise, repetitive and/or dangerous tasks. The office will become increasingly important as the focus of information, control and decision-making.

And so on, as far as the imagination can stretch. In the advanced nations, information technology is to the home, office and factory what the internal combustion engine was to mass transport; it is transforming practically everything, from societal patterns to the world economy. Those who wish to prosper from IT had better understand and master it.

IT and the chip

The integrated circuit (IC), to use its proper label, is a small chip of the semiconductor element, silicon.[1] Crystalline wafers (large thin discs) of

---

[1] Figure I.1 is a schematic illustration of the relationships between semiconductor materials and components, the various silicon IC generations and the main categories of equipment and systems.

silicon are the purest and most perfect solid material known to man, with countless billions[2] of silicon atoms each located at precisely the right place in the crystal lattice. Not untypically, the level of purity may be represented by one 'foreign' atom to every 10 million silicon atoms.

By subjecting the whole wafer to a highly sophisticated and precise series of chemical and physical processes, a complete electronic circuit of great complexity can be fabricated within a small area (typically 0.25 cm square) of the silicon, and this can be reproduced accurately all across the wafer, from one wafer to another within a production batch of wafers, and from batch to batch. Thus, very large numbers of identical, complex chips (i.e. entire circuits) can be manufactured at a very low cost per chip.

It is not just that the IC is the single most important and pervasive means by which the performance and cost of a wide variety of electronic equipments have been revolutionized; nor that many other equipments (such as electronic watches, portable calculators and personal computers) simply would not exist without the availability of low-cost microelectronic circuits (chips). An additional reason for conferring star status on the micro-chip in any chronicle of the IT industry is that the business triumphs and disasters in the electronic components industry reveal many of the key factors which have determined success or failure in the IT industry in general.

In other words, what is good for ICs is good for electronics. For such reasons, the early chapters are much concerned with the strategic impact of the various engulfing waves of component technology with which managers in the worldwide electronics/IT industry[3] have had to contend for the past 30 years or more.

The malady lingers on

The framework of this book is basically very simple. In Part One ('Seeds and Weak Beginnings'), key features of the underlying structure of the electronics/IT industries in the United States, Japan and Western Europe are highlighted by surveying the various strategic factors which have influenced the pace and direction of their growth up to the present time.

---

[2] Throughout this book, 1 billion equals 1000 million.
[3] In this book, the information technology industry is treated as synonomous with the electronics industry. Some observers would disagree with this simplification but the phenomenon of convergence (Chapter 6) implies that all such distinctions are becoming meaningless.

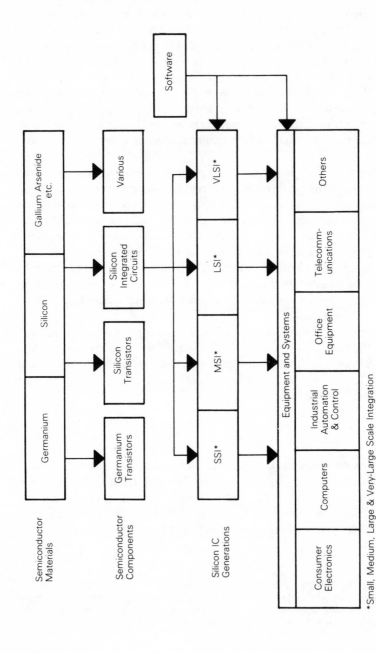

Figure I.1. The relationship between electronic components and equipment/systems.

*Small, Medium, Large & Very-Large Scale Integration

From a global point of view, there have been substantial differences between the continents in the response to the innovatory challenges of electronics technology. For example, the attitudes of management, commitment of resources, business strategies and production growth rates of IT products have been markedly different. Moreover, each region's (or country's) successes and failures can only be fitted within a common framework of business fundamentals if due weight is given to the particular circumstances prevailing at any given time in any given country. These intercontinental comparisons thus point up the markedly different routes by which America and Japan have achieved their current strengths, and illuminate the salient causes of Europe's relative decline.

Part Two ('Economists and Calculators') is essentially analytical in nature, albeit in 'macro', layman's terms. Quantification is the aim: first, to assess the size of the industry in general and, in particular, the size of Europe's capability gap in the IT sector; and second, to establish a credible, if approximate, method for estimating what the costs of catching up would be.

The fact is that at the core of Europe's high-tech syndrome, there beats a timid heart. The attitudes of previous managements and governments to meeting the multiplicity of resource needs of a demanding and revolutionary new technology have been unduly tentative. And the analysis shows that the catch-up costs are so much bigger than anything so far contemplated, or discussed publicly, that these incredible figures scream out for the support of a credible methodology.

In Part Three ('Trying the Measures'), various national strategies are assessed in terms of their capacity to effect a real and lasting renaissance of Europe's IT capabilities. All of those which have been tried so far are found wanting – including government support for research and development (R&D), inward investment by foreign high-tech companies and transoceanic technical linkages. Instead, the finger of analysis points to a crucifying lack of demand in Europe for the sophisticated products of the electronics industry, and to an urgent need for a strategy designed to create a much enlarged and cohesive European IT market.

The renaissance strategy proposed is inevitably expensive and bound to be controversial. None the less, the economic threat which IT now poses for Europe is real, immediate and daunting. It will be the ability of European governments to recognize the seriousness of this threat, and their determination to act decisively and collectively to counter it, which will determine Europe's prosperity in the third millenium.

PART ONE
Seeds and Weak Beginnings

There is a history in all men's lives,
Figuring the nature of the times deceas'd,
The which observ'd, a man may prophesy,
With a near arm, of the main chance of things
As yet not come to life, which in their seeds
And weak beginnings lie intreasured.

King Henry IV, Part II, W. Shakespeare

1 Genesis of the Information Revolution

The genealogy of the silicon micro-chip

This chapter is primarily concerned with the foundations of the present-day electronics industry, with particular emphasis on the successive generations of component technology. In this brief history a deliberate effort has been made to emphasize the social, commercial and geographical factors which have influenced the uneven pace of development of the electronics industry in different parts of the world. What emerges is that several of today's postulated conditions for success can be seen to have their origins in the early years of the electronics industry. These factors thus gain in credibility in comparison with some more recent, hotter (but sometimes half-baked) recipes for success.

THE PRE-TRANSISTOR PERIOD

Hot filament, cold start

The electronics era began in earnest with the invention, in the United States, of the thermionic triode valve (or tube) by Lee De Forest in 1906[1]. This allowed, for the first time, the amplification of very small electrical (i.e. electronic) signals or currents. At first, this device was, in modern parlance, a solution looking for a problem. Eventually, though, it found important applications, mainly during the inter-war years, in

---

[1] Patent application filed on 25 October 1906 for a three-electrode valve – a triode – for amplifying feeble electric currents.

telecommunications (for amplifying long-distance telephonic and tele-graphic signals), in communications (for providing the amplified signals for early radio transmissions) and in consumer electronics (i.e. radio receivers). A significant boost to electronics research and development (R & D) was produced in the Second World War through the needs of the military services for improved communications (telephone and radio) and defence (e.g. radar).

Although this 'thermionic era' is of limited relevance to the information technology industry of today, one or two illuminating comparisons can be drawn. In the first place, the rate of growth was leisurely by today's standards. Between 1920 and 1940, for example, valve (tube) production in the United States increased from $c.15$ million to $c.130$ million units per annum, a compound average annual growth rate (CAAGR) of 11.4 per cent. If that sounds substantial, a similar increase in the US production of micro-chips (from $c.9.5$ million to $c.134$ million units per annum) required only three years, from 1965 to 1968, representing a CAAGR of nearly 42 per cent.

Transatlantic parity

A second important feature of the thermionic era was that the race was run exclusively by American and European competitors, with Japan and the rest of the then-industrializing world more or less out of the reckoning. With the benefit of hindsight, this domination was based on the sim-ultaneous availability, in Europe as much as in America, of technological competence (including, importantly, the know-how of mass production), allied to the all-important numerate entrepreneur and what we would now call venture capital.

Thus, Europe at that time was still the cradle of science, although some European scientific talent was beginning to drift westwards in search of the perceived new freedoms of America, leaving behind the political and economic turmoil of Europe in the 1920s and 1930s. And, of critical importance to Europe, this indigenous technical strength co-existed with a strong native entrepreneurial spirit which had been at its zenith during the European empire-building of the eighteenth and nineteenth centuries. As the new century got into its stride, entire 'electronics' businesses were created by European inventors (some of whom, understandably, turned out to be unsuccessful businessmen), of whom Sebastian Ziani de Ferranti and Guglielmo Marconi were outstanding British examples, both of Italian extraction.

The third essential factor, as stated, was the existence of a breed of 'venture' financiers whose business ethos was founded on the premise that making money means risking money, and who were capable of understanding the businesses in which they invested, including the infant telephony and wireless industries. In this way, their forebears had financed the building of merchant navies and railroads, in America and Europe, and the deadening hand of socialism (a European invention), and its concomitant high rates of taxation, had yet to dampen the enthusiasm of the European risk-takers.

In short, on both sides of the Atlantic, success in the new 'thermionic' industry occurred exclusively in countries which simultaneously possessed the three essential attributes of exploitable technology, numerate entrepreneurs and venturesome financiers. Although these may not be the necessary *and* sufficient conditions for success in the high-tech industries of today, they are at least as important now as they were then.

In that pre-transistor period, the social impact of the new thermionic technology was relatively modest. While the use of telephones and radio sets was steadily increasing on both sides of the Atlantic, it was primarily the technology of the internal combustion engine which provided the enabling force of social change in the inter-war years. In other words, the era of information mobility was (had to be!) preceded by the era of personal mobility.

Solid prospects

By the end of the war, in 1945, the scientific and military communities, primarily in the US, the UK, Japan and Germany, had become acutely aware of the limitations of the thermionic valve. It was big and heavy; its heating element consumed energy in vast quantities relative to the size of the signals it was amplifying or switching; and it was fragile and unreliable. At the same time, scientists were understanding more and more about that curious class of solid-state materials, semiconductors, which conduct electricity in a highly selective way: not like metals, which are essentially without resistance to electric current; nor like insulators, which resist mightily.

Quite rapidly, there emerged in the minds of a few scientists the dream of inventing a solid-state (semiconductor) amplifier. This, they hoped, would obviate the need for the heater element of the thermionic tube, the vacuum which was essential to its operation and the glass envelope which sealed it all off from the outside world. And with them should go all of the other undesirable characteristics of this cumbersome component. Nowhere was this research pursued with such missionary zeal and creative imagination than at the Bell Telephone Laboratories at Murray Hill, New Jersey . . .

THE LIFT-OFF YEARS

So much has already been said and written about the invention of the transistor that it is certainly not necessary to repeat the story here. Nevertheless, there are some aspects of those years of lift-off (in more than one sense of the word, as will be seen), being mainly the decade of the 1950s, that are relevant to the circumstances of today.

The germanium decade

In the first place, despite swift recognition of the profound importance of the transistor, it still took about 10 years for it to become a significant factor – in either military or commercial terms. The theoretical hypothesis and experimental proof of solid-state amplification, by John Bardeen, Walter H. Brattain and W. Shockley[2] working co-operatively in Bell Telephone Laboratories, occurred officially on 23 December 1947. That research, for which these exceptional men were jointly awarded the 1956 Nobel Prize for Physics, was carried out using germanium, a somewhat rare and difficult element which was known to possess semiconducting properties. But it was not until about 1957 that Philco, later acquired by the Ford Motor Company, developed the so-called micro-alloy diffused transistor (MADT). This device could be manufactured in high volumes, at a low cost, and of adequate reliability and performance. The germanium transistor had truly arrived.

The reasons for the delay were many and varied. The most important was the fact that there was essentially no reservoir of production know-how on which to build. Germanium is a difficult material, and it became necessary to develop a whole range of new techniques; for example, to make reliable electrical contacts to it and to encapsulate the device so that it was adequately robust and physically isolated from the damaging effects of normal (i.e. somewhat polluted) room air.

Moreover, it can be inferred from what went on (or, more interestingly, didn't) in those years that the American military authorities, while exhibiting great curiosity about this wondrous new electronic device, were not convinced of its relevance to their own needs. Certainly they played a useful role in funding some of the early research, both in their own defence R & D establishments and in several industrial laboratories (including Bell Labs), but there was little evidence of great commitment.

---

[2] W. Shockley, How we invented the transistor, *New Scientist*, **689**, 21 December 1972.

In Europe, the story was similar, with the defence scientists, especially in Britain, showing great scientific curiosity, but little else. West Germany, Italy and, to a lesser extent, France, were still largely pre-occupied with recovering from the ravages of the war, in which their defence industries had effectively been destroyed. But Philips, in the Netherlands, had already started a significant programme of R & D centred on the germanium alloy transistor.

And in Japan, even in those very early years, there were signs of an unusual intensity of interest. Despite having been on the 'losing' side in the Second World War, and despite the horrific effects of the Hiroshima and Nagasaki atomic bombs, much of the Japanese industry was still intact. Moreover, cognisant of the social, economic and political dev-astation visited on Germany after 1918, one part of American policy was to steer Japan towards commercial, rather than military, exploitation of its industrial skills.

It may not be fanciful to suggest that one effect of these strategic forces was to heighten Japanese interest in an invention which represented a radical break with the past and which held a promise, albeit still latent, of a wholly new kind of industrial activity in which Japan would not be too heavily disadvantaged by its prevailing status (of being controlled, in effect, by the United States).

In any event, there was a rapid growth of semiconductor research activities in Japan. Also, the solid-state research laboratories of America and Europe gradually became accustomed to playing host to parties of visiting Japanese scientists, armed with portable tape recorders and an insatiable thirst for knowledge.

Designer coupling

During this period, when germanium technology was gradually becoming established, electrical engineers in many countries were struggling to understand how to use this strange new transistor. It was certainly not easy, but it naturally happened most rapidly in countries blessed with an existing establishment of solid-state scientists – whether based in university, military or industrial laboratories. Not surprisingly, America was in the vanguard, but Britain was not far behind, and they were followed closely by the Netherlands, Japan and West Germany.

The key factor here, to which further emphasis will be given later, was the effectiveness of the technical 'coupling' between those who were designing the components, and understood how they worked, and those whose job it was to design new equipment based thereon. All of this was given a considerable boost by the growing realization that the digital electronic computer (also, by coincidence, invented about 1947) could become substantially more effective and powerful if designed around the transistor rather than the thermionic valve. Thus the swelling army of computer designers – again, most evident in America and Britain – began to join the ranks of transistor enthusiasts.

Silicon takes over

Meanwhile, back at Bell Labs, reservations about germanium were gathering momentum. While no-one could yet be certain what were the critical questions, let alone the answers, the germanium transistor was still not exhibiting the high levels of reliability which would be required by the widespread telephone network of the Bell System, as it then was, if the changeover from electromechanical to electronic switching was ever to become feasible. Nor, it was clear, could this device ever operate satisfactorily at the higher temperatures routinely experienced by some items of telephone equipment (e.g. in strong, direct sunlight).

For these reasons, and also as a matter of pure scientific curiosity, research work into germanium's 'sister' element, silicon, had slowly been gaining momentum to the extent that, by the mid-1950s, a few dozen scientists and technicians, at Bell Labs alone, were working on the development of the silicon transistor and similar devices. This material was seen to have considerable inherent advantages over germanium. It could, in principle, continue to function as a semiconductor at much higher temperatures; and, as was eventually to emerge as a vitally important property, silicon is capable of developing an oxide 'skin', which is highly stable and can provide the underlying device with a degree of protection from external pollution.

Many different varieties of silicon transistor were developed, at Bell Labs and elsewhere and, by and large, they fulfilled their promise. The main problem with the silicon transistor, vis à vis its germanium counterpart, was its slow operating speed, but this disadvantage was overcome in one enormously significant technological leap (at Bell Labs, naturally) whereby the inherently high electrical resistance of the very pure silicon was significantly reduced by the so-called epitaxial process.

And so was born the Silicon Society, or the Age of Silicon, to use two of the many phrases (now clichés) coined to describe the electronics era which was built on the ashes of the germanium transistor, and which has continued ever since.

Space for expansion

Almost simultaneously, there occurred another event which was instantaneously and widely recognized as a major technological watershed. In October 1957 the USSR successfully launched the world's first orbiting satellite, Sputnik I, based on Russia's heavy emphasis on the development of very powerful rocket engines. Its impact on the American governmental/military/industrial establishment was massive. The only nation remotely capable of challenging America's general technological leadership had dramatically exhibited superior technical strength in one vitally important area, which raised serious questions about America's ability to compete with Russia's burgeoning military might.

The American response was swift and sure. Recognizing the long lead times which would be involved in developing competitive rocket engines, the US military authorities began to commit huge resources to reducing the weight of the payload to a level more in tune with the power of their available engines. And to this maiden's prayer, of course, the nascent silicon transistor was a well-nigh perfect answer.

In addition, to control their new space programme, and the satellites themselves, the American defence establishment found itself urgently needing more and more computing power. Computers, moreover, which were faster, bigger and more reliable than anything then available. This forced the computer companies (with International Business Machines – IBM – very much in the vanguard, even then) to accelerate the rate of changeover from thermionic to germanium to silicon technology.

As a result, there occurred a marvellously clear and effective manifestation of industrial synergy. The US Department of Defense (DoD) possessed essentially inexhaustible funds: they needed small, lightweight and reliable electronic components to put into their rocket payloads, and therefore provided industry with financial support for both R & D and for the establishment of transistor production facilities: the DoD also needed substantially larger and faster computers, and provided various forms of stimulus to the American computer industry to develop these new systems: and the computer companies, in turn, supplied the further stimulus to the components industry of a large and expanding market for the best devices they could produce.

Each industrial segment – defence electronics, computers and electronic components – therefore depended on, and was stimulated by, the others. This had two major effects. One was an astonishingly rapid closing of the techno-military gap which had seemed to open up with the first appearance of Sputnik. And the other was that, in all three industrial segments, US companies rapidly gained a domination of world markets, based on the best technology and the largest production volumes (and hence the most competitive production economics). These dominating US roles were maintained for at least two decades and only recently have some other nations begun to show signs of clawing a way back to some sort of parity with the Americans – Japan in computers and components, and Europe in defence electronics.

THE CHIP IS BORN

There is no need to repeat here the oft-told story of the invention of the integrated circuit (IC), popularly known as the micro-chip, nor to explain its technological complexities. Rather, the aim should be to describe, in layman's terms, some of the salient features of that critically important phase of industrial innovation, at the end of the 1950s, in order to provide a better basis for a strategic understanding of the electronics industry of today.

Westward, look, the land is bright

In 1954, Dr William Shockley had left Bell Labs and moved to northern California – more specifically, to the Santa Clara Valley, then a predominantly agricultural area, just south of San Francisco. His intention was to use his reputation and knowledge of semiconductor theory to create a new company, Shockley Laboratories, cheek-by-jowl with Stanford University and various new, small high-tech companies then coming into existence (e.g. Hewlett-Packard and Varian).

Although this venture was ultimately unsuccessful, it did represent a critical punctuation mark in the unfolding story of the electronics industry's development – in two respects. In the first place, Shockley's move was, beyond question, the starting point of what is now known as Silicon Valley, soon to become a seething mass of interrelated silicon-based corporations. Secondly, he was able to recruit a talented team of scientists and engineers to join him in California, some of whom came to play centre stage in the techno-economic drama on which the curtain was just being raised.

Of these, Drs Robert N. Noyce and Gordon E. Moore were most impressive examples of that combination of talents which was referred to earlier as the cause of much European industrial success two or three generations earlier. Both of these men were blessed with relevant scientific knowledge and creative insight and, of major importance, with business acumen which blossomed rapidly as they stepped easily and jointly into the role of scientific entrepreneurs. For their association with Shockley was brief and was followed, in 1957, by them obtaining corporate financing from Fairchild Camera and Instrument to establish the Fairchild Semiconductor Division.

This, also, was a seminal event because from that founder company has since sprung up a multitude of semiconductor spin-offs (the 'Fairchildren') of great variety. Indeed, having made a tremendous success of Fairchild, Noyce and Moore also moved on, about ten years later, to start another company from scratch, Intel, which was to become an even greater semiconductor success story.

Planar and simpler

In those not-so-far-off days of 1957, many semiconductor researchers, in several countries, had begun to recognize the inventive possibilities represented by the great stability of the oxide skin which readily grew on the disc-like, highly polished and incredibly pure and perfect wafers of silicon. One result, of catalytic importance, was that, in 1959, a wholly new technology was announced (by Fairchild) for making silicon transistors, known as the planar process. This allowed all of the transistor contact points to be brought to the surface plane of the silicon, thus greatly facilitating and simplying electrical connection.

The demonstration of this planar transistor led to a great burst of inventive activity, partly based on the perception that some of the ingredients now existed for building entire circuits (albeit simple ones) into the silicon. The notebooks of dozens of solid-state scientists of that era contained various jottings and sketches of possible 'solid-state circuits'. But credit for the invention of the 'monolithic' integrated circuit is usually given jointly to Noyce (for the basic silicon structure which still lies at the heart of modern micro-chips) and to J. S. Kilby who, at the research laboratories of Texas Instruments, first demonstrated a working 'solid circuit'.

The significance of the advent of the integrated circuit, or microelectronic circuit, or micro-chip, can hardly be overstated. In the first place, entire circuits (instead of individual devices such as the transistor), each carrying its own, integral pattern of (evaporated metal) electrical connections, could now be made within one pinhead-sized area of the silicon wafer, which at that time was typically a disc of $\frac{1}{2} - 1''$ diameter. Even more important was the fact that at first dozens, then hundreds (and now thousands) of these circuits could be manufactured simultaneously on one silicon wafer before being divided up into individual circuits, or chips, and then securely mounted in hermetic packages containing suitable wired connections to its external 'pins'. Moreover, such was the nature of key parts of the production technology that many silicon wafers could be processed together.

Thus, it became possible to process a whole batch of silicon wafers which could theoretically culminate in tens of thousands of individual, but identical, circuits. Even though the complexity of the production processes meant that the percentage yield of 'good' circuits was often quite low, the net result was still the manufacture of substantial quantities of good chips at a remarkably low cost (on a per-chip basis).

The tyranny of numbers

Of at least equal importance was the fact that the IC offered a badly needed solution to the systems problem of the 'tyranny of numbers'. One formulation of this averred that the greater the number of transistors and other components which had to be connected together via slightly unreliable interconnection points (such as solder joints and pressure contacts) the more unreliable must be the total system. Even by 1960, such was the level of concern, especially among designers of military electronic systems, about the long-term integrity of this kind of electrical connection that serious questions were being raised about a possible upper limit to the size of systems beyond which their overall reliability would become unacceptably low.

But the integrated circuit carries its own 'on-chip' pattern of evaporated-metal connections, the reliability of which eventually proved to be extremely high. This provided the answer to the 'tyranny of numbers' as more and more interconnections were carried by the ever-more-complex chips, thus permitting electronic systems which are both large and reliable.

In brief, a truly mass-production technology, with the added benefit of high intrinsic reliability, was now at the command of the electronics industry. The impact of this development was to be as profound as when, some 50 years earlier, Henry Ford first introduced mass-production methods into the manufacture of automobiles. For the electronics industry now had available to it (although, at the time, very few recognized the awe-inspiring magnitude of the breakthrough) the intrinsic ability to make entire circuits of greater and greater complexity, higher and higher reliability and lower and lower cost. This was the spark which ignited the revolution in information processing, which is still in its infancy.

Numerous practical manifestations of the revolutionary impact of this new technique of mass production are discussed in Chapter 2.

Money, men and Murray Hill

Although in Europe, also, there were several examples of contemporaneous musings about circuits contained within solids, it is an
incontrovertible fact that all of the critical early inventions relating to the
integrated circuit were made in the US. Clearly, the national spasm which
followed the launch of Sputnik I, and the defence-derived R & D funding
which ensued, were major factors in stimulating this incredible outpouring
of coast-to-coast American research and development.

But, equally clearly, it could not have been simply a matter of money.
For one thing, there had to be, all ready and waiting, so to speak, a
small army of R & D scientists and engineers poised to exploit the new
technology. That this was uniquely the case in America can largely be
attributed to the fact that the transistor was invented at the Bell Telephone
Laboratories and that, at the time, its parent company (American Telephone & Telegraph, or AT&T) was a regulated telephone utility with
little opportunity or motive for profiting from selling the transistor in
external (i.e. non-AT&T) markets. One result of this fortuitous genesis
was that, in 1952, Bell Labs generously licensed its semiconductor technology to essentially any organization which could pay the modest fee of
$25,000.

A more vital benefit to America at large, however, was Bell Labs' role
as a reservoir of skills which could be tapped by companies anxious to
try their hand at the commercial exploitation from which AT&T was
effectively barred. Since Americans rarely emigrate (indeed, the inward
flow of immigrant scientific talent, mainly European, was accelerating –
the so-called 'brain drain'), it was natural that these Murrary Hill skills
should be recruited almost exclusively by US companies.

Although innovation has obviously been a major strategic factor in the
growth of the international electronics industry, and will continue to be
so for the foreseeable future, the key elements of innovation are development and marketing, not basic research. In fact, there has been very
little correlation between the commercial success of a US semiconductor
company and the quality and size of its basic research programme,
an ability to recruit key personnel having been much more important
historically.

In this matter, the US possessed a major advantage in the fortuitous
combination of a high rate of personnel mobility and the existence of Bell
Labs, plus several other highly capable R & D laboratories, which acted
as national generators of technology and technologists. Thus, in the US,
the diffusion of technology occurred mainly through the diffusion of

people, and the commercial exploitation of new ideas was rarely inhibited for long because the innovator and the would-be exploiter could not make common cause. Moreover, the bulk of these commercial marriages were consummated in one or other of the fertile skill centres, such as Silicon Valley and Boston's famous Route 128, with which the United States was becoming so well endowed.

The process of knowledge dissemination was further reinforced, moreover, through the rapid creation, by several professional institutions, of many first-rate scientific and technical conferences – located, again, in the US – which served the vital function of providing forums for the ongoing exchange of knowledge.

Apart from the availability, and mobility, of this pool of talent, the other essential factor in encouraging America's accelerating investment in microelectronics technology was the early stimulation of markets by the computer and defence industries, as already mentioned. Given a ready market for their products, and blessed with the existence of a growing band of technically informed and well-funded venture capitalists, many American entrepreneurs set forth on the road to riches which they believed had been opened up by the advent of the integrated circuit.

Thus was the 'chip' conceived, gestated and born, all in the United States. And the industrialized world everywhere was eventually to learn that this lusty infant represented, in about equal proportions, enormous opportunities and massive threats.

2 America in the Saddle:

Harnessing the Power of the Micro-chip

TAILS-UP TECHNOLOGY

At the beginning of the 1960s, the US electronics industry was already in a position of great strength in relation to its foreign competitors. Indeed, the most recent similar example of one nation so dominating a major new industrial technology was probably Britain in the nineteenth century, with its decisive commitment to steam technology in railways, ships and general manufacturing. (Interestingly, there was an important element of industrial synergy in this case, too, since Britain had also achieved a leading position in the latest technology of steel-making.)

Apart from the defence area, the other business segments where America was dominant (silicon components and digital computers) were not yielding much early profit, however, from non-military markets. In the case of components, this was because most of the commercial applications of transistors at that time were in the embryonic consumer electronics industry (e.g. cheap, portable radios). The nation which seized this opportunity most effectively was Japan, which possessed at that time the considerable advantage of low labour costs, although Europe (and Philips in particular) was also in the vanguard.

In the United States, on the other hand, the consumer electronics industry was already showing signs of technological atrophy (of which more later), and the component industry's emergent entrepreneurs – heavily committed to silicon technology by this time – were seeking markets which were responsive to the impressive ICs they were now able to produce. And, lucky for them, they found one – namely, in the fast-expanding *commercial* applications of computers.

Demand pull

The formative role played by IBM in this period probably warrants a separate, in-depth treatment. Suffice it to say that, from its first major silicon transistor procurement contract (with Texas Instruments) in 1958, IBM has played a vital part in stimulating demand for leading-edge component technology. Although the company was blessed with far-sighted management, coupled with privileged insights stemming from its proximity to the US Department of Defence, it is nevertheless to its great credit that it took considerable initiatives (and some risks) in spurring the advance of silicon technology. While it was obviously not alone in these perceptions, its growing procurement muscle power was of great significance in the 'demand pull' factor which gave the American IC producers the confidence to invest, and invest, and invest again in ever more sophisticated production facilities and ever more expensive R & D.

Nor was it only IBM. The whole of the US electronics industry seemed to be aware of, and involved in, what was going on. So demand pull came not only from the DoD and IBM, but also from the many other companies which were determined to be successful in computers, and in the new technology generally. Even at the highest levels of management, there was often an air of commitment and excitement. Expansion, aggression and growth were the buzz-words of the American electronics industry at that time, and confidence was further reinforced as, in many cases, the world's high-tech markets fell captive to this new, tails-up, silicon-suckled breed of management.

THE MYTH OF AMERICAN MANAGEMENT

But, it must be said, it wasn't really a case of (Texas) roses all the way – even if it sometimes appeared so to the frustrated, baffled managers of non-American electronics companies.

In the first place, these high-tech, high-growth US entrepreneurs were invariably high spenders, too, and often with unimpressive profitability records. Whatever the margins (usually modest, anyway, in such a swash-buckling, competitive business), the growth rates were so dizzily high that new investment demands (in production facilities and R & D) could rarely be funded from net profits. In fact, it is relevant that Intel, probably the most famous name in components technology, has never paid a dividend since it was incorporated in 1968 – and this is by no means unusual in American high-tech companies.

Fortunately for them, these entrepreneurs operated in a sophisticated investment environment, in which even non-professional punters had been conditioned by the (well-informed) media to enjoy capital growth as a more-than-adequate substitute for dividends. And the venture capitalists and investment trusts were more than happy to be judged by a portfolio of stocks at stratospheric price-to-earnings multiples rather than by the more prosaic criterion of dividend income.

Contrary to most non-American perceptions at that time, however, many US managements proved to be inept at riding these large waves of new technology. Brief reference has already been made to the decline of the American consumer electronics industry, for example, but it warrants further comment. From a position, around 1960, where US firms supplied the vast majority of America's markets for radios and television sets, more recently only RCA and Zenith remain as American-owned television manufacturers of significance. Apart from the sales by Philips (through its acquisitions, Magnavox and the television portion of Sylvania), and the television sales of the US companies, the bulk of America's enormous current appetite for entertainment electronics is now supplied by Japanese-owned companies – either as imports or from US-based production facilities, many of which were acquired cheaply as some of the once-powerful American companies bit the dust.

The tragicomedy of entertainment electronics

The intriguing question, of course, is why, despite the catalogue of successes achieved by the American electronics industry, the area of consumer electronics should be an exception.

The main responsibility, without doubt, must lie with the senior managements of those companies at the time when all the technological turmoil was beginning, in the mid-to-late 1950s. For the fact is that most of these American consumer electronics companies simply ignored the transistor. This was to such an extent that even in 1965 (by which time both Japanese and European companies, such as Sony and Philips, had amply demonstrated the appeal of radio portability, based on the transistor), it was very difficult to buy an American-made transistor radio.

It is probably not without significance that, in most cases, these US consumer electronics firms were located in the American mid-West (e.g. Chicago), whereas the technological action was mainly taking place at the coastal extremities of the United States (i.e. along the Eastern seaboard, from Philadelphia to Boston, and in Silicon Valley, near to San Francisco). The development of these polarized 'skill clusters' was already becoming an important factor in the efficient diffusion of technological know-how, designer coupling and management 'feel', and it is clear that isolation from such concentrations of skill, knowledge and technical interaction can impose crippling disadvantages. There was insufficient recognition of this effect in the American consumer electronics industry of the 1960s, just as there is still inadequate understanding of it today in the minds of some European (and other) policy makers.

If technical myopia was one reason for failure, blindness to the salient importance of export markets was another. Without exception, the leading US consumer electronics companies (and, indeed, a large population of US firms in other industrial sectors) concentrated on supplying the domestic, North American markets, to the virtual exclusion of all others. And this at a time when the accelerating impact of technological change was already resulting in more complex (and expensive) designs and abbreviated product life cycles, thus underlining the importance of economies of scale.

As it happened, this concentration on the fat and happy domestic market not only deprived the US consumer electronics companies of some scale benefits (at the margin) but, probably a much greater debilitation, also isolated them from the full blast of the competitive winds emanating from Tokyo and from Eindhoven, in the Netherlands, where Philips has its headquarters and substantial R & D and production facilities. Had they been competing head-on in the less comfortable, non-American markets where consumer electronics Titans were battling head-to-head, and under fair competitive conditions, it is difficult to believe that these American managements would not have been alerted (before it was too late) to some early warning signals, such as falling market share.

In short, it seems clear that at the heart of the failures of the American consumer electronics companies lay complacency. They had had it so good, for so long, that managements became intellectually atrophied, a condition induced by geographical isolation and compounded by plain ignorance.

Macro micro failures

Even in the IC business itself, things were often not as perfect as they sometimes seemed when viewed from across some vast ocean. Take, for example, General Electric and Westinghouse. Around 1960, these two large companies together dominated the US electrical engineering industry. Both were moving heavily into nuclear engineering; both had established large central research laboratories plus development facilities (usually linked to specific product divisions) with substantial teams working on semiconductor devices; and both were confident about, and publicly committed to, becoming large and successful in the blossoming micro-electronics business. It would have taken a brave man, indeed, to have predicted that *both* of these electrical behemoths would fail utterly in a business segment for which they seemed ideally suited – in terms of technology, talent and financial muscle power.

But, of course, they did. And so did Honeywell and Sylvania; and so – almost – did RCA and Hughes and a welter of other multi-product electrical/electronic conglomerates which seemed, in principle, to have a lot going for them in high-tech generally, and microelectronics in particu-lar. It is important, therefore, to appreciate the business fundamentals in this complicated industry, to try to understand why things went so horribly wrong for so many would-be American participants.

The most obvious reason is that there simply wasn't enough 'market space' for the number of companies which wanted to set out their stalls. Or, in an analogy with the California gold rush of a century earlier, a natural consequence of the 1960s 'silicon rush' of US companies pros-pecting for semiconductor profits was that some, not surprisingly, found that their mine shafts missed the rich seams of new technology.

Capsized by waves of change

However, this doesn't explain the GE and Westinghouse failures, since these two companies, in principle, could simply have shouldered their way to positions of prominence (both, in fact, tried to do just that at some stage). For additional clues it is instructive to examine Table 2.1. This lists the top ten US manufacturers of electronic components at five year intervals from 1955 to 1985[1], thus not only covering a total span of 30 years but, more to the point, embracing various waves of component technology. These stretch from the original vacuum-tube (thermionic) era, through the periods when germanium and silicon transistors each reigned supreme, and to the stage where the original bipolar[2] integrated circuits have now been overtaken (in market size) by the newer, MOS forms of ICs.

What can be seen from this table is that only a few of the leaders in one technological generation succeeded in making the transition to the

---

[1] 1985 data estimated at the time of going to print.
[2] The descriptor 'bipolar' was coined to reflect the fact that this type of transistor operates by a judicious mixing of two radically different kinds of electronic currents, of opposite polarities. On the other hand, metal:oxide:silicon (MOS) chips are basically simpler and involve only one type of electron flow (i.e. unipolar) in each MOS transistor on the chip.

Table 2.1 Leading US electronic component merchant manufacturers

	Tubes/Valves	Transistors	Semiconductors			Integrated circuits		
	1955	1955	1960	1965	1970	1975	1980	1985 (est.)
1	RCA	Hughes	Texas Instruments	Texas Instruments	Texas Instruments	Texas Instruments	Texas Instruments	Texas Instruments
2	Sylvania	Transitron	Transitron	Motorola	Motorola	Fairchild	National Semiconductor	Motorola
3	GE	Philco	Philco	Fairchild	Fairchild	National Semiconductor	Motorola	Intel
4	Raytheon	Sylvania	GE	General Instruments	Signetics	Intel	Intel	National Semiconductor
5	Westinghouse	Texas Instruments	RCA	GE	National Semiconductor	Motorola	Fairchild	Signetic (Philips)
6	Amperex	GE	Motorola	RCA	AMI	Rockwell	Signetics (Philips)	AMD
7	National Video	RCA	Clevite	Sprague	Raytheon	General Instruments	Mostek	Fairchild
8	Ranland	Westinghouse	Fairchild	Philco/Ford	Rockwell	RCA	AMD	RCA
9	Eimac	Motorola	Hughes	Transitron	RCA	Signetics (Philips)	RCA	Harris
10	Lansdale Tube	Clevite	Sylvania	Raytheon	General Instruments	AMI	Harris	Mostek* (United Tech)

* Being taken over, at the time of going to print, by Thomson, of France.

next. Only one of the top ten US vacuum-tube manufacturers in 1955 (RCA) survived as a significant producer of transistors and integrated circuits.

The reasons for this high rate of wastage are numerous. Boards of directors and managements, for example, which have made heavy financial commitments to a particular technology tend to be reluctant to admit that they backed the wrong horse. In other cases, some senior managers find themselves incapable of again learning from scratch the different techno-economic subtleties of a new technology. And then there are the cases where clinging too long to an outmoded technology simply drives the company into bankruptcy.

The inescapable conclusion from Table 2.1 is that, contrary to popular opinion, US companies in general do not have a good track record in the management of electronics technology. A few, however, have obviously exhibited very impressive abilities and growth, and it is these successful companies, of course, on which the American domination (and management reputation) has been based. What it all adds up to is that the overwhelming success of American companies in the electronic component business was, not unexpectedly, something of a lottery. With so many companies starting up, in such favourable conditions, some at least were likely to succeed in a big way. And many certainly did.

There are some other advantages that US semiconductor companies, in particular, have enjoyed. An analysis of this industry, particularly over the two decades between about 1960 and 1980, shows that the distinguishing organizational feature of the successful companies was that they were geared to react swiftly to new developments. In many cases, as has been said, they also had the tremendous advantage of being led by an impressive new breed of technical entrepreneurs skilled at their trade.

Although it is a truism, the electronics industry, like every other, depends on the right people being given the right tools, and the right motivation, to do the right job. In this sense, the US had considerable early advantages over Europe and Japan since the evidence is very strong that entrepreneurial drive and freedom were essential conditions for success in the formative years of the electronics business, and these characteristics seem to thrive preferentially in America's relatively *laissez faire* economy.

Certainly the evidence is strong that the IC ventures of General Electric, Westinghouse and others in the 1960s were stifled by the heavy hand of central, corporate managements unskilled in the art (and it was indeed an art form in those days) of constructing strategies for success in the fiercely competitive, wholly American semiconductor business of those days.

This hypothesis is further strengthened by the fact that Motorola, one of the very few companies which succeeded in the IC business despite having its primary roots in another segment of the electronics industry, had the good sense to start up its semiconductor venture in Phoenix, Arizona, well removed from its corporate base in Chicago.

All of this, of course, does not constitute a unique indictment of American management, but does suggest that, like their counterparts in other countries, American managers are just as fallible.

TECHNOLOGY PUSH

As already described, the American computer companies in general, and IBM in particular, exerted a highly beneficial influence on the US semiconductor industry during its formative years, especially in providing a demand for the highest-performance, lowest-cost devices which the semiconductor manufacturers could produce. This 'demand pull' was a vital factor during the earliest years, when the entrepreneurs and their financial backers needed the conviction to back their courage in ploughing more and more investment into new production facilities and new products.

Moore's Law

The truly revolutionary nature of the integrated circuit was now becoming clearer, however. To some of the men (very few women were involved) at the heart of this new IC business came the dawning realization that they had within their grasp a technology so latently powerful that its eventual limitations could not be foreseen. For example, in 1964, Dr Gordon Moore[3] first observed that the number of components (e.g. transistors) contained within a single state-of-the-art IC was roughly doubling every year, a relationship which has held true enough over 20 years or so (see Figure 2.1) for it now to be known as Moore's Law.

Moreover, it was also coming to be realized that, once a new product or process refinement had 'bedded down', the cost of producing an unpackaged chip was almost independent of its complexity provided the (small) area of silicon used remained more or less constant. And, such

---

[3] Quoted by R. N. Noyce in 'Microelectronics', *Scientific American*, **237**, 63.

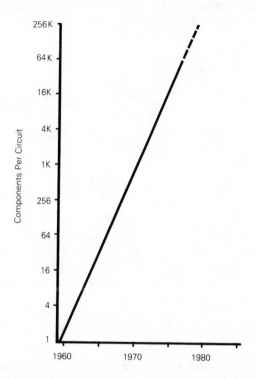

Figure 2.1. Moore's Law: the systematic increase in chip complexity (after Warner & Grung, *Transistors*, copyright 1983 by John Wiley & Sons Inc., with permission).

was the pace of technological progress, Moore's doubling of complexity per annum could be achieved without significant expansion of the silicon area per chip. In other words, a doubling of chip complexity need imply no increase in chip cost – which was a pretty startling conclusion to an industry which, like most others, had naturally assumed that the more you get, the more you pay.

The virtuous circles of microelectronics

Nevertheless, in the minds of the more astute thinkers in the IC industry certain key relationships began to be recognized which, while certainly not unique to microelectronics, are particularly effective and powerful in this case. The business strategies of the leading IC manufacturers came to be influenced profoundly by these relationships, which can be represented by two interlocking virtuous circles (Figure 2.2), viz: (1) higher

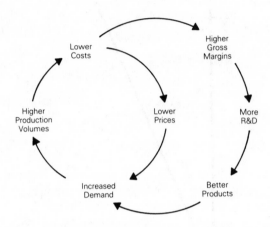

Figure 2.2.   The virtuous circles of microelectronics.

production volumes lead to better manufacturing processes and higher manufacturing yields, which lead to lower costs, which allow lower prices, which stimulate demand and lead to yet higher production volumes; and (2) these lower costs (stemming from higher production volumes) also lead to higher gross margins; which permit higher investment in R & D, which produces better products, which again stimulate demand and lead to yet higher production volumes.

Of particular importance was that these new economic facts of life were first evident to the aforementioned breed of young *American* semiconductor entrepreneurs (not, in the main, to the Boards of Directors of companies in electrical engineering or other segments of the electronics industry); *and* to their venture-capitalist partners; *and* there was, in any event, a government-stimulated blossoming of demand; *and* the growing designer-coupling activities guaranteed an enthusiastic user reception to new, improved ICs; *and* permeating all of this was a healthy US economy, a high level of business confidence and a national penchant for new ideas and new products. The latently revolutionary seed of microelectronics thus fell on to optimumly fertile *American* soil.

Forward pricing: more for less

One result of all this was that some of the leaders of the American IC industry, confident of falling costs if production volumes could be increased, set out to stimulate market growth through aggressive, forward pricing. That is, knowing their production economics, and driven by ambition and the exciting competition for growth, they deliberately chose to maximize the long-term expansion of markets at the expense of short-term profits.

And it worked beautifully. Indeed, it is such a perfect example of the constructive operation of the entrepreneurial, competitive, free market that it deserves more attention from the theoretical economists than it has so far received.

Because it is so fundamental a strategic factor in the global domination of commercial IC markets which US producers achieved throughout the 1960s and early 1970s, but at some risk of repetition, this phenomenon can be described in other words. Namely, that the IC entrepreneurs used 'technology push' to create a demand for their products – a demand which would have developed less swiftly, and in some instances not at all, had they not first understood, and second, practised the massively effective economies of scale offered by microelectronics technology.

Three groups benefitted from the thirst for business growth of the archetypal, high-rolling, hard-riding, white-hatted cowboys of the American IC industry of the 1960s. *They* did, of course, except for those who couldn't stand the punishing pace. (The history of the American semiconductor industry is littered with famous alcoholics and divorcees).

And their key employees benefitted too. Generally through the mechanism of stock options, thousands of employees in the American IC industry have made substantial capital gains from the increasing value of their companies' shares; the number of dollar millionaires created by the US semiconductor industry alone (i.e. excluding the rest of the electronics industry) is probably well in excess of 200 already, and there are more to come.

The others to benefit were the users of components – in other words, the designers and producers of equipments and systems. These, by and large, constituted a relatively more conservative, traditional community, and yet they were remarkably quick – in America – to recognize the advantages of embracing microelectronics technology in their equipment and to enjoy the performance 'highs' offered by the silicon pushers. Given efficient and reasonably inexpensive communications (i.e. by air and/or by telephone within the continental United States), makers of equipments got together with the vendors of advanced microelectronic components, and learned not only about the breathtaking performance capabilities of each new generation of ICs but, equally impressive, of alluring price projections.

The maker–user interface

The whole process of designer coupling now began to loom impressively in reinforcement of America's high-tech hegemony. Designers of leading-edge ICs could not bring their prototypes to production-ready perfection without significant, frequent and intimate interactions with leading-edge users. And these users, of course, needed to know what was in the minds of the leading IC designers in order that their equipment prototypes could take optimum advantage of the best and the cheapest chips.

This coupling of the skills and needs of the makers and users of ICs was exceedingly fruitful in the US. The exchange of knowledge and experience during the development process enabled both the component and equipment companies to fine-tune their ultimate products, with obviously beneficial results on general market acceptability. It was, and still is, one of the 'secret' ingredients of America's success.

The sharing of information involved in designer coupling requires reasonably close physical proximity between the maker and user, and is most efficient if it occurs within a skill cluster. It also demands that they speak the same language. For these reasons, it has occurred to only a very modest degree in Europe, as we shall see. In Japan, however, which has dense concentrations of industrial activity in places like Tokyo and Osaka, designer coupling became a major factor in its gathering IT strength once its IC producers eventually established a world-class capability (see Chapter 3).

The result of all these facets of technology push was that many of the equipment makers in the United States leapt even further ahead of their non-American competitors. In short, almost the whole of the US electronics industry began to enjoy rapid growth fuelled primarily by microelectronics, and the men who managed this growth were almost invariably young, technically trained and, as will be seen later, increasingly aware of the strong economies-of-scale effect and concomitant need to capture non-American markets.

So technology push worked marvellously well – in America, by Americans, and for Americans. It worked because all of the ingredients of success existed – in America. But outside America, as will become clear, many of the lessons to be learned from this scintillating example of high-tech free enterprise have, even yet, to be fully assimilated.

ENTER THE MICROPROCESSOR

As the decade of the sixties swung by, it was a case of 'all (American) systems go'. Makers of computers, instruments, office equipment, military systems and industrial control systems were jumping on the silicon bandwagon, generating new products and capturing new markets. Together with their component suppliers, they became a small but seething part of the US economy, with total (electronics) sales in 1970 representing about 2.5 per cent of the gross domestic product. The electronics industry was on its way.

But, no matter how much senior managements may regret it, and fight it, and try to ignore it, technologies tend to develop their own momentum, especially one as radical and revolutionary as IC technology. Thus, as soon as one major technical hurdle has successfully been leapt, the dictates of competition, and the ambitions of designers to stretch the technology to its limit, rapidly bring the next hurdle into view.

The commonality conundrum

Not surprisingly, then, a cloud, no bigger than a micro-chip, appeared on the horizon in the late 1960s. Stated baldly, the IC industry had, through the combination of its innovative skills and mass-production economics, painted itself into a corner. Integrated circuits were capable of being made extremely cheaply, but only if they were made in enormous quantities. On the other hand, as the circuits contained within the chips became progressively more complex, the number of applications for which each IC design was suited became progressively more restricted.

This effect is illustrated in Figure 2.3, which shows qualitatively how the commonality of applications decreased as chip complexity increased through the various IC 'generations' of small-scale integration (SSI), medium-scale integration (MSI) and large-scale integration (LSI). But, as the figure suggests, help was at hand, and it came in 1971 in the form of the microprocessor, yet another seminal invention in the continuing development of the microelectronics industry.

The microprocessor sprang from the same Fairchild/Intel intellectual powerhouse as had so many other crucial semiconductor inventions of the 1950s and 1960s, which is to say that behind it lay the guiding philosophies of Drs R. N. Noyce, G. E. Moore and A. S. Grove. In essence, what the microprocessor had which was entirely new, was a degree of 'on-chip programmability', which is an ability for its on-chip memory to be programmed by software, *after complete manufacture*, to

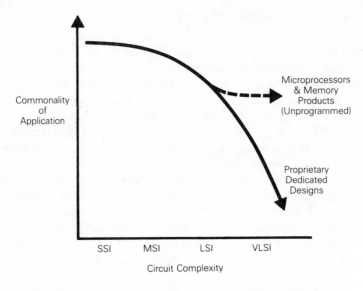

Figure 2.3.   Commonality of IC applications *versus* chip complexity

carry out a variety of different logical operations. Thus, at a stroke, the vicious circle of greater complexity:reduced commonality:higher cost was broken, and the IC industry was set free to resume its unfettered growth.

The first microprocessor, needless to say, was a relatively simple device. In the jargon of the trade, it was a 4-bit processor, meaning that it had the capability of performing logical operations involving the use of four binary digits of information. But, such is the power of the innovatory forces acting in the IC industry, it was not long before 8-bit and 16-bit microprocessors were developed, and, more recently, 32-bit microprocessors have made their appearance.

With each new generation, the microprocessor became capable of performing logical functions (i.e. computing) more rapidly and more cheaply, to the point where it achieved, more or less on its own, a computing capability (on a $\frac{1}{4} \times \frac{1}{4}''$ sliver of silicon, it needs to be remembered) which was comparable to that of the physically large, power-hungry computers of the early 1960s. It offered, and still does, as big a step forward for digital systems as did the original integrated circuit.

MEMORIES ARE MADE OF THIS

As well as the ability to perform logical functions on streams of digital data, the process of computing requires the capacity to store, or remember, some of these electronic signals. This memory function had long been a targetted market for the semiconductor industry and, as far back as the early 1960s, memory ICs had been designed with the ability to store a modest number (typically 16, 32 and 64) of binary digits (i.e. bits). These early semiconductor memory chips, however, were designed around the then-prevailing bipolar process, although this was not proving to be entirely suitable for all of the memory tasks which had to be performed.

MOS: the process with the mostest

Fortunately, towards the end of the decade the metal:oxide:silicon (MOS) process was coming to the fore and it became evident that this type of structure was particularly well suited to the job of making memories. In particular, the MOS process was conducive to the design of both read-only memory (ROM), whereby the appropriate memory configuration is permanently etched into place on the silicon chip, and to random-access memory (RAM), in which the electronic state of any element in a grid can be set or interrogated individually. Moreover, designs were produced for both static RAMs (in which the state of the memory is maintained permanently, provided that the electrical power is not interrupted) and dynamic RAMs (which, in the absence of 'refresh' signals, only retain the memory pattern for a few micro-seconds).

Despite this apparent drawback of MOS dynamic RAMs, their basic memory cell structure is so simple that they could be manufactured very cheaply and in relatively high-density single-chip configurations. For this reason, considerable design talent in the United States – in both the computer and IC companies – was invested in devising system solutions to overcome the problem of the transient nature of the memory. Such was the advanced state of the designers' art by then, that answers promptly emerged.

The real breakthrough of the IC makers into the memory business – and the event which spelled the death-knell of the then-ubiquitous ferrite-core memory – came with Intel's announcement, in 1970, of the first 1024-bit dynamic RAM, the famous 1103 1-kilobit RAM. This device had the massive, dual impact of bringing widespread respectability to both MOS technology and to the use of semiconductor memory. It ranks, therefore, as yet another major milestone in the onward march of IC technology.

The arrival of the very cheap, standardized, high-capacity memory IC also represented a major new strategic factor in the development of the electronics industry in general, with substantial effects not only in the United States but in Japan also, as will be seen later.

Before the advent of the Intel 1103, some of the more far-sighted IC producers in the United States had begun to question whether their phenomenally high growth rates (typically 18 per cent per annum average sales growth over, in many cases, six to ten years) could be sustained for long into the future. Where were all these memory bits and logic elements ('gates'), which they were becoming so proficient at producing, going to be used? Where were the (new) applications? Who would be the (new) buyers?

What no one realized at the time was that the world (the industrialized, relatively wealthy parts of it, that is) had a latent capacity to use electronic memory to an almost unlimited degree – provided it was cheap enough. And here, fortuitously, was the MOS memory, designed around the simplest kind of transistor structure, and capable of being densely packed and made very cheaply. In other words, the IC industry now had a true 'commodity' product.

Although this evolving story of the (mainly American) semiconductor industry might already seem too full of 'gung-ho' events to be wholly believable, yet another 'unbelievable' milestone had been reached. Because it wasn't just the computer industry which leapt at the opportunity to build new kinds of electronic data-processing systems designed around the availability of massive quantities of very cheap memory. The portable calculator manufacturers (very much in their infancy in the early 1970s) gradually came to recognize the tremendous product-enhancement possibilies of cheap memory. And so did the designers of electronic watches and clocks, and electronic instruments, and telecommunications products, and electronic typewriters (soon to evolve – using memory – into word processors), and consumer electronics generally, and video games, and so on, and so on.

The cost revolution

The combination of this immense growth in demand for MOS memory ICs and the dominating influence of economies of scale in the IC industry, resulted in an unprecedented tumbling of costs, to the extent that, in the

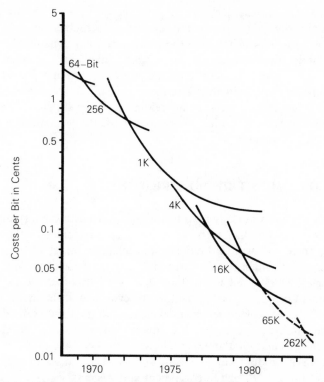

Figure 2.4. The tumbling costs of semiconductor memory ICs (after Noyce, copyright 1977 by *Scientific American*, with permission).

course of ten years or so, the cost of producing one bit of MOS memory fell by a factor of at least 100.

This astonishing process has been well documented by Noyce[4], who first produced the series of curves shown in Figure 2.4. This portrays the cost-per-bit dropping from a level of about 2 cents in 1968 (for the 16-bit chip), to a level of about one-hundredth of a cent in 1985 (for the 256-kbit chip). Thus, over approximately 17 years, memory ICs (with the actual chip size remaining fairly constant) increased in complexity over 400 times while, *at the same time*, the cost-per-bit dropped by a factor of about 200.

It is difficult to find appropriate words to describe this monumental

---

[4] R. N. Noyce in 'Microelectronics', *Scientific American*, **237**, 63.

achievement to the layman without seeming to verge on the hysterical. Fortunately, the facts more or less speak for themselves. Moreover, the process is far from finished, and the 1 and 4 megabit dynamic RAMs are already under development. If, as is highly likely, the semiconductor industry can continue to develop techniques for improving the resolution of the hyperfine lines which determine the density of transistor structures on the silicon chips, there is no reason to believe that the next 17 years will not witness similar progress in both the size and the cost of semiconductor memory.

SEMI-CUSTOM: A TAILORED RESPONSE

Although this is specifically *not* a history of the semiconductory industry, much emphasis has had to be given to microelectronics in these early chapters since this was undoubtedly the major enabling technology, or force of change, which operated within the international electronics industry during the 1960s and 1970s. Indeed, it is still true that the continuing development of ICs (as exemplified by the evolution of the memory chip, described above) remains an essential element in the future growth of the electronics industry generally. For this reason, it is useful to conclude this brief chronicle of the *American* IC industry, with mention of the latest wave of product innovation — one which promises to provide yet more fuel for growth of the equipment and systems segments.

'Commodity' economics versus custom needs

One of the drawbacks of microelectronics technology, as explained, is that its full economic potential is only realized when it can be used to manufacture enormous quantities of identical chips. There are many potential applications for ICs, however, where either the electronic performance required is so particular, despite high-volume usage, or a special performance is required *and* the requirement is for only a small number of chips, that the standard approach of designing the equipment around 'catalogue' ICs cannot be used.

In the former case (i.e. special performance, but high-volume usage, of which the automotive electronics industry can provide some good examples), it is often worthwhile to have a special (i.e. custom) IC designed for that specific purpose. Indeed, an ever-increasing number of electronic equipment companies now feel justified in setting up their own in-house IC design and wafer-fabrication facilities in order to give them the ability to produce their own custom ICs.

There has been a serious problem, however, in satisfying the needs of the latter kind of users; that is, those who need special-performance ICs but only in relatively modest numbers (of which the defence sector is a good example). One solution has been to evade the problem by adopting a different design philosophy – one, that is, that starts with the assumption that catalogue ICs *must* be used. But this usually entails cost penalties, and it is sometimes impossible to achieve the required overall performance (e.g. the speed of processing the data signals) without putting more of the total system on to single chips. Fortunately, the inherent power and flexibility of IC technology again provides a solution.

Customization by connection

In this case, it had been realized since the early 1960s that it should be possible in principle to produce a chip containing an array of identical, finished but unconnected logic elements, and then to design the final interconnection pattern according to the particular logic function which was required from the number of elements available. In fact, such a technique had been in use for several years in the production of the MOS read-only memory (ROM) chips.

By this means, it was reasoned, the final product would benefit from combining the very low costs which can be achieved by manufacturing large quantities of identical circuits, with the 'customized' performance obtained by tailoring only the final, interconnection-defining step of the total fabrication process.

The problem lay, however, in the task of actually designing this final, interconnection pattern. This was not too difficult in the early days, when only 50–100 gates had to be connected. In fact, most of the pioneering work in this area was carried out by the British electronics company, Ferranti, whose Semiconductor Division carved out what was claimed to be about 30 per cent of the 1980 total world market for what it calls uncommitted logic arrays (ULAs), and what are known generically as semi-custom ICs.

Design automation

As the per-chip gate count increased to hundreds and thousands, however, the design options and constraints became too onerous to be handled efficiently by the human brain. The solution, of course, was to apply the immense logical ('number-crunching') capabilities of computers to the job of laying out the interconnection pattern, taking account of the plethora of design rules which had gradually evolved. And this conceptually simple step of using computer-aided design (CAD) proved to be the real take-off point for semi-custom ICs, creating the small irony of computers designing circuits many of which would be used incestuously in other computers.

An additional small irony (but one with strong reflections of geographical differences towards risks, technology and business strategies in general) was that Ferranti, coincidentally one of the world's first manufacturers of digital computers, held back from making the same whole-hearted investment in the large and expensive CAD systems (which were becoming essential for creating the customized interconnection patterns) as some of the Johnny-come-lately semi-custom IC producers of the US and Japan. The discussion of the European electronics industry (Chapter 4) will show that this sort of lack of investment, often more a matter of financial poverty than management choice, is a common thread running through its decline since about the mid-1960s.

Instead, it was Silicon Valley which – once again – showed the way ahead, this time led by a 1980 semiconductor start-up company, LSI Logic, founded by W. J. Corrigan. And to illustrate just what *can* be done with a new technology or product, if well managed and properly funded (and, to be fair, located in the US), at the end of only its first full year of operation (1982) LSI Logic achieved total sales of *c.*$5 million and surged to *c.*$160 million by 1985. Meanwhile poor (literally poor: i.e. starved of funds) Ferranti had increased its ULA sales from $60 million to about $100 million.

It wasn't only the US semiconductor industry which identified, and vigorously responded to, the business opportunities represented by the advent of semi-custom ICs of sufficient complexity to excite substantial user interest and demand. Nevertheless, once again the old American formula worked: a viable 'new' technology, plus informed (and substantial) customers, plus skilled managements, plus adequate financial investment, plus a *willingness to take risks*, equals success.

This generalized formula for achieving profit from an industrial technology hasn't changed for generations, but what does seem to have changed is the main geographical location where all of these ingredients of success are simultaneously present. It used to be Europe, but drifted westwards to America. Now, as will be seen, there are signs that the focus is moving further westwards towards Japan.

In any event, despite losing some of its total domination of world markets during the late 1970s/early 1980s, the US semiconductor industry continues to exhibit an impressive resilience. And while that remains the case most of the other parts of the American electronics industry can take comfort from their physical, intellectual and philosophical proximity to these sometime silicon cowboys.

FROM SMALL BEGINNINGS

To round off this outline of the rise and rise of the American electronics industry, it is merely necessary to record that the powerful engine of microelectronics[5] hauled into the last quarter of the twentieth century a gigantic train of chip-dependent equipments and systems. As one measure, during 1983 (see Chapter 5) total US factory shipments of electronics goods were valued at approximately $144 billion, which meant that the American electronics industry was then about three times that of Japan.

By way of comparison, US factory shipments of automobiles in 1983 amounted to about $70 billion, and the Gross Domestic Product of France was approximately $520 billion (at average 1983 exchange rates).

This very substantial American 'sunrise' industry had grown, in only 20 years or so, from economic insignificance to represent about 20 per cent of the total manufacturing sector of the US economy[6], and had overtaken all the 'smokestack' segments. Its products ranged from minute precision-engineered parts for micro-circuit packages, to gigantic number-crunching mainframe computers (such as the Cray 2); from cheap and cheerful $5 watches to new public switching systems costing upwards of $1 billion to design; from simple but highly reliable silicon solar cells to hair-thin optical fibres capable of carrying almost limitless numbers of simultaneous telephone calls; from 'spreadsheet' software packages to Space Invaders; from word processors to voice synthesizers; from electronic dashboard displays to laser diodes; and from sophisticated sensors capable of monitoring the sharp end of an oil drill to a cheap, 'go-anywhere' telephone handset.

Moreover, it had spawned important new business – for example, in designing software (for computers and for more mundane purposes, such as video games) and in the specialized distribution and marketing of mass-produced products such as the personal computer.

---

[5] As Cicero wrote, *omnium verum principia parva sunt* (the beginnings of all things are small).

[6] *The World in Figures* 4th edition, published by the Economist Newspaper limited, 1984.

3 Land of the Rising Sunrise:

Japan's Leviathans capture the high ground

Numerous books have attempted to analyse and explain the post-war Japanese economic 'miracle', so there would be little point in going over the same ground here. Nevertheless, certain key elements of this enviable surge of industrial growth are germane to the electronics sector specifically, and need to be fitted into place in building a comprehensive picture of the principal players in the international battle for IT markets now in progress.

MIGHTY MITI

With hindsight, it is clear that, in the 1950s, Japan was a nation possessing a number of vital (albeit, still latent) advantages. Probably the most important of these was a cohesive population of over 100 million, unified in its commitment to the restoration of national honour following the traumas of 1945. Furthermore, the exchange rate for the yen was such that Japan's labour costs were very much lower than those of all the other major industrialized countries, and the prevailing social mores led ineluctably to a highly disciplined work force.

But there was another powerful weapon in the Japanese industrial armoury – the Ministry of International Trade and Industry (MITI). There is now widespread acknowledgement of the influential role which MITI has played in the industrial renaissance of Japan, and nowhere has this been more clearly manifest than in the electronics sector.

It has certainly not been a case of MITI throwing Japanese taxpayer's money at a problem, however. Indeed, in most cases its direct financial contributions have been modest. Nor has it been required to function as a national planning body in the sense of setting specific five-year targets and marshalling resources to achieve them.

Its critical role, which it appears to have played with consummate skill, has been to orchestrate national strategy and to tease out a concensus from otherwise-competing Japanese companies. And, from all of the evidence so far available, MITI seems to have possessed quite remarkable insights, not only into technology, product and market trends across a wide spectrum of industrial activity, but also into the relative strengths and weaknesses of Japan's international competitors.

As will be seen, the influence of MITI permeates the success story of the Japanese electronics industry. Although its touch has invariably been light, its impact on the orientation of R & D investments, and its occasionally catalytic effect in bringing together – and partially funding – a major national effort (as in the VLSI) programme, discussed later), has been of incalculable benefit.

THAT'S ENTERTAINMENT

Given the evidence of its omniscient perception, it is not difficult to believe that MITI identified, very early on, the consumer electronics segment as the soft underbelly of American high technology. Here, they may well have reasoned in the 1950s, was the beachhead from which Japanese electronic goods might fan out to over-run market territory occupied by Americans. If so, of course, MITI would simply have been repeating the same strategy (penetrate on a narrow front; secure the logistical/political base; then broaden the attack) which had served Japan so well in the international markets for products as diverse as ships, motorcycles and cameras.

Sounds of the sixties

In any event, the companies which first identified a promising market niche for portable music and which first marketed on a worldwide scale germanium-based transistor radios were overwhelmingly Japanese. Their rewards came swiftly, as the younger generation, in particular, reacted enthusiastically to the muscial outpourings of the 'Swinging Sixties'.

It was Sony, followed by a host of Japanese industrial companies, who rushed to fill this rapid international upsurge in the demand for electronic entertainment of expanding versatility. For this was the period when the

emancipated world began the irreversible shift away from seeking collective amusement outside the home to staying in to enjoy its chosen
form of electronically delivered entertainment.

Television was now coming of age and, largely thanks to RCA in
America, was just being blessed with the extra dimension of colour. The
record industry was switching pell-mell to the new 45 and 33 rpm vinyl
records, while the world's pop song writers strove to feed an apparently
insatiable appetite for on-demand music. And all of this heady growth
was made possible by the fact that, in America, Europe and Japan, full
employment and rising prosperity granted the common man, for the first
time, sufficient discretionary income to gratify his craving for variety,
excitement and music.

It is possible, of course, that it was simply good fortune that the
Japanese electronics industry struck just the right note at the right time.
But the American consumer electronics companies, despite their natural
advantages in the world's biggest cohesive market, blew it – as already
noted. Europe, although led by the redoubtable Philips, and containing
(then-thrusting) enterprises of the calibre of Grundig, Telefunken, Thomson and Thorn, generally failed to see (or, having seen, to act upon)
the immense economic implications of this new technology-based social
revolution. Indeed, even the colossal energy and creativity of the British
pop music industry in the 1960s (fortuitously sharing a common language
with the vast American consumer population) failed to stimulate UK
electronics companies into making the kind of financial commitments
which were clearly warranted by the immense business potential. No
signs of synergy there.

And yet even MITI, back in 1960, could hardly have been percipient
enough to realize just how vast this business potential really was. First
there is what can loosely be called the audio segment, embracing radios,
'hi-fi' components (such as tuners, record and cassette-players and loud-
speakers) and 'Walkman'-type personal stereo systems. Starting from the
humble transistor radio, and excluding peripheral products such as in-
car entertainment systems, blank and pre-recorded media (such as records
and cassette tapes) and the 'software' activities of the substantial pop
music industry, the worldwide audio hardware industry had grown to
the point where aggregate sales in 1984 reached about $30 billion[1].
Clearly, the demand for on-demand music has been music in the ears of
the equipment makers – overwhelmingly Japanese in this first phase of
market growth.

---

[1] Valued at street (retail) prices, in contradistinction to the data in Part Two, which are in
terms of factory prices.

Quality and quantity

The television business, however, posed new strategic problems for MITI and its Japanese industrial colleagues. By the 1960s there had emerged three entirely different systems for colour-television broadcasts, none of Japanese origin. America introduced the first, NTSC-TV[2], which suffered somewhat from early development in that its colour quality was generally inferior to the subsequent systems patented in West Germany (PAL) and France (SECAM). Japan, under the post-war American influence, had adopted the US 525-line TV standard, and this led it also to adopt the NTSC colour system.

Later, when colour-TV broadcasting started in Europe in the mid-1960s, the Europeans were able to employ the PAL and SECAM patents to control the Japanese attack on the European colour-TV market, although only to a limited extent, as we shall see later.

Japanese companies were quick to recognize that, in view of the self-evident economies of scale involved, inter alia, in the production of colour TV tubes, a domestic colour-TV industry could only succeed in a big way by capturing substantial foreign markets.

This they did first in the US where it was easier to penetrate the NTSC colour-set market, since this was the type of set being produced in high volume for the Japanese domestic market. Gradually the Japanese built up exports to the US, but in the mid-1970s, the Japanese colour-TV set imports into the US leapt dramatically. This caused an outcry from the American TV industry and forced the US government to negotiate an Orderly Marketing Agreement (OMA) with Japan to limit set imports to a mutually acceptable level. Leading Japanese TV manufacturers then quickly established US manufacturing facilities (sometimes by acquisition) to surmount this barrier.

Although domestic US manufacturers have subsequently been able to retain a major share of the US market, it has been a bloody fight with severely reduced margins in recent years.

In Europe, AEG-Telefunken (which held the patents on the PAL colour-TV system adopted by most European countries) was able to limit the Japanese penetration of European markets in the way it granted licences to Japanese set manufacturers. The most significant restriction was to disbar them from manufacturing sets with picture tube sizes greater than 19 inches (diagonal) because, in the early colour-TV market

---

[2] Sometimes claimed by industry wags to be an acronym for Never-the-Same-Colour-Twice Video.

development phase in Europe, the biggest market share was taken by large-screen sets.

This, however, was still not sufficient to limit Japanese set imports into certain European countries to levels that were acceptable to the European industry (i.e. below ten per cent of the market). As a result, OMA deals were struck between MITI and various national bodies to limit TV-set imports from Japan to these levels.

A major reason for the Japanese success was that the TV manufacturers in Japan had acquired an image of building sets with a high level of performance and reliability. This allowed the Japanese to command a higher price for their TVs, given that they were only permitted a minority market share. The ironical outcome was that Japanese manufacturers enjoyed substantial profits from a restricted market share, whereas many European setmakers were making losses on their colour-TV activities despite retaining the bulk of the market.

In order to counter their relatively poor-quality image, certain European setmakers launched crash programmes to match the Japanese in quality, but it was too late. Even today, many years after these early manoeuvres, Japanese sets are still able to command higher prices due to the image they were able to establish earlier.

From their experience of trade friction with the US over TV imports, several Japanese manufacturers started to establish European manufacturing bases early on, anticipating the imposition of more stringent tariffs and quotas. And although still requiring a PAL licence fee, European-manufactured TV sets are now free from the screen-size restrictions. However, the PAL patents expired in Germany in 1985, and will expire in the UK in 1988. They will then no longer be an obstacle, either to the Japanese or to other Far Eastern countries such as Korea.

The Japanese have therefore achieved a very significant commercial success in the colour-TV business through a combination of Japanese production techniques and domestic plus offshore (i.e. non-Japanese) manufacture. In 1984, Japanese companies produced a total of about 15 million colour-TV sets worth in aggregate $c.\$3.5$ billion at factory prices, and representing approximately 25 per cent of total world production.

In such a manner, then, did the small army of Japanese consumer electronics companies burst out of their original, tiny, product beachhead and roll on to capture major sectors of the entertainment electronics marketplace. But there was another gigantic piece of virgin territory, still in the entertainment electronics segment, for which the battle lines had first been drawn up some ten years earlier . . .

FOR THE RECORD

Back in the late 1950s, the R & D laboratories of many consumer electronics companies, in many countries, had begun working on systems, analogous to audio records and tape cassettes, by which it might be possible to play (and, perhaps, record and play back) video programmes via a television set. Most of these efforts were centred on magnetic recording techniques, similar to those used in today's computer memory tapes and audio cassettes.

The birth pangs of video

The main problem was the very much larger frequency bandwidth required by television (video) signals in comparison with audio. Thus, while a bandwidth of 15 kilohertz will allow the reproduction of music of reasonably high fidelity, an acceptable television picture requires about 3 megahertz, or 200 times as much bandwidth. This frequency requirement translates into the size and quality of the recording medium (e.g. vinyl tape coated with ferric oxide) and into the speed with which this material passes the signal-sensing device ('head') used to pick up ('read') the electronic signals recorded thereon. For this reason, acceptable audio quality can be obtained from tape travelling at the relatively low speed of a few centimetres per second, whereas video tape needs to be travelling at the much higher speed of several metres per second.

This requirement presented the erstwhile video-recording innovators with formidable technical and cost problems. One aspect of their dilemma was that, even if such tape speeds could be achieved, anything less than a very large reel or cassette of tape would be used up so rapidly that only a few minutes of programme material could be viewed (or recorded). And the inevitable corollary was the problem of somehow condensing the sheer quantity of magnetically coated tape (or disc) needed so as to bring the costs down to the point where a mass (consumer) market might be feasible.

The first successful solution was developed by the US company Ampex. It used a high-speed rotating drum holding four recording/replay heads scanned across a 2-inch wide magnetic tape that travelled relatively slowly past the head assembly. This achieved the very high head-to-tape 'writing' speed needed for the video signals. However, tape consumption was very high and was only justifiable for broadcasting purposes, as indeed was the very high cost of the recorder itself, which occupied a substantial amount of floor space. It was obviously still necessary to reduce the cost and size of the equipment, and the tape consumption, to levels that would be acceptable to domestic users.

For such reasons, the early days of experimentation on video recording techniques were difficult and contentious. Many researchers put their bets on some form of magnetic disc on which, they hoped, the signals could be recorded (and subsequently 'read') more densely. Others stuck to tape, with which much more experience had been accumulated in audio applications. And Philips was already beginning to think of a radical shift from (analogue) magnetic to (digital) optical recording techniques, of which more later.

Got it taped

The real breakthrough came with the successful development, by Toshiba in the early 1960s, of the so-called helical-scan system. This relied not on electronics technology but on a meticulous, mechanical engineering refinement of the original Ampex rotating head techniques. A $\frac{1}{2}$-inch wide magnetic tape was made to follow a helical path around a rapidly spinning drum a few centimetres in diameter to which two video recording heads were attached. While not achieving superb performance, it did allow acceptable-quality video pictures for non-broadcasting applications.

The Japanese had thus succeeded in reducing the video recorder from a very large piece of equipment, which needed to be operated and maintained by skilled engineers, down to a suitcase-sized box that could be placed on a tabletop and used by almost anyone. The video tape rcorder (VTR) could record around an hour of video on a 7-inch diameter reel of $\frac{1}{2}$-inch wide tape which cost $30, a small fraction of the broadcast-system tape cost.

However, the VTR itself at around $1500 at 1960 prices, was still too expensive for most consumers, and the helical-scan VTR was therefore directed mainly to educational and commercial users throughout the 1960s. Nevertheless, it is clear that the major Japanese companies were at this time refining the product with a view to a major attack on the consumer market.

The development efforts were primarily focussed on two key facets of the problem: major reductions in the cost of the helical-scan system itself, and housing the videotape in an easy-to-use cartridge or cassette. By achieving both of these objectives, of course, video recording would at last come within the reach and technical competence of the ordinary customer.

And that is just what happened, but not in the gentle, orderly way in which most of the world's business is conducted, but in yet another example – probably the electronics industry's most spectacular so far – of gung-ho explosive growth.

The actual technical achievement came from a costly and painstaking process of marrying sophisticated electronics with precision mechanical engineering, with great emphasis on value engineering. The first practical VCRs on the consumer market were produced by Philips in 1971 but, fatally as it turned out, too soon for the average consumer. Although the Philips' VCR was configured with all the features necessary for the consumer that had not previously been embodied in the Japanese professional VTRs (e.g. a built-in tuner for TV-programme reception, a timer to allow unattended recording, and easy connection to the antenna input of the TV), both the VCR itself and the tape-cassette costs were still too high for most consumers, and the 1-hour maximum recording time was a serious limitation.

In the mid 1970s, the Japanese companies Sony and JVC had refined the video-recording process to the point where a smaller quantity of video tape, in a paperback-book-sized cassette, could record 2 or more hours of video (later to be extended to 8 hours). The recording cost had now dropped to a few dollars per hour, and the Sony Betamax system and the JVC VHS system were quickly adopted by several other Japanese consumer electronics corporations.

Based on their vision and conviction that the era of video recording was about to burst wide open, enormous investments were then made by these Japanese companies in heavily automated factories for the production of VCRs. Prices of the equipments were now down to more acceptable levels and, to put the cap on it, several of the leading non-Japanese consumer electronics companies (such as RCA, Thomson and Thorn) were persuaded to market VHS machines on an own-label basis, through their powerful and well-established distribution channels. The fact that VHS gained increasing support from both Japanese and non-Japanese companies in the late 1970s led to its faster penetration of world markets, steadily gaining market share and achieving a dominant position against Betamax and the Philips European VCR system.

The victorious VCR

The rest, as they say, is history. Despite valiant rearguard actions by Philips and Sony, their VCR systems, although generally competitive in terms of price and performance, gradually lost worldwide market share to the massive onslaught of the VHS 'club' to the point where, in 1984, almost 75 per cent of total VCR sales were of the VHS format. Even

Philips was forced in 1984 to swallow the bitter pill of starting up production of a VHS machine, thus adding – albeit not significantly – to the competitive pressures opposing its own improved V2000 model.

Two aspects of this absorbing tale merit an additional word or two. The first is the meteoric rise of the VCR as a product of major economic significance within the global electronics industry. From modest world-wide sales of about 400,000 units in 1976, eight years later total sales of VCRs (all formats, all countries) had reached the staggering rate of 24 million units per annum, with an estimated total sales value (at factory prices) of about $10 billion. Since most of these were manufactured in Japan itself, and assuming a higher-than-average productivity figure of about $60,000 per worker per annum, it means that around 170,000 Japanese *direct* jobs were created, in only eight years or so, and all based on a single new product. Need the question ever again be raised as to why, and how, Japan has managed to avoid the high chronic unemployment levels which disfigure the economies of many of its OECD partner nations?

The second aspect, obviously, is the critical role played in this saga by strategy: not technology *per se*, nor production economics necessarily – but simple business savvy. There is, of course, a myriad of consumer products where standardization is irrelevant. Soap powder, cigarettes, handbags and the shape of wine bottles come to mind. But, it seems, when the cost of the product is dominated by economies of scale, *and* when it is technically complex, *and* when it is marketed internationally, *and* (perhaps most importantly) when the consumer must himself match a key component to its appliance, standardization becomes paramount. Thus, electric light bulbs are partly subject to these criteria and are therefore partially (i.e. at least nationally) standarized. Likewise with razor blades, batteries and refills for ballpoint pens. But it is in consumer electronics – most acutely in audio and video cassette machines – where these criteria apply with greatest collective force.

The intelligence of MITI and a majority of the Japanese electronics industry in recognizing this as a key business factor, in advance of most of its competitors, should serve as an object lesson. In fact, it is to be hoped that this message has now been so well absorbed in the minds of the captains of (the consumer electronics) industry that no major new consumer electronics product (such as electronic home movies) will ever again be fully launched without prior international agreement on standardization.

But, as will be seen, the salient importance of international standardization has yet to be fully recognized by some of the politicians and officials who devise government strategies in some parts of Europe, and other laggard regions.

NIPPON CHIPS IN

Despite its early research activity, Japan's role in the international semiconductor business was low key during the 1960s. Certainly a number of leading Japanese electrical/electronic conglomerates (mainly Hitachi, Matsushita, Mitsubishi, Nippon Electric Company and Toshiba) had developed sufficient IC capability to supply, collectively, more than half of the national demand for relatively simple microelectronic circuits, but the Japanese IC industry was far from being a competitive threat to America's domination. In particular, neither in terms of design skills nor production economics did the Japanese IC manufacturers bear comparison with the leading US semiconductor companies.

And then, at the beginning of the 1970s, something happened which was to initiate a perceptible shift of power – away from California, and towards Japan. Although dramatic in its ultimate impact, it began very quietly. And no-one who was not there could possibly know precisely how it happened.

What can be surmised from the available evidence is that a concensus emerged in Japan – probably, again, orchestrated by MITI – that the national urge to excel in electronics could not be sustained without an indigenous and fully competitive IC industry. Indeed, this would not have been a surprising conclusion since it had been much discussed, publicly, in Europe, and the innovative heartland of the American electronics industry was by then widely recognized to lie in the semiconductor laboratories of the sunbelt states of California, Texas and Arizona.

The VLSI programme

In 1971 MITI announced an LSI (large-scale integration) programme, which was, however, modest in both size and scope. But four years later the pace hotted up considerably with the start of MITI's successor programme on VLSI (very large-scale integration). This brought together six leading Japanese electronics companies to concentrate resources on the task of bringing their IC technology up to par with that of the leading US companies by the early 1980s.

As usual, the absolute magnitude of financial support directly from government (i.e. MITI) was not enormous. In this case, it was probably about $65 million (in 1978 dollar values) per annum over five years, which is less than the microelectronics support programmes currently being funded by one or two individual European countries. Again, however, the Japanese VLSI programme was constructed on an impressive foundation of knowledge of the sector, resulting in an overall national strategy which took due account of the particular strengths of the individual participating companies, which set realistic but challenging performance objectives, and which established mechanisms for encouraging the essential co-operation between the industrial partners.

It is worth noting, particularly in light of current trends in Europe, that the VLSI programme was emphatically focussed on the *development* of specific products and processes. Armed with these, it was assumed, the participating companies would then compete with each other and the rest of the world. In other words, government showed no signs of worrying about (competing) companies co-operating on projects close to commercial exploitation.

While it is clear (and is much discussed later) that national differences in Europe make this approach more politically hazardous, it is doubtful whether any government support programme will be successful which lacks MITI's robust attitude to such perceived sensitivities.

Overtaking America

As it happened, a contemporaneous shift in the underlying economics of the IC industry gave great support to MITI's VLSI strategy. In brief, the design costs of state-of-the-art commodity ICs – being mainly microprocessors and memory circuits – were escalating inexorably as the complexities of the chips increased. Furthermore, this upward trend in up-front costs was reinforced by the ever-increasing cost of building competitive new 'wafer-fab' facilities. Each quantum increase in the size (diameter) of the silicon wafers, each new generation of better (but more expensive) production and test equipment, put up the price of chips in the world's most expensive poker game.

The net result was a shift in the balance of advantage – away from the fleet-of-foot entrepreneur and towards the well-heeled corporation. Thus one of America's greatest advantages in the IC industry became a waning asset, while the intimate financial:industrial linkages so common in Japan began to assume great importance.

The stunning success of the VLSI Programme has been widely commented on, and two specific parameters can be used to measure the magnitude of this achievement. The first is the timing of the introduction of major new semiconductor products. In the 1971–3 timescale, the leading Japanese companies lagged one to two years behind their American counterparts in first marketing such 'milestone' ICs as the 4-bit microprocessor and the 1k and 4k dynamic RAMs. But, with typically single-minded concentration, and bolstered by the VLSI Programme, the Japanese companies focussed on memory circuits so that, by 1984, they had achieved something like a full year's lead in this area over the most advanced US companies[3].

The other key parameter is worldwide market share. Although the relatively closed nature of the Japanese IC market introduces an element of distortion into this parameter (and, incidentally, means that the battle for supremacy between the US and Japanese IC producers is being fought out primarily in the relatively open markets of the US and Europe), it is nevertheless valid to use any *change* in market share as a measure of the shifting balance of power.

On this basis the Japanese progress represents a daunting challenge to its competitor nations. For Japan's share of world IC merchant markets increased from roughly 17 per cent in 1975, to 24 per cent in 1978 and 30 per cent in 1982 (approximately $3 billion sales out of a global total of *c*.$10 billion)[4]. And, on present trends, Japan and America will be running neck-and-neck by the early 1990s, which would mean that, on a per-capita basis, Japan would be out-producing the US by a ratio of about 2:1.

For the rest of the world, there are both good and bad aspects of this chronicle of Japanese success. The good news, of course, is that what Japan can do today, some other country could, in principle, do tomorrow. But the bad news is that, with two very powerful nations now having a stranglehold on the world's IC markets, it will be even harder for any third party to achieve a reasonable piece of the action. The consequences of this for Europe, in particular, are dismal, and are discussed in due course.

THE SWITCH TO INFORMATION PROCESSING

This initial attack by Japan on the American domination of the IC business was concentrated unequivocally on the memory market (shades,

---

[3] Nippon Electric Company, NEC, began mass production of 256 k DRAMs in December 1983, about 12 months before similar levels of production were reached by any American manufacturer.

[4] These percentages would be somewhat lower if based on figures for *total* IC production, since captive (i.e. non-merchant) sales are significantly higher in the US. Nevertheless, the trend of increasing Japanese competitiveness would still be very evident.

again, of the 'spearhead' strategy!). Although this product segment is quite narrow, it seems inevitable that, some time during the late 1980s, Japanese companies will expand from this base to become fully competitive – even dominant, perhaps – in all mainstream IC product segments, including microprocessors and semi-custom ICs. There is some evidence, in fact, to suggest that for MITI, at least, the all-important task of establishing a world-class IC industry in Japan is now close to completion.

So, with the most important enabling technology now well nigh mastered, and with domination established of most of the consumer electronics markets, the question the world should be asking is what Japan will do for an encore. From what follows the short answer seems to be: everything.

Mainframes under control

Going as far back as the early 1960s, the electronic data processing (EDP) or computer segment has been fingered for special attention by MITI, and attendance on the needs and aims of the Japanese mainframe-computer companies can be seen to run like a continuous thread through each phase of MITI's initiatives in the electronics sector. This was especially true in the case of the VLSI programme, and several other government programmes have been structured so as to assist the computer industry, most recently that on so-called fifth-generation computers.

The reason, of course, is that whereas IC technology holds the key to product innovation, performance and cost in the electronics sector generally, in terms of economic importance (e.g. direct employment) it is very much a lightweight compared with, inter alia, the computer segment. Moreover, just as ICs lie at the heart of, and pervade, information (data)-processing systems, so do computers, of one sort or another, represent the working guts of a very wide range of other electronic equipments and systems – from modern digitial telephone exchanges, through factory automation systems, to the relatively humble word processor.

As might be expected, therefore, with typical commitment, concensus and clarity, MITI long ago set about creating conditions favourable to the emergence of a viable Japanese computer industry able to compete on equal terms with that of the United States, and success is already tangible.

In fact, at the larger end of the spectrum of computer systems (which range from small personal computers to enormous number crunchers), Japanese companies such as Fujitsu and Hitachi are already a match for their American mainframe counterparts such as Control Data and Cray

Research. Japan does not, of course, have a company to approach the size of IBM, the computer colossus – but then, it seems unlikely that any country will ever again witness the emergence, other than by acquisitions, of an electronics company of such awesome proportions [5]. Nor is Japan yet as powerful a force in the world's mini-computer and personal-computer markets as it threatens to become.

Beyond that, it is to be expected that Japan will become increasingly successful in product areas contiguous to, and synergetic with, segments where it has already achieved world standing. Thus, towed along by the successes in the IC industry, Japanese companies are now becoming a major force (in fact, threaten to take over from under the noses of the Americans) in the strategically, economically and technologically important segment of semiconductor production and test equipment. Another example is the rapid growth enjoyed by Japanese manufacturers (such as TDK) of magnetic tape, riding on the backs, to some extent, of the Japanese hegemony over audio- and video-cassette players.

The Japanese office

Electronic office equipment seems, on the face of it, an odd mixture of success and failure for the Japanese, although this mixed bag of results can be understood relatively easily. In electrostatic copiers, on the one hand, Japanese producers such as Ricoh, Canon, Sharp, Toshiba, Minolta and Konishiroku have already bitten heavily into the market domination once enjoyed by Xerox and its close partners, Rank Xerox and Fuji Xerox. The US Xerox plain-paper copier market share, despite the heavy protection afforded by a small mountain of patents on the original xerographic process, dropped from about 96 per cent in 1970 to 46 per cent in 1980, during which period the production by Japanese copier manufacturers increased by over an order of magnitude – from $c.30,000$ units in 1970 to $c.340,000$ in 1980.

This, however, was not as impressive an achievement as it might at first seem because, by the mid-1970s, the Xerox business empire had begun to exhibit some of the sclerotic symptoms of corporations which have grown too old and too fat. Moreover, the patent protection was wearing a bit thin. All that the Japanese companies had to do was to develop an array of copiers which out-performed the Xerox range, were

---

[5] In 1984, IBM had sales of about $45 billion representing 11–12 per cent of the total, worldwide, all-products electronics market, in many segments of which, of course, IBM does not currently trade at all.

cheaper and of higher intrinsic quality and reliability; and then go out and market them globally with skill and dedication.

Obviously, it is easier said than done, even against such a cumbersome and slow-witted adversary as Xerox then was. Nevertheless, it wasn't, in the main, the European companies who successfully attacked this vulnerable giant, nor even the Americans. It was the Japanese – again!

The other side of the office-equipment coin is the relative failure of the Japanese companies – so far, at least – in the general area of text-processing equipment (electronic typewriters and word processors, in the main). A plausible explanation is the difficulty which the Japanese are bound to encounter in designing electronic equipment which is intimately linked to the Roman alphabet. This cryptographic hurdle is undeniably a serious obstacle for the ideograph-indoctrinated Japanese design engineers to overcome. Nevertheless, once the Japanese companies succeed in developing a fully viable Kanji-based text processor (as they will), enormous business opportunities will lie before them, not only in Japan and South East Asisa, but also in China as this vast market opens up and grows (as it must).

There is another sense in which this 'Kanji syndrome' could turn out to be a stimulus to major new developments. This could arise because of intensive Japanese concentration on developing techniques for character recognition and generation (i.e. because of the Kanji problem). If (or rather, when) this occurs it would give Japanese companies the ability to leap-frog over the more cumbersome (and expensive) text-processing methods currently used by Western companies. And that, naturally, would result in a strong Japanese attack on the worldwide text-processing market, as well as yielding substantial technical advantages in other equipment areas likely to be receptive to the advent of optical recognition techniques (e.g. industrial automation).

TELEPHONE EXTENSION

In recent years, the telecommunications business in many countries has started to become electronic in nature, having at last broken free from the shackles imposed by its electromechanical origins. These ancient switching techniques have served society well for many decades but have become far too unreliable, noisy and slow to meet the needs of the information era.

The transformation to digital telecommunications networks and sophisticated digital exchanges (public switches), for both voice and data traffic, is now well under way in most of the world's industrialized nations. Nowhere is this changeover more advanced, and more imaginatively planned, than in Japan.

Broadband bonanza

The clearest evidence of this lies in the publicly announced development of Japan's Integrated Network System (INS). Although this is not the place to go into great detail, INS is ultimately planned to be a fully integrated broadband network based throughout on high capacity, fibre-optic cables with the capability of carrying a wide range of services. Thus, in the mid-to-late 1990s, it is expected that essentially the whole of Japan – e.g. homes, offices, factories, theatres, cinemas, hospitals, hotels, golf courses, telephone kiosks, computer bureaux and dentists – will be 're-wired' so that all of these premises will be connected together via a vast broadband communications network which will encompass all of the relevant new electronics technologies.

Once this network is in place in most of the country, communications will become radically cheaper (the price charged for point-to-point connections will probably tend to become less distance-independent), and a large range of new services (many of them two-way, or interactive) will become available and affordable. In this way, the videophone will at last become a commercial reality; shopping-from-home and banking-from-home (tele-shopping and tele-banking), based on expanded use of television 'terminals', will become commonplace; working-at-home, using personal, intelligent work stations (i.e. computers with data, graphics and text-processing capabilites) will begin to become significant enough to presage a reduction in business travel (by road, rail and air); and the local fibre-optic cables, still with multiple megahertz of spare capacity, will probably also deliver a full range of entertainment services, including public-service television, pay TV to cater for a wide variety of entertainment, sporting and educational needs, and high-fidelity audio programmes.

In short, Japan will then be in a position to benefit from very cheap and very extensive communications facilities, including the rapid processing of information of all kinds. Business efficiency and productivity will increase inexorably, Japanese companies will become even more competitive, and Japan will become the first fully paid-up member of the Information Society.

Which, for the occidentals, would be worrying enough, even if all of this new telecommunications-based economic activity was confined to Japan. But it won't be. There is now a trend in an increasing number of countries to the deregulation and privatization of the telecommunications carriers, who usually fall within the aegis of each country's posts, tele-phone and telegraph (PTT)[6] authority. Thus the old AT&T in the US has been denuded of most of its domestic operating (i.e. telephone) network, which now exists in the form of seven, independent, regional 'carrier' companies; in the UK, British Telecom has been sold off to the public to the tune of 50.2 per cent of its equity, and its procurement policies are gradually being broadened to weaken the links with its classical (almost wholly British) suppliers; and even in Japan, meaningful steps are being taken towards the privatization of Nippon Telephone and Telegraph (NTT), which was originally modelled to a considerable extent on what AT&T was like in the 1950s.

This combination of events presages a competitive explosion in the international telecommunications business such as to shake the foun-dations of even the largest corporate structures. For Japan's postulated surge ahead in broadband, interactive networks (and also by inference, in the large variety of domestic and business terminals which will be connected to it), coupled with the opening up of hitherto closed markets for telecommunications equipment and terminals (e.g. the simple tele-phone) in Western Europe and the United States, will give the Japanese manufacturers unparalleled opportunities to hijack the biggest and (soon) most rapidly growing market segment of the whole electronics/IT sector.

The threat to AT&T

If that happens, America is likely to witness a significant further reduction in the power of AT&T, until recently the world's biggest (and, some would say, best) company. This will be because AT&T, as newly con-stituted, is heavily dependent on its massive manufacturing arm, Western Electric (now called AT&T Technologies). This, in turn, *has* been totally dependent on preferred-procurement contracts from the once-captive Bell system operating companies and, to a lesser extent, the US Department of Defence. But these operating companies, representing the source of the huge revenues with which to purchase new telephone exchanges and all the ancillary equipment (and whose protected, public-service margins allowed the old Western Electric to grow fat and happy), are now truly independent. The criteria by which their managements will be judged no

---

[6] In many countries, the postal and telecommunication services are provided by a single organization, generally called the Post, Telegraph and Telephone (PTT) authority. For the sake of brevity, PTT is used here as a shorthand notation for the national tele-communications network provider even when, as in the UK, it comprises two independent private enterprises, BT and Mercury.

longer imply any loyalty to Western Electric. Clearly, if Japanese companies can supply the best goods, at the best price, and of the best quality (which is what shows up in the tea leaves), then they will get the business.

Given the great importance of economies of scale in this segment (as in most) of the electronics industry, the loss of sales by Western Electric – already struggling to adapt itself to the fiercely competitive commercial world into which it was abruptly dumped in 1984 – could cause it to go into an accelerating tail-spin of losses. This, in turn, could cause parent AT&T to economize on its R & D burden (i.e. the re-named Bell Telephone Laboratories would have to retrench drastically), the seed corn would have been eaten, and America's sometime technological showpiece, the company which really got the whole electronics thing started, could be reduced to an also ran.

Of course, to Americans in general, and AT&T executives in particular, this scenario will probably sound preposterous. Look at all this new energy and enterprise, they may say, oozing from each pore of the AT&T body corporate. If, however, the company is indeed to survive and prosper, that and much more will be required. Because even massive companies sometimes fade away – and this one happens to be in the path of what could become the biggest Japanese high-tech juggernaut of all.

ROBOTS GALORE

To fill in the remaining salient gaps in the Japanese picture, it is appropriate to dwell briefly on three other important segments: industrial automation, defence electronics and software engineering.

As will come as little surprise, the general area of robotics, automation, computer-integrated manufacture, computer-aided design and straightforward industrial control is expected to grow at a very heady rate for the foreseeable future. The companies which succeed in this segment will need, as well as the more general attributes for high-tech success, additional skills and experience in marrying advanced electronics technology with precision mechanical engineering.

It will be clear that Japan, in general, now has established an impressive capability in electronics, and its leadership in the manufacture and use of computer-controlled machine tools of many kinds is well documented. For instance, in 1983, Japanese companies were reported to be using about 40 per cent of the world's total population of robotics in their own manufacturing operations (although many of these are machines endowed with relatively simple intelligence), while the worldwide market for all types of robot equipments (*c*.$1 billion in 1983) is estimated to have been dominated by Japanese suppliers to the extent of 60 per cent.

With such an unchallenged right to the pole position, it is a safe bet that Japan will win the race to capture the bulk of the world's market for all kinds of computer-integrated manufacturing (CIM) systems, which will probably amount to about $40 billion in total by the end of the century.

DEFENCE ELECTRONICS UNDER ATTACK

So far as the defence sector is concerned, many Western observers argue that, despite some recent small increases, Japan's modest military commitments and concomitantly low R & D expenditure on defence electronics, will prove in the long run to be that country's high-tech Achilles heel. But they are wrong, for the reasons which follow.

The most probable source of this misconception is the (now) widely recognized stimulus which the American Department of Defence provided to its US suppliers in the formative years of the electronics industry, as described in Chapter 2. That support was critically important at that particular time, of course, and was without doubt the single most important factor in lifting the American electronics industry to its early, dominating position in the free-world markets.

Since those early days, defence electronics has become of much reduced relative economic importance within the electronics sector as a whole. It is notoriously difficult to get a true reading of the size of the defence electronics business – because of secrecy, of course, but also because much of the electronics content of military equipment tends to be submerged in high-value, non-electronics hardware such as aircraft, ships and tanks. But 1984 market estimates of approximately $45 billion are probably not far off the mark. In that case, the defence segment represented only about 12.8 per cent of the total 1984 worldwide (i.e. free-world) electronics market of *c*.$350 billion.

Obsolescent technology

There is another, more fundamental reason for believing that the modest size of Japan's activities in this area is more of a blessing than a curse. This is because it is in the nature of modern defence/military systems, particularly those of great sophistication, for the gestation period to be generally much longer than for commercial systems of similar complexity. Sometimes the reason lies in the need to evaluate and compare alternative products from rival suppliers before going into full production; sometimes it lies in the need to make new equipment compatible with older, or other new, equipment; sometimes it lies in the painstaking negotiations (for example, in NATO) to standardize multi-nation requirements around an agreed performance specification in order to maximize the production run against which the (usually very high) development costs can be amortized; and sometimes it lies in the need to ensure extremely high levels of reliability.

For whatever reasons, it is now usually the case that, except for certain military-specific technologies, such as infra-red imaging, the level of electronics technology used in defence and aerospace equipments *in production* lags instead of leads that in comparable non-military equipments. Or, to put it another way, whereas erstwhile defence electronics – even in production systems such as the first Minuteman missiles – were usually leading-edge, with the non-military sectors carried along on its technical coat-tails, today the situation is largely reversed.

Cost cushions

This trend has been reinforced progressively as the ability of electronics technology to produce very low-cost, high-performance products has become inexorably clearer. Of all the different segments of the electronics industry, the defence area (usually for good and proper reasons) is the least sensitive to costs. Thus, unlike the personal-computer industry, say, defence-systems' designers rarely demand the most avant-garde components with the lowest per-bit component cost. Indeed, the 16 k-bit DRAM, for example, will still be on the active procurement list of the DoD (and its European equivalents) long after the majority of non-military systems are centred on the 1-megabit (and bigger) memory chip. In short, the military sector no longer represents as important a demand pull effect as it did in the formative years of modern electronics.

Before driving too many defence scientists and military experts to the point of apoplexy, it is perhaps important to add that there still are, of course, many military/defence problems which demand – and get – the application of the most advanced technology available, and some where cost is paramount. As examples of the former, battlefield communications come to mind, in which the use of sophisticated, state-of-the-art techniques is essential to provide secure and reliable systems. Likewise with missile guidance systems, submarine detection, 'stealth' bombers, satellite surveillance, and so on all the way to the 'Star Wars' concept.

But the main point remains valid – namely that, unlike the 1960s, the world of electronics is now dominated by commercial and industrial systems applied to commercial and industrial problems (i.e. the Information Society), and the defence sector in general is no longer anywhere near as significant as a source of technology push or demand pull.

Talent dilution

There is yet another reason why Japan may be considered to be better off unencumbered by a substantial national defence industry. At the present time, all high-tech industries, in most countries, are talent-limited. The educational establishments, by and large, have not been able to keep up with the ever-growing demand for what are known in the UK as qualified scientists and engineers (QSEs) – or, more generally, as 'third-level' science and engineering graduates. Because of the glamour of, and high salaries which can often be paid by, defence electronics companies, they tend to cream off a disproportionate share of the top talent, thereby denuding the commercial segments of both the quantity and quality of skills it needs. In Japan, it will be clear, this is not likely to be a serious problem.

FIRMER SOFTWARE

Lastly, there is need to take a hard look at software. By way of a layman's definition, software is merely a means of delivering instructions to the hardware so that it can actually do something useful. In this sense, an audio cassette carries the software which instructs a magnetic head to generate particular electronic signals, which are then 'processed' by the conglomeration of ironmongery and electronic components which constitutes the hardware. These signals are instantaneously manifest as music or speech.

In the same way, computer software is merely a short-hand term for the set of instructions (usually delivered by a magnetic tape or disc) which tells the mass of electronics just what to do: e.g. what data are needed, where they can be located, what to do with them and where to store them, display them or print them out.

In the early days of the computer, 'software' was a simple matter of programming a data processor to carry out certain arithmetic calculations in a specified order. But as processors rapidly became much bigger and faster, controlling them – by means of software – was elevated into a vital and complex constituent of the total system. Indeed, software engineering has become such an essential element in the fast and cost-effective operation of large systems that it is now generally ranked, together with microelectronics, as one of the key 'enabling technologies' of the information-technology industry.

Weakness into strength

As the relative importance of software loomed larger and larger, it began to put about that this was a skill in which the Japanese were especially weak. This emanated not only from Western experts, looking with some disdain at the early products of the Japanese computer industry, but also from Japan itself. Numerous speeches by eminent Japanese politicians and industrial leaders lamented this national deficiency, and some commentators (both Japanese and other) went so far as to associate this shortcoming with the widely held view of the Japanese as being 'no good at research'.

All of this has been based, it will eventually be seen, on a profound misjudgement of the innate qualities of the Japanese people. Research, for example, can be thought of as the creation of something new from the imaginative use of existing knowledge, and no-one who has tried to appreciate some of the subtleties of Japanese art and architecture (to say nothing of literature, music, theatre and films) could deny the presence of an impressive national streak of creativity. Moreover, although the scientific knowledge base in Japan was not strong enough, in the immediate post-war years, to provide a climate in which scientific research could flourish, Japanese research laboratories are now trail-blazing into relatively unexplored (electronic) territories such as artificial intelligence, and much less is heard about their creative and research shortcomings.

And as for software itself, the very fact that a national deficiency has been recognized and acknowledged means that, given the long, strong arm of MITI, it is already halfway to being solved. It must surely be clear by now that one of the most impressive attributes of Japanese industry is that, having pin-pointed a salient weakness, or targetted an important objective, it works cohesively, intensely and unremittingly until the problem is overcome.

As in text processing, however, it is certainly the case that having an ideograph-based written language is a major Japanese handicap in view of the fact that much software must usually be written in the form of numbers and the Roman alphabet. But again, in the longer term, this may prove to be an advantage in providing Japan with an additional spur to develop high-level languages by means of which the man:machine interface will become significantly easier (or user-friendly, in contemporary argot). In other words, the applications software (as distinct from the machine codes and operating systems which are internal to the computer, and which are opaque to most users) will increasingly be based on voice communications, towards which achievement Japanese companies will be drawn as a means of overcoming the 'Kanji syndrome'.

Taking a balanced view of all such factors, the rest of the industrialized world, it seems clear, has no choice but to assume that Japan, despite these difficulties, will soon become as competent at software engineering as it already has become at the equally generic technology of microelectronics. Or, to put it another way, they should take little comfort from the much-discussed Japanese lag in software: where there's a (Japanese) will, there's likely to be a (Japanese) way.

NIPPON RAMPANT

It is a great frustration, in writing a book such as this, to have to omit so much material which, strictly speaking, is relevant to the question in hand. There has been no mention, for instance, of the fascinating and instructive success stories of highly entrepreneurial, courageous and imaginative Japanese companies such as Kyocera, Oki, Seiko and Sharp, to name but a few; too little stress has been given to the important role played by management insistence on high levels of product quality in the marketing strategies of Japanese electronics manufacturers, in many different segments of the industry; the advantageous financial circumstances of most Japanese companies (e.g. relatively low interest rates, high debt-to-equity ratios) clearly deserve more attention; the influence of Japan's trading policies (e.g. in devising subtle protectionist measures against imports of 'strategic' goods) is evidently a factor of great importance, as well as being a source of much anti-Japanese sentiment; and the pros and cons of Japan's geographical proximity to both South-East Asia and China ideally need to be taken fully into account in assessing the long-term prospects of Japan becoming a full-blooded competitor in the worldwide electronics business.

Nevertheless, since the overall objective is to concentrate on the problems of the high-tech laggard nations, it must be sufficient unto the day to confine discussion of the high-tech leader nations to those *key* factors which, in aggregate, represent the foundation of their success. This should not only provide insights into any special circumstances which have contributed importantly to their successes, but should also give a reasonably coherent picture of what makes the electronics industry tick (as a whole), and provide pointers to special factors which the current 'losers' might want selectively to emphasize in devising effective renaissance strategies.

Enough has been said to confirm the gathering strength of the Japanese electronics industry across the board. Taken as a whole, Japan is already a contender for leadership in some segments of the electronics product spectrum, and it has long since swung from the role of imitator to innovator. This is clearly manifest by its ambitious plans for the new broadband Integrated Network System (INS), discussed earlier and, even more dramatically, by its initiative in starting the curiously named[7] fifth-generation-computer project. This national programme, with which international collaboration has been invited, is effectively the pacesetter in the race to develop commercially viable systems based on artificial intelligence (AI), such as 'seeing' robots, voice-instructed machines, automatic translators and, closer to exploitation, 'expert-systems' which have an in-built ability to consult an extensive 'knowledge' memory in order to make decisions about abstruse problems (e.g. whether to perform a particular surgical operation) based, inter alia, on previous related experiences.

In fact, strong evidence has been presented in these pages for the emergence of Japan as the world leader in electronics and IT generally. No significant weaknesses have been discerned in any of the segments examined (albeit briefly), other than the 'Kanji syndrome'. And even this can be postulated as eventually delivering yet more industrial power into Japanese hands as technological necessity becomes the mother of commercial invention.

Building on the colossal technological foundations constructed predominantly by the American electronics industry in the third quarter of the twentieth century, Japan looks well placed to set its international competitors, including the US, a blistering pace as the huge IT markets of the twenty-first century loom up invitingly.

---

[7] 'Curious' because there is a wide disparity of views among computer experts as to what constitutes a computer 'generation' and how many of them there have been.

4 Europe – The Uncommon Market:
A continent misses the message

BRITAIN RULES THE (ELECTROMAGNETIC) WAVES

Until about 1960, Europe was in reasonably good shape vis à vis American technology, and tended to be quite scornful of Japan's first imitative electronics products. In many product segments, it was Britain which possessed the best 'European' technological capability although, ironically, the UK at that time[1] was not much inclined to think of itself as European.

The special relationship

Britain's lead, understandably, was based primarily on the technology-push factors which had been particularly evident during the latter years of the 1939–45 war, allied to the fact that, a multitude of bombsites notwithstanding, most of its industrial capacity had survived the war intact. The UK was also aided somewhat by its military links with America, although (with the obvious and overwhelming exception of the Manhattan Project, devoted to the development of an atomic bomb) the technology-transfer aspects of the Anglo-American alliance were conspicuous mainly by their absence.

In any event, due to the technological stimulus of war and to the relative weakness of most of the continental European nations during the 1950s, Britain alone had any valid claim to match America's smouldering,

---

[1] The Treaty of Rome had been signed in 1957, and the six founder members had – not surprisingly – taken umbrage as Britain distanced itself from this embryonic European Community.

ready-to-erupt technological capabilities across the board. In jet engines, military aircraft, radar, high-power electron tubes, radio, television, telephony, radio astronomy, electronic components generally and a host of other 'high-tech' products, Britain stood, with America, at the very frontiers of scientific discovery and technical know-how. Its research laboratories – industrial, university and defence – enjoyed universal respect, its 'high-tech' industrial facilities were comparable with all but the very best in the US, and its workforce was skilled and well practised in the technology of war.

How all of this scientific aptitude, technical knowledge, national self-respect and industrial capability was allowed to crumble gently into the ruins of the 1980s is a horror story worth recounting in its own right. However, for present purposes, the discussion will be confined, in due course, to just the principal characteristics of Britain's techno-failure, and mostly in a European context.

REVANCHIST EUROPE

Meanwhile, the other nations of Western Europe were busy trying to feed themselves, rebuild their cities and reconstruct what would now be called their smokestack industries. New shipyards, steelworks, coalmines and car factories began to appear; energies and resources were largely absorbed in restoring the same kind of industrial capabilities as had existed before the war; new technology was not afforded much pride of place.

Except, that is, in Germany, Holland, and to some extent France. Although the impressive wartime cadre of German scientists had largely been destroyed or dispersed, the feeling for technological excellence had so pervaded the West German industrial culture that the surviving residue of technical talent soon floated to the top. Within ten years, Siemens had again become a respected name among the international community of research physicists, and a rebirth of national self-respect, allied to a cowed (and therefore disciplined) workforce, led to an industrial renaissance in which 'new' technology was a welcome ally.

In the Netherlands, Philips, effectively saved from wartime devastation by a temporary (and complicated) evacuation of control to the US, set about rebuilding its business of manufacturing light bulbs, consumer products and components. Unencumbered by an inheritance of 'heavy' engineering, this company was intrinsically alert to the possible exploitation of anything new in 'light' engineering which happened to come its way – or emerge from the rapid expansion of its own research facilities.

And in France, there was a clear perception that some new things were bound to happen in the realm of industrial technology. If for no other reason than a restoration of French military might[2], it would be unwise for the Fourth Republic to stand aside from new developments.

Transient parity

In the long sweep of history, 15 years is not a long time. And yet, by about 1960, continental Europe had largely completed the process of industrial and economic restoration. More particularly, Britain, Holland and West Germany had cottoned on to the burgeoning importance of transistor technology and were regarded by American semiconductor scientists as warranting close attention; transistor production had also started up in France and Italy; and throughout most Western European countries there was a growing realization that the industrial world was basking in the gentle rays of a new technological dawn. The sun was rising.

In fact, the European electronics industry at the close of the 1950s appeared to be in an excellent state of health:

- In 1960, Western Europe as a whole was basically self-sufficient in all aspects of electronics technology then in a commercially exploitable state, and enjoyed a strong, positive trade balance in electronics-based goods.
- Whether or not the forerunner of today's computers (that is, electronic, digital computers employing stored program control) was invented in the UK, that country was undoubtedly in the vanguard of computer science, and was the only country outside the US capable of designing and manufacturing state-of-the-art digital computers.
- The pre-eminent Dutch electronics company, Philips, led the world in the production of the (then) most important semiconductor device, the germanium transistor.
- When looked at in aggregate (although they were, and still are, far from being aggregated), European companies were vigorously pursuing new electronics technology and products across the full range of research topics, and important new electronics developments (such as the aforementioned PAL and SECAM colour-television systems) still emanated, to no-one's surprise, from European laboratories.

In short, although Britain was still ahead of its continental competitors

---

[2] The disemberment of the French Empire (specifically Indo-China and Algeria) had yet to gather momentum.

in many segments of the electronics industry, Europe as a whole was gaining ground and – again looked at as a whole – had the appearance of a formidable potential competitor to America's innovative and thrusting electronics companies. But, just like Britain, the other nations of Europe (astonishingly, without exception) also failed dismally to benefit from this promising start.

CHRONICLE OF FAILURE

The stark, economic dimensions of Western Europe's colossal failure in the electronics sector are presented in the following chapter. For now, however, it is sufficient to note just a few of the more important events by which this steady decline was punctuated:

- During the 1960s, IBM achieved effective dominance over the free-world markets for electronic data-processing systems, and even the American also-rans (computer manufacturers such as Burroughs, Control Data, Honeywell and Sperry) became very much larger than even the biggest of the declining number of European computer companies.
- In the mid-1960s, as the revolutionary impact of microelectronics grew ever more apparent, the European nations became progressively less innovative in this critical field, and utterly failed to make the necessary investments to maintain anything like research or production parity with the American IC companies.
- As the essential driving force of a large, innovative, successful, indigenous components industry slowly waned during the 1970s, the European electronics equipment companies continued to lose ground. Thus the hi-fi and audio-equipment market became totally dominated by Japanese producers; the European television industry (despite the protection afforded for many years by the PAL patents) increasingly lost market share to Japanese rivals; and in all existing product segments, from office equipment to numerically controlled machine tools, non-European companies took over the running.
- Enormous (and entirely new) growth opportunities in electronic calculators were generally ignored by the Europeans, and even those brave efforts which were made (going back as far as 1967) were invariably under-resourced.
- And the European (especially Swiss) watch and clock industry was incomprehensibly slow to accept that a revolutionary change had occurred in the basic technology for making accurate and cheap timepieces.

The catalogue of failure is endless. Excluding specialist, niche products, essentially all of the 'open' (i.e. unprotected) markets for electronic goods of all types came to be swamped by non-European producers. Only in the 'old-fashioned' technologies (e.g. electron tubes) and in the heavily protected public-sector markets (telecommunications and defence), did European suppliers maintain market share, and even then those small successes invariably stopped short at the national frontiers.

For a balanced picture, however, it is important to note that this dismal record is mitigated to some extent by an occasional success story – even if the success needs to be measured in devalued European terms. Although it is invidious to select examples of European companies which bucked the trend, names such as Ericsson (Sweden), Matra (France), Nixdorf (Germany), Olivetti (Italy), Philips (Netherlands) and Racal (Britain) come to mind as manufacturers who, even in the most advanced areas, managed to create a fair measure of commercial success out of electronics technology. Their accomplishments are placed in a global context in Chapter 7.

COMPONENTS OF COLLAPSE

In attempting to diagnose Europe's high-tech malady, it is clearly essential to assemble all of the crucial evidence before reaching a final verdict. If this sounds blindingly obvious, it needs to be said that too many half-baked diagnoses have already inspired too many half-hearted government 'cures'. It is an important enough question in all conscience, and so late in the day to boot, that all due care and attention seems justified.

The problem, of course, is that the scope of failure is so vast – the virtual collapse of Europe as a tenable competitor in the most important new industrial technology of the century – that it is not a simple matter to select out the salient causes of decline from the multiplicity of candidates. Nevertheless, there is a number of key factors, generally common to all of the major European countries, on which much blame can unequivocally be laid.

Nothing with chips

The first, most obvious aspect of Europe's general deficiency, is the extraordinary delay in appreciating the overwhelmingly revolutionary nature of silicon technology and the IC. Enough has been said already about this tidal change of technology: what needs explanation is Europe's

Canute-like devotion to its belief in the immutability of the discrete, germanium transistor.

Geography, in all probability, played an important part, as in the 'Chicago syndrome', previously discussed, with which the US consumer-electronics industry was afflicted. Between Paris and San Francisco there is normally a time difference of nine hours; in the early 1960s, even the fastest civil aircraft required about 14 hours to traverse haltingly these 6000-odd miles. And all the evidence suggests that knowledge, like the beam of light from a torch, fades with distance.

It would not be surprising, therefore, if the remoteness of Europe from the semiconductor hot-beds of Texas and California was one factor, at least, accounting for Europe's lethargy. After all, it is a matter of record that even in the Bell Telephone Laboratories, a mere 2500 miles away from the main action, there was a profound, lingering scepticism about the long-term viability of the integrated circuit. And, as we have seen, the American East Coast technical community, with only a few exceptions, was also uncertain how to treat this wave of (mainly) West Coast technology coming, as it did, hard on the heels of much recent East Coast innovation.

So it is not difficult either to understand or to forgive Europe's inability to appreciate instantaneously the awesome magnitude of what was happening in far-off Silicon Valley. What remains impossible to condone is the very long time which it took for the message to be received.

Any number of reasons might be proferred, but only one withstands the test of historical scrutiny. Which is that in Europe, the captains of industry, university professors, directors of research and government officials alike were intellectually incapable of keeping up with the blistering pace of technological change set by the silicon establishment of the Golden West. To minds hardly attuned, as yet, to the original rumblings of America's volcanic innovatory spasm, whose epicentre was the transistor, the advent of the planar process, the IC and their combined potential for mass-produced electronic intelligence, could have seemed almost incomprehensible. It must have been of some comfort to them to act on the head-in-the-sand assumption that each of these radical new developments was merely one more small step in the headlong, helter-skelter pursuit of change for the sake of change imposed on a rational world by the 'whizz-kid cowboys' of the sunbelt States.

In retrospect, it all seems very understandable, very human. But there *were* voices being raised about Europe's lethargy; the message *was* being broadcast. So the receivers must be blamed – those, as defined above, whose job it was to keep Europe on its toes. From this indictment, the opinion-formers of 1960s Europe cannot escape. And from their failure have stemmed many of Europe's subsequent IT deficiencies.

The management gap

Practically everyone who had some power and authority to influence industrial policy must therefore share in the blame for Europe's debilitating neglect of the chip in the 1960s. For the industrial leaders, specifically, who contributed to this benign neglect, it was clearly a case of the self-inflicted wound.

The technology/industrial decision-makers, however, were uniquely responsible for ignoring other vital aspects of the revolutionary changes in management techniques which were happening in the very business sector, electronics, which had been entrusted to their stewardship.

One particular failure of the European managements was their blinkered view of the rapid changes which were taking place in the industrial economics of high-tech products. Nor was this simply a failure to appreciate the growing importance of economies of scale generally, although this, more than anything else, lay at the heart of most of the other stultified management attitudes prevalent in Europe (and in some US companies) at that time.

For it was the case that the more enlightened leaders of America's electronics companies were pioneering – in a highly visible way – any number of new cost-reduction techniques. Of these, one of the most important was the use of ever more complex printed circuit boards, combined with increasing investment in automatic (i.e. 'computer'-controlled) machines for inserting electronic components therein. Another was recognition of the substantial savings which could accrue from shifting labour-intensive operations 'offshore' – i.e. to regions of the world where labour was significantly cheaper than in the US. In fact, the first decisive use of offshore assembly labour in the American electronics industry was by the Fairchild Semiconductor Division, in setting up its Hong Kong facility in the mid-1960s. Ten years later, it was still possible to meet senior industry executives in Europe – in ICs, television and other labour-intensive product segments – who had yet to recognize the significance of this shift.

For those who were in a position to observe, more or less simultaneously, the quality of 'high-tech' management decisions during the 1960s on both sides of the Atlantic, the differences were startling. In America, the thrust in the better companies was towards more technology (hence better products), lower costs (hence cheaper products) and growth (hence more products). By comparison, in Europe (despite some honorable exceptions), and in the less successful US companies, the general attitude of managements seemed to be uninformed, lethargic and reactionary, resulting in critical loss of time before attempts (even then, often half-hearted) were made to emulate the economic and technological innovations of the leaders of the US electronics industry.

Market economics

In the other area where Europe was massively disadvantaged right from the start, the bulk of the blame must be assigned to the politicians of the day (and their official advisers) for failing to press irresistibly for the creation of a common EEC market for high-tech products.

The European Economic Community was conceived in a German haystack, born in a French vineyard, and suckled on Italian olive oil. During its entire history, agriculture and the Common Agricultural Policy have been the prevailing preoccupations of its politicians and officials. What little time, money and energy was left over for industrial matters were primarily invested in the smokestack industries as the EEC countries were forced to adjust to living (co-operatively) with a reduced share of the global market in these sectors, coincident with substantial increases in productivity.

Only in the 1980s has the Commission of the European Communities (CEC) begun to exhibit a serious interest in electronics and high tech generally. While this might have been of great significance in 1960, today (so far at least) it must be regarded as yet another case of too little, too late.

Of course, in the field of high-tech products, back in the 1960s every nation was still under the impression that it could go it alone. In the absence of strong signals from its industrialists about the paramountcy of economies of scale and the concomitant need for larger markets than any single member state could offer, the politicians and officials can perhaps be excused for failing to see the strategic necessity of a harmonized EEC high-tech marketplace.

The lack of a truly common European market for high-tech products increasingly led the managers of electronics companies in continental Europe to cast envious glances at the enormous, open market which lay across the North Atlantic. The concensus European view seemed to be that, so dispiriting were the difficulties of selling to their foreign-tongued, chauvinistic and rather strange neighbours, it would be easier to attempt to push up sales by attacking the US market.

This marketing strategy was reinforced by the fact that, mainly through the pervasive influence of the Americans, English had become firmly established as the international language of electronics. It seemed a simpler matter, therefore, for the French, German, Italian, etc. manufacturers to enter a marketplace which at least spoke their second language, than to go to the trouble (probably for little reward, such was the prevailing sentiment) of hiring 'foreigners' and translating data sheets, etc., into 'foreign' languages. This 'easy option' was further reinforced by the fact that, because most European companies had already conducted negotiations with Americans (regarding matters such as licences, joint ventures and distribution agreements), they had become relatively familiar with US legal and commercial practices.

And for the British, of course, trading preferentially with the United States was wholly natural. The UK was not yet a member of the European Community, and America – particularly during the lengthy duration of the Kennedy influence – was often first-choice partner in matters political, diplomatic, military, cultural, business and technological.

Unfortunately, this policy was rarely successful, even when reinforced (as was occasionally the case) by European acquisitions of American electronics companies. The reasons, more often than not, were that the Boards and senior managements of most European electronics companies in the 1960s were still insufficiently acclimatized to the heat and swirling changes of the high-tech entrepreneurial business breezes, were too handicapped by the inadequancy of their products and their marketing techniques, and were too ignorant of the dictates of the learning curve and economies of scale to stand much chance in the most fiercely competitive high-tech market in the world.

As for their failure to penetrate neighbouring European markets, it is often argued, even today, that the lack of a harmonized 'common' market is no excuse. After all, goes this theme, it is clear that being non-European has not stopped any number of American (and, more recently, Japanese) companies from achieving a high degree of sales success in these unfamiliar, foreign marketplaces. In short, it is said, since IBM (and Hewlett-Packard, Hitachi, Motorola, National Semiconductor and all) can sell successfully all across Europe, it should be even simpler for European companies, who enjoy easy access, by definition, to at least one national market.

This argument, however, is both simplistic and fallacious. It ignores the fact that the non-European companies *never* attack the European markets until after their manufacturing base has been made large and secure on the basis of prior successful penetration of their own domestic markets. Indeed, it is precisely that availability of a large, responsive domestic market – which patently does not exist in Europe – which gives the non-European companies the economic foundation to succeed, even against local competition, in each national market in Europe.

So, in all fairness, it needs to be recognized that the European managers of the 1970s and beyond, inheriting the consequences of their pre-decessors' shortcomings, faced acute marketing difficulties. Generally alert by this time to the overriding importance of economies of scale and to the need, in order to be fully competitive, to compete whole-heartedly in the global market, they could rarely find a way of leaping over the marketing hurdles. In other words, their 'national' sales were too small to yield them the benefit of competitive economies of scale; neighbouring European national markets had the appearance of bloody battlegrounds, with wounded 'National Champions' trying to fight off the invading transoceanic hordes; and the American market well nigh impenetrable because of their lack of credibility and competitive goods.

But, to return to the starting point, it need not have turned out so. If Europe's captains of industry in the 1960s had indeed recognized both the new technological *and* economic forces at work, if the political leaders had been pressured thereby into creating an open, harmonized market for high-tech products within the EEC, and if industry had then made the investments appropriate to their much-enlarged 'home' market, we would now, without doubt, be looking at a European electronics industry able to compete effectively against all-comers. Whether (and, if so, how) such a renaissance can still be achieved, despite the lateness of the hour, is what the remaining chapters are all about.

These, then are the three major causes of the European disease – the failure to appreciate the revolutionary nature of the micro-chip, management deficiencies, and the absence, particularly during the con-solidation years of the 1960s and 1970s, of a large 'home' market. The diagnosis would not be complete, however, without touching on the other significant contributory factors even if, as is sometimes the case, appropriate remedial actions have already begun.

Science supreme

Europe, as every schoolboy knows, is where modern science really got started. Names like Leonardo da Vinci, Copernicus, Newton and Einstein come to mind as merely a few of the peaks of a veritable mountain range of scientific talent, with its foothills in ancient Greece.

For present-day Europe, it might be thought, this can only be good. Europe is engaged in a desperate struggle for economic survival because it missed a trick or two in the formative years of a new, gigantic, science-based industrial revolution. Its scientific heritage, scientific culture and its excellent scientists themselves, must surely represent, therefore, at least one entry in the assets column of Europe's information-technology balance sheet.

But perhaps not. It is, after all, not uncommon to suffer from too much of a good thing. And science, *per se*, is not where the problem lies. By and large, the quality and quantity of Europe's capabilities in *pure* science (or 'unfocussed' research) bear comparison with the best in the world. The real problem lies in *applied* science – applied, that is, to the creation of new products, jobs and economic activity generally.

What Europe has needed, in other words, and still needs, is an enhanced ability at the exploitation of science and, in fact and by definition, this is not what Europe's community of pure-research scientists is good at. If your whole training, work ethic and intellectual culture are targetted on creating new knowledge, you are unlikely to absorb the kind of *savoir faire* relevant to creating new enterprises.

This wouldn't matter much if, as in the United States, the research community was merely one link in the long chain of capabilities available to transform scientific discoveries into profit. But if, as is arguably the case in Europe, science has a disproportionately strong voice in the affairs of state, a judgemental imbalance is introduced into the decision-making process, to the detriment of commercial success.

Again, the example of defence electronics comes to mind. Europe's scientists were, and still are, magnificently capable in this realm because, when faced with the problem of simply doing something novel and better, they are as good as the best. Where they have failed, however, is in gaining a full appreciation of the business ramifications of their work.

It is, of course, not their fault. If anything, it is the fault of an elitist educational system which has conditioned them to believe implicitly in the purity and beauty of scientific research in the quest for knowledge and understanding. Indeed, woe betide any nation which denies a role for such pursuits. But it is a question of balance. If, on matters pertaining to advanced technology, the voice of the (uncommercial) pure scientist is the only one which is powerful enough to reach the ears of the opinion formers and decision makers, then that is the message which will register. And that is the way it has been, for much too long a time, in most of Europe.

In contrast, the US has managed to produce, as mentioned earlier, a unique breed of entrepreneurial scientists – men and (now) women with their educational roots in pure science but with their hearts and minds committed to the pursuit of fame and fortune. So powerful have they become that their views are listened to, with respect, in the innermost chambers of Congress and the White House. As a result, pure scientists, and academe in general, are only used in their proper, proportionate role in matters which are primarily of industrial importance.

Whether or not a nation is 'better' for placing its business builders on a higher pedestal than its intelligentsia is a matter beyond our present scope. What cannot be denied, however, is that such entrepreneurs set the standards, like it or not, which others must match if their countries are to earn a respectable place in the technology-dominated world of this century and the next. Because electronics, and high technology in general, is an international business. If economic isolation was ever a viable strategic option, technological isolation is certainly not.

Nothing ventured, nothing gained

For such high-tech entrepreneurs to start their businesses rolling naturally requires the lubrication of money – much more, usually, than for conventional manufacturing businesses. This, for unaccountable reasons, is a fact of commercial life which failed to penetrate the minds of European political, financial and industrial leaders for an unconscionably long time.

In the 1960s, as the electronics juggernaut really got under way, and when budding European high-tech entrepreneurs should actively have been encouraged to start new enterprises, it was virtually impossible to obtain venture capital in Europe. Most clearing banks were willing to provide overdraft facilities, but only with appropriate guarantees based on the personal assets of the founder(s). Even then, new enterprises were expected to become profitable quickly, and the overdraft level was rarely allowed to become significantly out of line with net asset value.

These conditions, however, are difficult to meet in the electronics sector. Generally based on a complex product and/or technology, high-tech start-up companies not infrequently need a gestation period of a year or more before winning their first sales. Achieving profitability usually requires a good deal longer. In such a conservative, unenlightened and unsupportive investment climate, it is not surprising that the vast majority of new European enterprises during the 1960s and 1970s were confined to 'low-tech' manufacturing (which even bank managers could understand) and to the service sector (which is rarely capital-intensive, particularly in the early years).

In the meantime, America as usual had been showing the rest of the world how it should be done. Venture capital first became a significant factor in high-tech start-ups during the late 1950s, mainly (again) in California and the region around Boston, Massachussets. As the fortunes being made by those early venture capitalists became more and more visible, the high-risk, high-reward investment business in the US really exploded. Indeed, apart from an hiatus caused by a retrogressive change in the tax laws, American venture funds have exhibited strong growth right up to the present day.

A key factor in his readiness to invest, of course, was the US venture capitalist's (and his backers') ability to realize his capital gains (or offset his losses) relatively easily, through the medium of the over-the-counter (OTC) market. This is essentially a market for gambling in shares of, in the main, small, lightly documented, relatively volatile, risky and (often) high-technology companies.

It effectively serves the needs of three communities. The venture capitalists and their backers are not locked in to their investments for the lengthy period necessary to obtain a major Stock Exchange listing; the punters (public and private) can buy into companies they fancy at an early stage, with the prospect of mouth-watering capital gains; and the entrepreneurs can tap into a large capital market which is fed by investors who are usually fully aware of the risk:reward possibilities.

All of this has been abundantly clear for 20 years or more, even when viewed through the bottle-glass windows of financial institutions in Frankfurt, London, Milan, Paris and Zurich; and many 'high-tech' European voices have preached the venture-capital gospel since the late 1960s, if not earlier. It is appalling to contemplate the brake thus applied to the latent entrepreneurialism which undoubtedly existed in Europe in the critical, take-off years of the 1960s and 1970s.

The principal blame must lie with those who then ran Europe's financial institutions – namely, the clearing banks, merchant banks, pension funds, investment trusts and insurance companies. Conservative, blinkered men on the whole, interpreting their responsibilities too narrowly and virtually oblivious to technology or to the tremors emanating from the American-led electronics revolution.

But this oblivion was itself caused by the wet blanket of incomprehension thrown over the potentially inflammable topic of high-tech free enterprise by those previously indicted European leaders of industry, government and academe. And where were the media during this crippling do-nothing decade? Who can point to the tub-thumping, attention-getting, convincingly argued articles which might have opened the sleepy eyes of the financial community a vital few years earlier?

In at least two European countries, this is one inhibiting problem which, at last, is now evaporating. In the UK, the venture-capital business began to take off rapidly during the early 1980s (enormously stimulated by the setting up of the Unlisted Securities Market, or USM) and has recently reached the state where, despite being very small relative to the US, there are probably more venture funds available than there are worthwhile ventures to fund. A similar growth in the number of venture capitalists can also be observed in the Federal Republic of Germany, although some two years behind the UK; and there are signs that France has recently recognized that the combination of venture capitalism and an OTC/USM type of market is an essential factor in breeding the new high-tech enterprises which can become the high-growth employers of tomorrow.

Thus, with varying degrees of intensity, the blame for Europe's failures in the electronics sector can be laid at the door of the politicians (for failing to create a common, EEC high-tech market), executive managements (for, basically, incompetence), the pure scientists (for having too much influence), the financial community (for failing to get to grips with technology, and for delaying the availability of venture capital), and the leaders of industry, academe, the media and just about everything else (for not seeing, soon enough, the gigantic innovatory power of the chip).

There is, needless to say, much else which could be blamed, and some relevant pointers are encapsulated in the brief reviews of the different pace and scale of events in the US and Japan (Chapters 2 and 3, respectively). Nevertheless, there is only one other salient feature of the international electronics industry which warrants particular attention, before turning to a discussion of the future. This is the question of industrial structure.

Illusory skill clusters

In the matter of skill clusters, Europe suffers badly by comparison with the US and Japan. Although it contains several excellent laboratories, and its scientists, as stated, are well up to par, neither they nor Europeans generally exhibit the same willingness to get-up-and-go (somewhere else) as prevails in the US. This inhibits not only the spread of know-how but, probably more critical, the concentration and build-up of expertise to a degree where it would constitute a skill cluster.

The 'Silicon Valley' effect has long been recognized by European governments. In particular, leading officials in France, Germany and the UK, dazzled by the concentrated industrial incandescence of such regions, have pitted their persuasive powers (reinforced, of course, by their tax-payers' wallets) against the free-wheeling dispersive nature of the typical high-tech entrepreneur. Thus, around Grenoble, Munich and the Scottish Lowlands have begun to appear the first embryonic signs of the high-tech concentrations. But it isn't happening big enough or fast enough.

In the first place, it is not always understood that many inward investors do not rate very highly the need to locate their European offshoots in rudimentary skill clusters. Technical infrastructure (the availability of skills and materials, for example) is obviously important, but *their* skill centres are back at home. A multitude of other parameters loom larger in deciding where to locate their subsidiaries.

This has been clearly demonstrated in the UK, for example. In the 1970s, it was the policy of British Governments to encourage investment (preferably high-tech, but anything, in truth, would do) in economically deprived areas such as 'the North East' (e.g. Liverpool). Considerable fiscal incentives were approved and publicized, even including a publicly financed venture-capital fund orientated specifically towards such depressed areas. The end result, not surprisingly, has been not very much.

The reason why it is not surprising is obvious. The vast majority of inward investors in Europe have so far been American. In their case, they expect (not unreasonably, it might be argued) that a free society must be based on mobile people, not stagnant populations[3]. It takes an awful lot of fiscal incentive, therefore, to shift an American CEO (Chief Executive Officer) from a choice of location which his experience and instincts suggest is right for *his* company.

It is probable, in the case of Japanese companies, that carefully programmed computer models play a more influential role in plant location decisions than managerial instinct. For this reason, they tend to be most populous, in the UK, in the development areas of Scotland and Wales, where the financial risks are underwritten to a significant extent by the Treasury.

The net result of all of these contradictory forces is that, ironically, it is the non-subsidized regions around Cambridge and the Thames Valley, not the incentive-laden development areas of Britain's geographical extremities, which are slowly developing the kind of technical communities (and incipient hubris) of genuine skill clusters.

Even then, unfortunately, they are no nearer than their continental counterparts to achieving the extraordinary peaks of technical interactivity which confer such blessings on areas like Silicon Valley (and Boston, and Dallas, and Tokyo, and Osaka). The gap, it must be said, should be *lived* to be believed.

---

[3] The social price that must be paid for such policies, in such cities as Detroit, is beyond our present scope. It is not argued that there isn't a price to pay; merely that the overwhelming importance of creating economic wealth through technology must take first priority. Then, and only then, will it be possible for a nation to afford to ameliorate the worst effects of the unplanned, free-enterprise world of technological opportunism.

SURVIVAL OF THE BIGGEST

It is an interesting fact that, by and large, the biggest European electronics companies today were already among the biggest companies 25 years ago. In other words, 'national champions' never die, although they do (like the 'old' AEG-Telefunken) sometimes fade away.

This impressive longevity should not necessarily be ascribed, however, to high-quality managements since supportive governments have usually been a much more important influence.

Considering Europe specifically, some governments slowly began to wake up, mainly during the mid-1970s, to the fact that things were perhaps not going as well in their electronics industries (particularly in microelectronics) as they had hoped and expected. Their simplistic response was to assume that industry was not doing sufficient R & D, a problem which could be solved, they thought, by throwing money at it.

But when the officials looked around for worthy recipients of this largesse, it was generally only the straightforward electrical giants which came into view. In the absence of venture capital, and all the other attributes of high-tech success which have already been discussed, there were very few small, entrepreneurial companies around, and those that were appeared to be doing very little R & D in the classical sense.

Human nature being what it is, allied to common sense, the officials allocated most of these support funds to those companies which appeared best able to make use of them – clearly, the big 'electricals' with their existing research laboratories.

Even in the Federal Republic of Germany, committed for decades to the philosophy of the free market economy, it has been Siemens, the quintessential establishment company, which has enjoyed the largest dollups of taxpayers' money to subsidize its R & D. And hardly surprisingly, Siemens has grown bigger – but not necessarily stronger in relation to its international IT competitors.

Usually, these great Euro-survivors are also heavily involved in one or more of the public-sector markets (defence and telecommunications). This tends to enhance their dependence on, and closeness to, government and further emphasizes their apparently essential role in the nation's techno-military-industrial establishment.

What is clear, then, is the causal relationship, in Europe, between government support and the survival of the biggest. Because of this, plus some of the other factors previously discussed, it is inevitable that the vast bulk of Europe's current IT capability resides in electrical/electronic conglomerates. These are large, national (mainly), highly-structured companies, of which GEC and Siemens (again) are excellent examples. (A French representative company is more difficult to pin down because of the massive industrial restructuring which went on in the French electronics sector in the early 1980s.)

Such companies also tend to be vertically integrated to some degree, meaning that their activities can range from electronic components, through various kinds of equipments to large systems. They are multiproduct companies, in contradistinction to mono-product, specialist or niche companies operating on a very narrow product and/or market base.

In Japan, also, the electronics industry is not dissimilar to the European heavyweights. Although government support programmes have again contributed to this situation, it has been strongly reinforced by the intimate links which exist between the financial and industrial sectors in Japan. In other words, a company like Mitsubishi, with its roots firmly in classical electrical engineering, has systematically and convincingly moved into high-tech electronics (including state-of-the-art IC memories) aided and abetted by the kind of advantageous financial relationships which were described briefly in Chapter 3.

By slightly different routes, then, the structures of the European and Japanese electronics industries in the mid-1980s have turned out to have much in common. But in the US it is clear from studying the history of the electronics industry that most of the running in the 1960s and 1970s was made by companies which were primarily focussed on just one product segment and which were independent of any major industrial group (i.e. were not in a vertically integrated company). In this way, it is clear, these specialist companies were able to preserve the advantage of entrepreneurial fleetness of foot which has evidently been of paramount importance in such a highly volatile business environment.

The apparent disadvantages of vertical integration were heavily underscored during the 1970s when the 'specialist' companies (such as Digital Equipment Company in minicomputers, Intel in ICs, Atari in video games and, in Japan, Sharp in electronic calculators and Seiko in electronic watches) were able to run rings around companies which ventured to move into their speciality market segments. So Intel, National Semiconductor, Texas Instruments (TI) and others failed miserably in electronic calculators and watches; GE and RCA failed expensively in computer mainframes; and Honeywell failed (yet again) in microelectronics. And in the early 1980s, TI (again) failed spectacularly in personal computers.

It would be easy to reach the conclusion, therefore, that vertical integration, by and large, is a snare and delusion, and that the typical multi-product, multi-market European or Japanese electronics conglomerate is doomed to failure.

In fact, at this stage two quite fundamental questions need to be recognized since they will bear heavily on the future path which the European IT industry should take. The first, based on historical facts, is why, if the Japanese electronic conglomerates have been able to compete successfully against the free(er)-wheeling Americans, have the Europeans not?

This can be ascribed relatively easily to the dispiriting catalogue of European shortcomings outlined above (see page 69): chip blindness, management sclerosis and market dispersion being the three most important. What it adds up to is that the structure, *per se*, of the European companies was not a salient cause of failure. Which is not to say, of course, that things will not change in the future.

This leads to the second question, which concerns the *future* balance of advantage, disregarding national factors, between the large, structured, vertically integrated electronics conglomerate, and the entrepreneurial, specialist company (which will also be smaller, if only by dint of trading in a narrower market).

It must be clear that the answer will have profound ramifications for the development strategies of electronics companies wherever they may be located. But the question cannot be tackled convincingly until we have considered the influence of the various forces of change discussed in Chapter 6.

EUROPE ROUNDED UP

There can be, should be, no equivocation about the state of the European electronics industry in the mid-1980s. Collectively, it has failed abjectly to keep up with its main international competitors, the US and Japan, and it is now further threatened by new and determined competitors located in South-East Asia.

Part Two demonstrates the magnitude of the problem which Western Europe in general (the EEC specifically) must face up to if it is to eradicate the technological cancer threatening its economic future. For now, it is convenient to summarize briefly Europe's state of health in each of the main product segments of the IT sector as a whole.

Micro malady

Despite the tremendous changes of the last 25 years, microelectronics is still the most important of the enabling technologies. Acting through the designer-coupling effect, a leading-edge fully competitive European IC industry would be of great significance in lifting the indigenous equipment and system companies to substantially better, more timely and more competitive products.

The evidence, however, is chilling. With the exception of a brave attempt by Philips and Siemens acting jointly (the Mega Project) to try to keep up with the blistering pace in semiconductor memory products being set by the Japanese, most of the other European IC producers seem to have limited their ambitions to keeping a toe-hold in niche markets. A few (SGS, Thomson) are striving to catch up with Europe's 'big two' by attacking the sector on several fronts (an expensive business at the best of times), but most companies have clearly opted out of trying to play in the first division.

As an illustration of this decline, from a position in 1978 when the top five European nations commanded about 14 per cent of the global markets for ICs, by 1984 this had slipped to a disappointing nine per cent. Many of these ICs, moreover, were not products at the leading edge of microcircuit technology.

It has always been true, is still true, and is worth repeating yet again, that Europe can have no hope whatsoever of competing successfully in the wider IT markets until it contains within its borders a number of world-class IC businesses able to match the best of the global competition in terms of product performance and price.

Consumer electronics in peril

From the foregoing pages it will already be clear that Japanese companies have achieved a startling domination of the world's consumer electronics markets. In terms of main-line video products, only Philips is comparable in size with the Japanese majors, and even this doughty Dutch company has failed badly in its attempts to capture a reasonable portion of the world VCR business.

It is difficult to imagine Western Europe without the kind of strong, indigenous consumer electronics industry which it has harboured for the past half century, particularly since it represents a vitally important market for 'local' suppliers of components – both high-tech and low-tech varieties. Nevertheless, it is known that even Philips, driven into corners by remorseless pressures from its competitors on all product fronts, has recently considered withdrawing from this segment in order to better fight in others. (It has said it will continue to fight on, however).

One gleaming hope is the Philips-invented, laser-based compact disc (CD) technology (and its video equivalent, laservision). This technology, which has some features in common with ICs, is now promising to oust conventional 45 and 33 rpm records; Philips has a leading position in the technology and market and has established access to a powerful software library; the company also seems nowadays to have learned the lessons of its past mistakes. Nevertheless, it faces massive and escalating competition from Japanese CD producers.

So, as the world of audio shifts irresistibly to compact audio systems (including portable and in-car entertainment systems), supported by slow but steady growth of video-disc systems, it is just possible to believe that Philips (using Marantz, its Japanese subsidiary, as the production base) will lead Europe back to its earlier position of strength in this segment.

Numbers crunched

Back in the 1960s, there were about 15 European companies manufacturing mainframe computers. Today, excluding personal computers (PCs) and specialist (e.g. military) machines, the EEC contains no more than six (Bull, ICL, Nixdorf, Olivetti, Philips and Siemens).

Unfortunately, this consolidation process has merely nibbled at the edges of the economy-of-scale problems which lie at the heart of the matter. Combined sales of the six companies in 1984 amounted to about $7.5 billion which, even with the aid of some discreet preferences given for public-sector procurements, only adds up to about ten per cent of the world computer market.

To quantify the problem further, each of these six companies would have to be spending, on average, 40 per cent of its sales on R & D merely to match the level of its average second-rank US competitors (that is, excluding IBM). A saner, but equally unattainable alternative, would be for this average European mainframe company to increase its sales by 400 per cent and spend the same percentage on R & D.

What this adds up to is that the world computer business has moved ahead at much too smart a pace for the European companies – certainly too fast for them to consolidate into larger groups *and* to design and produce the stream of new products which is the first prerequisite for increased market share.

Given the central position which computing techniques occupy in the gamut of IT products and services, and the critical role played by designer coupling in this segment, too, it must be a mandatory element in any IT renaissance policy to effect a substantive restoration of the European computer industry.

Office scandal

Europe's failure in the office automation segment is two-fold. In the first place, it is not investing sufficiently in productivity-enhancing tools for the office worker, such as word processors, intelligent copiers, personal computers and intelligent work stations. For example, 1984 per capita expenditure on office equipment in Western Europe was only about 16 per cent of the equivalent figure for the US.

This is clearly worrying in its own right. It provides dispiriting evidence that senior executives and office managers in Europe's IT-user communities (i.e. the non-electronics commercial and industrial sectors in general) fall well behind their American counterparts in being aware of the inherent advantages of office automation.

And in the second place, Europe's performance as a producer of electronic office equipment is also very poor. Out of a total 1984 production of c.$15 billion for the US, Japan and Western Europe combined, the European share was only about 15 per cent, and even that included substantial contributions from the European factories of non-European multi-nationals, such as IBM.

The two most consequential mass markets for electronic goods are in the home and in the office, and it is the latter which is likely to exhibit the fastest growth in the future as many new products and services are developed. On current form, Europe will have to stand aside as other nations seize the profit from equipping its workforce with the essential tools of the Information Society.

Busy lines

There are currently about nine European manufacturers of public switching systems (telephone exchanges), and all of them are in the process of converting from the old electromechanical systems to digital electronic switches. The cost of developing a world-class digital exchange, using stored program control (SPC), is generally agreed to be well in excess of $500 million. If all of these companies achieved one-ninth (11 per cent) of the total available market in Europe for such switches, plus a modicum of exports, they would all be losing money like a drunken sailor. It is hardly necessary to point out that this is commercial madness.

So far as trade statistics are concerned, the telecommunications segment – thanks to the protective umbrella of public procurement – *appears* to be one of Europe's more successful IT businesses. But in reality the situation is fraught with difficulty. There are plainly too many suppliers, but some of these, being national champions, also double as holy cows. And while dog eats dog in Europe, a free-wheeling, entrepreneurial competitor is harvesting orders from many countries, including the US. The company, Northern Telecom, is Canadian and benefits very little from its national public-sector market.

Tailpiece

The rest of the European IT industry resembles the proverbial curate's egg – good in parts. In printed circuits, passive components, certain kinds of instrumentation, automotive electronics, high-power silicon transistors and a number of niche product areas, Europe is more or less holding its own. The problem, however, is that most of these segments are low-tech and low growth (excluding automotive electronics); Europeans do all right in these areas because, by and large, its competitors don't care.

Reviewing, then, the debris of the once-proud European electronics industry, we can identify very little to offer hope for a better future. Indeed, the projections of the following chapter suggest that, unless something rather startling happens, the game will have been lost irretrievably by the century's end. Clearly, something needs to be done about IT.

PART TWO
Economists and Calculators

But the age of chilvalry is gone. That of sophisters, economists, and calculators, has succeeded; and the glory of Europe is extinguished for ever.

Observations on a Publication,
'The Present State of the Nation', Edmund Burke

5 Signposts to Sunset:

Intercontinental comparisons of IT performance at end-century

To this point, the historical foundations of the Information Era, and the principal forces which led to the different nature and pace of developments in the US, Japan and Western Europe, have been described largely in qualititative terms. It has been concluded that:

- The US, thanks to its overwhelming early advantages, is still in a strong position overall, but wilting somewhat against escalating trans-Pacific competition.
- Over the course of the last 25 years, Japan has come from virtually nowhere to achieve or threaten domination of many of the world IT markets where the US has been accustomed to reigning supreme.
- In Europe, with very few exceptions, the electronics industries within the diverse nations have slowly but inexorably declined in international competitiveness and lost global market share.

In this chapter, we begin the process of adding a quantitative dimension to the analysis by making carefully analysed projections to the year 2000 of recent historical trends.

EXTRAPOLATION EXCUSED

No self-respecting analyst needs to be told that the extrapolation of past trends is fraught with uncertainty. No matter how consistent the historical changes may have been, no matter how beautifully the data may fall on to a straight line, no matter how many terms in an empirical series may progress systematically from one to the next, there can be no guarantee that the *following* event, or whatever, will conform to these reassuring trend lines.

For it is a fact that, unless the trend is founded on one of the great laws of science, it is entirely possible that the next event will be influenced by a random effect not present earlier, or by a new force of change not previously of significance. Indeed, it is precisely because it has no great laws, too many variables and too frequent appearances of unanticipated phenomena, that economics must always be treated as an inexact science.

The extrapolator can usually take some comfort, however, from those handmaidens of predictability, momentum and probability. Many of the matters with which this book deals have a massive momentum of their own: the devotion to television of billions of viewers; the technological advances emanating from the continuous expenditure of countless billions of R & D dollars; and the total dependence on computers of most of the advanced world's industrial and commercial enterprises. These and many similar factors provide the IT industry with an in-built momentum which ensures that the future will bear a sensible relationship to the past.

The influence of probability is much the same. So well documented are the telephone users in some advanced countries, for example, that future traffic patterns can be predicted with almost the same actuarial precision as death itself. Also predictable on purely statistical grounds (although less precisely) are matters such as the number of photocopies required per annum by each category of office worker, the number of new vehicles fitted with electronic ignition, and the global sales of colour-television sets stemming from new and replacement purchases.

Superimposed on this substrate of IT predictability, however, are the business booms (and sometimes busts) which frequently emanate from very major, sometimes unexpected and wholly new products. Some recent examples are the electronic calculator, the video cassette recorder, digital watches, video games, CB radio and the personal computer.

The impact of most of these seachange products cannot be predicted well in advance, but the overall effect (despite the bursting of an occasional 'CB-radio' bubble) is invariably to sustain the high growth rates for the IT industry generally. The only realistic conclusion, therefore, is that IT growth will remain high just as long as the industry carries on producing new, better and cheaper goods. Looking at the new areas ripe for electronic exploitation (e.g. the potentially vast realm of artificial intelligence), this seems a wholly reasonable assumption.

With these caveats in mind, we shall use the simple tool of extrapolation to obtain a glimpse of what some key numbers may look like by the end of the century.

THE SECTOR DEFINED

No purpose is served in this book by drawing fine distinctions between electronics and information technology. This was mentioned earlier and will be further justified by the later description (Chapter 6) of the convergent forces which are acting within this sector.

Nevertheless, for the sake of accuracy and clarity, in the analyses presented in this chapter, the sector is defined to include:[1]

- electronic components;
- communications equipment (including defence);
- consumer electronics;
- control and instrumentation;
- electronic data processing (EDP);
- medical and industrial;
- office equipment; and
- telecommunications.

Each of these segments is assumed to embrace its own software content in the market or production statistics quoted.

Because it is radically different in nature from the hardware-based segments of the IT industry, on which this book is mainly focussed, the independent software business is not included in this analysis, although it is taken fully into account in the later discussions about policy alternatives. Another justification for this simplification is the fact that, in the year (1977) at which this present analysis begins, the software industry was very much in its infancy. Its inclusion would therefore have introduced an extraneous and confusing element of growth.

BASIC METHODOLOGY

The end objective is to be able to make valid comparisons of the historical growth of IT markets and production, and changes in parameters such as IT productivity, between each of the three main countries or regions – the US, Japan and Western Europe. The growth rates so obtained can then be extrapolated to indicate the projected figures for the year 2000.

For such comparisons to be meaningful, however, it is first necessary

---

[1] This segregation is based primarily on the Standard Industrial Classification (SIC) codes, as used by most of the official sources of trade statistics.

to correct historical data for past inflation rates in the 'local' currency (e.g. yen), so that the growth rates are all in constant-value terms. Moreover, to make valid international comparisons, all of these local values must be normalized to a single currency (e.g. the US dollar), and further corrections made for historical variations in exchange rates. This results in real, comparable growth rates, and the projections would then be based on the unlikely but unavoidable assumptions that future inflation rates would be zero (long-term inflation, in any event, is not predictable), and that the other currencies will maintain their 'normalized' values in relation to the dollar. Which is merely equivalent to saying that the projections are in constant-value terms (i.e. the 1983 US dollar).

The analytical process begins, therefore, by taking *actual* data – in Japan, Western Europe and the US – for electronics production and markets. The longest recent span over which self-consistent data are available (for each 'country'), which are also mutually comparable, is 1977–83.

The overall methodology is described in detail in Appendix A, but can be explained here briefly by means of an example – in this case, Japan. The inflation index in yen increased from 118 in 1977 to 150 in 1983, giving an average annual Japanese inflation rate over the six years of 4.1 per cent. Over the same period the yen appreciated against the US dollar by an annual average of 2.1 per cent (see Table 5.1).

Reliable market and production data are available from the Electronic Industries Association of Japan (EIAJ) in current values for the years covered.[2] In the case of markets, and in terms of EIAJ's definitions, the value increased from Y3683 billion in 1977 to Y6775 billion in 1983, giving an apparent growth (in yen) of 10.7 per cent per annum.

Now, however, it is necessary to use a bit of simple algebra to convert the apparent growth rates into real rates. For the purists, the full derivation of the formula is given in Appendix B, the application of which gives a real growth rate for the Japanese electronics market as 8.6 per cent per annum. This rate (assuming that it remains constant in the future) can then be applied (Table 5.1) to the 1983 market of $28.5 billion to give a projected value in the year 2000 of $115 billion. A similar procedure can be followed for making projections of IT production.

While all of this may seem a little convoluted, it is the only way in which valid extrapolations – and, more importantly, valid *comparisons* – can be made, as we see in the following section.

---

[2] *Electronic Industries in Japan*, 1984 edition. Published by EIAJ.

Table 5.1 Corrections to growth rates for the Japanese IT markets

	1977	CAAGR	1983*	CAAGR	1985*	1995*	2000*
Inflation index	118		150				
Inflation rate		4.1%					
Exchange rate							
(Y = $1.00)	269		238				
Exchange-rate							
appreciation		2.1%					
Markets (Y bn)	3683		6775				
Apparent growth							
(in Y values)		10.7%					
Real growth							
(in $ values)		8.6%					
Markets ($ bn)	13.7			28.5	8.6%	33.6	76.3	115

* Constant 1983 US dollar values.

INTERCONTINENTAL COMPARISONS OF PROJECTED IT MARKETS AND PRODUCTION

Using the methodology just briefly outlined over and over again (details in Appendix A), it is a simple matter to derive similar projections, all in terms of 1983 US dollar values, for markets and production in all three 'countries'. Table 5.2 shows the actual starting values for 1983 plus, for the sake of completeness, the approximate market and production figures for the 'Rest of the World' (RoW).

The results of the growth rate calculations are shown in Table 5.3. Looking at the apparent rates in columns I and II, there is a clear, if surprising, implication that Europe is growing faster, in terms of both production and markets, than either of its intercontinental competitors. All of the growth rates, moreover, are apparently in double figures, with Japan bringing up the rear.

But the real growth rates (columns III and IV) show a very different picture indeed. Now, as we can see, it is the Japanese who are surging ahead in real (dollar) terms, with production, for example, increasing at a rate almost 80 per cent faster than America, and nearly five times the European rate.

Table 5.2   World electronics trade in 1983

	Markets	Production	Trade balance
Japan	28.5	53.3	24.8
US	145	144	(1)
W. Europe	85.5	76.7	(8.8)
Sub-total	259	274	15
RoW	*c.* 44	*c.* 29	(15)
Total	*c.*303	*c.*303	0

All figures in terms of 1983 US dollars (billions).

Table 5.3   Intercontinental growth-rate comparisons

Country or region	Growth rates (% per annum)			
	Apparent		Real	
	I Markets	II Production	III Markets	IV Production
US	16.3	15.3	7.1	6.1
Japan	10.7	13.1	8.6	10.9
W. Europe	17.7	15.8	3.0	1.3

Figure 5.1 portrays graphically the market and production trend data already given in the table. The most vivid message from these projections is the way Japanese IT production is soaring up towards the US level (despite, it will be remembered, a 2 : 1 ratio of population in favour of America). In fact, if these growth rates are maintained (6.1 and 10.9 per cent for the US and Japan, respectively), Japan will catch up with America in the year 2006 when IT production output (in 1983 values) in both countries will reach about $570 billion.

Perhaps the second most startling feature of Figure 5.1 is the huge IT trade surplus ($194 billion) projected for Japan. There can be no doubt that this is what the analysis projects; there must be considerable doubt,

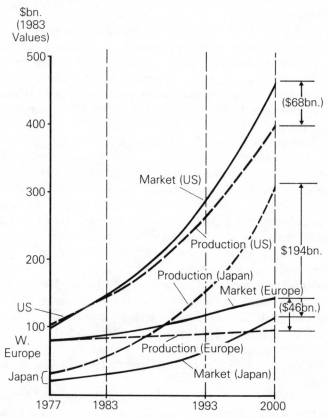

$bn.
(1983
Values)

500
400
300
200

US
100
W.
Europe

Japan

Market (US)

Production (US)

Production (Japan)

Market (Europe)

Production (Europe)

Market (Japan)

($68bn.)

$194bn.

($46bn.)

1977   1983   1993   2000

Figure 5.1. Projected electronics production and markets in Western Europe, Japan and the US.

however, whether Western governments would stand by and allow such an enormous trade imbalance to develop. Unfortunately, if these trends truly reflect the future capacity of these three 'countries' to produce IT goods, the political ramifications (e.g. on the General Agreement on Trade and Tariffs, GATT) of corrective actions are likely to be deeply disruptive to international trade generally.

If a Japanese IT trade surplus of $194 billion seems an improbable figure, incidentally, so would a surplus of $25 billion in 1983 have seemed preposterous viewed from the perspective of 1970.

Turning to the US, the evidence of its performance between 1977 and 1983 suggests that America's IT markets are growing at a real rate of 7.1

per cent per annum, whereas its production is increasing at only 6.1 per cent per annum.

A first comment is that these sort of annual growth rates (six to seven per cent) are substantially less than the 15–20 per cent range which the average American electronics executive probably perceives his sector to be growing at. The difference, of course, is US inflation, which has averaged about 8.5 per cent per annum over this period, although it is rarely remembered to take this into account when commenting on growth – particularly in America, natural habitat of the 'bull'.

The effect of this one per cent difference between the growth rates of markets and production is sufficient to amplify the US trade deficit in electronic goods from just less than $1 billion in 1983 to $68 billion in 2000. Whereas the American electronics industry has become accustomed, during the 1980s, to seeing its once large trade surplus gradually melt away, it is doubtful if a deficit of such magnitude would be politically acceptable. But then who, in the 1960s, could possibly have imagined the US running a budget deficit in 1985 of *c.*$200 billion coupled with an overall trade deficit of around $140 billion?

Undoubtedly the most dispiriting feature of Figure 5.1 – to European eyes at least – must be the quite remarkably slower growth of both markets and production in Western Europe, compared with Japan and the US. And if there is any doubt about the validity of the projections, the relative trends are illustrated clearly enough by the historical data, where the constant-value European IT production rate can be seen to be almost flat.

From Table 5.3 it can be seen that the real, historical growth rates have been merely 3.0 and 1.3 per cent for markets and production, respectively. Extrapolating to the year 2000 suggests that by then European IT production will be only about two-thirds of its own market, resulting in a sector trade deficit of about $46 billion.

In all of these analyses, the production data implicitly include the contributions from 'foreign' multinationals with factories in the 'country' under the microscope. Although this is a marginal factor in Japan and the US, it is significant in Western Europe where there has been considerable inward investment by non-European IT producers over the past 20 years or so. Despite their contributions, Europe's IT trade balance has deteriorated from a deficit of about $400 million to approaching $9 billion in 1983.

Parenthetically, it will be clear that the balance of IT trade in 2000 will be absorbed by the rest of the world (RoW). On the basis of present trends (i.e. neglecting the effect of any successful European IT renaissance), world electronics trade in 2000 (measured, again, in 1983

US dollar values) could appear roughly as shown in Table 5.4, with RoW producing about $120 bn of electronics goods, but buying *c*.$200 billion worth.

Table 5.4 Projected world electronics trade in the year 2000*

	Markets	Production	Trade balance
Japan	115	310	195
US	465	395	(70)
W. Europe	140	95	(45)
Sub-total	720	800	80
RoW	*c*.200	*c*.120	(80)
Total	*c*.920	*c*.920	0

* In the absence of any effective IT renaissance plan in Western Europe
All figures in terms of 1983 US dollars (billions).

EMPLOYMENT AND PRODUCTIVITY COMPARISONS

Three other parameters are of considerable interest in comparing the historical and future performance of Japan, the US and Europe. As discussed fully in Appendix A, from the data for population, IT production and markets (see above) and IT employment, it is a simple matter to calculate IT employment per head of population, IT productivity and per-capita spend on electronics/IT.

This latter figure, of course, is obtained from the *total* spend on electronics goods, including expenditure on items such as new telecommunications equipments, defence electronics, transportation electronics (e.g. new civil radar or blind-landing systems), instrumentation and factory automation, as well as the more evident electronics products in the home, the office and the automobile.

Comparative data for the three 'countries' are shown in Table 5.5, covering the years 1983, 1995 and 2000. They make fascinating reading, but a word of caution is in order. Detailed research has shown that the IT employment numbers can be regarded as only an approximate guide,

Table 5.5   Intercontinental comparisons of IT employment, productivity
and per-capita spending on electronics

		Japan	US	W. Europe
IT productivity	1983	53.8	86.4	41.5
(1983 $ k)	1995	80.0	94.0	52.0
	2000	95.0	97.0	57.5
IT employment	1983	0.99	1.66	1.85
(millions)	1995	2.30	3.13	1.73
	2000	3.25	4.08	1.65
IT employment per-	1983	0.82	0.72	0.53
capita (% of	1995	1.81	1.22	0.47
population)	2000	2.48	1.53	0.45
Per-capita spend on	1983	237	625	244
electronics (1983 $)	1995	600	1290	335
	2000	880	1740	380

whatever the country or the year. It seems that a definition of IT employment has not yet been agreed internationally, in the absence of which each country tends to use its own. While the data are still comparable, year on year, for any one country, they may not be fully reliable for making exact country-by-country comparisons.

In any event, assuming that the Japanese statistics for IT production and IT employment are mutually compatible, simple division yields an apparent, historical growth of productivity in Japan of 7.6 per cent per annum. This, corrected as before, translates into a real growth rate of 3.4 per cent, which then projects to a productivity figure growing from about $54,000 per IT worker in 1983 to $95,000 in 2000. And dividing that number into the projected production output of $309 billion, gives prospective Japanese total IT employment of 3.25 million in the year 2000 – i.e. 2.25 million more than in 1983 despite the projected large increases in productivity. In a similar way, IT employment per-capita in Japan is projected to increase from about 0.8 per cent in 1983 to almost 2.5 per cent by 2000.

The historical IT employment data for the US show an increase of about 450,000 over the six years from 1977 to 1983. The resultant IT productivity growth, once the effects of inflation have been removed, is unimpressive at 0.7 per cent per annum. A real increase at that rate would take the US from its excellent 1983 IT productvity of c.$86,000 to a figure of $97,000 in 2000 – competitive but no longer significantly superior to Japan.

Working this productivity figure back into the projected 2000 production output of $396 bn, gives a postulated total IT employment by then of nearly 4.1 million, an increase of almost 2.5 million on 1983. Similarly, the per-capita IT employment in total will have increased from about 0.7 per cent in 1983 to c.1.5 per cent in 2000. By smilar means, the per-capita spend on electronics in the US is projected to increase from about $625 in 1983 to over $1700 by 2000, a figure which is almost double that of Japan's.

The calculated European IT productivity in 1983 is at the low level of $41,500 and has been increasing at an average real rate of 1.9 per cent. Extrapolating this to 2000 gives a projected productivity of $57,500.

At this level of 1.9 per cent the real historical European rate of productivity increase falls almost midway between that of the US (0.7 per cent) and Japan (3.4 per cent) – which means that it hasn't been all that bad. But because the rate of production increase, at 1.3 per cent, is lower than the increase in productivity (the only 'country' where this is so), the inevitable result is a projected *decrease* in European IT employment, to a level of about 1.65 million by 2000.

With the largest population, it is not surprising that Western Europe has the highest current level of IT employment (1.85 million in 1983) in absolute terms. However, as a percentage of the total population it is already very low at c.0.53 per cent, and is projected to fall to 0.45 per cent by 2000. The relatively modest real growth of markets (3.0 per cent per annum) also implies that the European per-capita expenditure on electronics is projected to grow slowly, from about $250 in 1983 to $380 in 2000.

Table 5.5 reinforces the exceedingly poor European performance which is illustrated graphically in Figure 5.1. In every parameter, Europe is losing ground – grindingly, inexorably – against its two major IT competitor nations. At the same time, in every parameter Japan is either catching up with or overtaking the current pacemaker, America.

METHODOLOGY REVIEWED

It is worth stressing again that while an extrapolative exercise of this kind has a perfectly respectable place in the armoury of predictive methodologies, it is obviously only as good as the underlying assumptions. In this case, one important assumption is that the 'base' years, 1977–83, were reasonably typical, both for the electronics industry itself and for the world economic system as a whole.

A reasonably affirmative answer can be ventured in both cases. Given the enormous glitches which nowadays seem so often to threaten world economic stability (e.g. wars, droughts, currency crises, national insolvencies, oil price changes, harvests too small or too big), the years between 1977 and 1983 seem to have been relatively uneventful. Certainly they embraced no more, one would think, than a usual number of cataclysms per annum.

During these years, the electronics industry itself powered forward in its usual irresistible way, reinforced by a glittering array of prize-winning new products. In particular, the VCR was really getting up steam and the personal computer (PC) market was exhibiting hell-bent growth. (The PC market growth actually slowed down a bit – the vendors' version of the Day of Judgement – in 1984–5.) Indeed, the year-upon-year growth of the combined markets in America, Japan and Europe, over the six years was about 15 per cent in current-value terms ($113–259 billion), which is a very typical apparent growth rate for electronics generally over most of the past two decades.

The final comment on the methodology concerns the validity of the basic source data, about which two quick points can be made. The first is that, given the complexity, volatility and high growth rates of the IT sector generally, it is unlikely that the official statistics will ever be precisely correct for any one year, or precisely comparable from one year to another or from one country to another.

On the other hand, the sources quoted in Appendix A *are* the most authoritative for each country, and the definitions used are reasonably consistent from year to year for each source. Some variations of definition tend to appear between the different sources, however.

It seems safe to assume, therefore, that the trends for all of the 'countries' are sufficiently accurate to justify extrapolation, but that significant differences may arise in comparing absolute values. In other words, when these trends are compared graphically, as in Figure 5.1, the slope of the lines can be regarded with much confidence, but the separation of individual lines with less.

As will be clear, it is the trends, fortunately, which are by far the most important in making projections about any country's performance.

EUROPE EXTINGUISHED

Edmund Burke's observation, with which Part Two begins, that in an age of sophisters, economists and calculators, Europe's glory is extinguished, has about it the smack of premonition. For it is a melancholy future indeed that the data of Figure 5.1 and Tables 5.3, 5.4 and 5.5 predict for the Europe of 2000.

- It will suffer from a trade deficit in IT products to the tune of about $46 billion (probably much larger in the reduced dollar values of 2000).
- Its per-capita IT production will be almost an order of magnitude less than Japan's ($260 *versus* $2360, respectively).
- Of its roughly 370 million population, less than 0.5 per cent will be employed directly in the IT industry against an average for Japan (*c.*2.5 per cent) and the US (*c.*1.5 per cent) more than four times higher.
- Its per–capita outlay on electronic goods will be less than half that of Japan and a quarter that of the US, reflecting less investment, inter alia, in communications, office electronics and industrial automation, with concomitant adverse implications for Europe's efficiency, productivity and competitiveness in most areas of commercial and industrial activity in which a free market pertains.
- Europe's productivity in the IT sector will be only some 60 per cent of that in Japan and the US.
- Compared with an additional 2.2–2.4 million jobs created directly in the IT industries of Japan and the US, Europe – unbelievably – will have *destroyed* about 200,000 jobs.

And all of this grisly picture, it should be emphasized, assumes that the 'European' IT industry will still contain, at the century's end, the same proportion as now (roughly 50 per cent) of non-European companies producing IT products, as inward investors, in European factories.

If there are to be any accusations about too much purple prose; if the industry's leaders, politicians or government officials claim that things aren't really so bad; if the managements of ensconced non-European multinationals seek to convince us that all is for the best in the best of possible worlds, and cast doubts on the severity of Europe's demise in information technology; in all these cases, the onus must be on he who doubts to show cause why these projections will not turn into reality.

There has been talk for years of Europe's fading capabilities in the electronics sector. The limp-wristed, knee-jerk responses have been almost wholly ineffectual – for the reason upon reason heaped high in Part One of this book. But now we can begin to see where it is all leading us (government support notwithstanding): to technological oblivion.

Something must clearly be done. Something new and big enough to turn the European trend lines up. And yet something which Europe can afford.

There is some reason to believe that it can be done, given the destruction of a few shibboleths, and a possible strategic plan is outlined in Part Three. In the meantime, it is useful to consider some of the forces of change which may themselves render the future somewhat different from the projections of the simple-minded extrapolator.

6 Forces of Change:

Key factors influencing the future international balance of advantage

History does not repeat itself – at least, not in the electronics business. It is an industry which is driven by, thrives on, and profits from change.

The complex nature of the forces inducing this change is illustrated by the consistency of the sector's growth rate over about two decades (Figure 6.1), despite the magnitude of the intervening macro-economic shock waves which have engulfed less vigorous industries. This steady rate of growth is primarily due to the fact that a multitude of factors is constantly at work. If this were not so (i.e. if the number of growth influences were small), the overall progress of the sector would be erratic as one or more of these dominant forces waxed or waned.

There is good reason to believe, therefore, that the sector will continue to grow smoothly in the years ahead, perhaps along the constant-value trajectories projected in Chapter 5. But it is not sufficient to leave it at that. New forces of change are looming which, in principle, could radically alter the structure, economics, markets and business strategies of IT companies as the twenty-first century approaches. These forces therefore need to be assessed for their potential relevance to the high-tech plight of Europe, as graphically demonstrated in Figure 5.1. Such an assessment, albeit briefly, is the aim of the present chapter.

THE NATURE OF CONVERGENCY

The word convergence has recently been much in vogue in the electronics industry. It is usually employed to describe the gradual merging of the computer and telecommunications segments as more and more public networks carry combined voice and data, and as everything from local

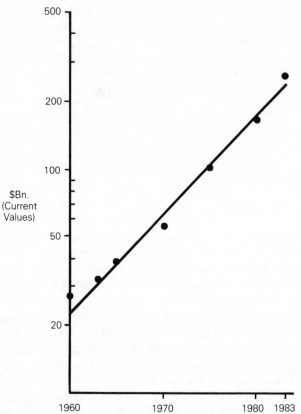

Figure 6.1.   Growth of the electronics market (US, Japan and Western Europe).

area networks (LANs) to communication satellites blur the once-clear distinctions between two businesses with disparate histories, structures and economics. (The combination of computers and communications is sometimes regarded as the true definition of information technology.)

But there is a more profound and far-reaching trend in progress, which can be called product de-segregation, and of which convergence, as defined above, is a sub-set.

About 15 years ago, a common view of the way the electronics sector was segmented is depicted in Figure 6.2. Plotting the number of units shipped (e.g. per annum) against the average unit price (AUP), there was a clear progression of discrete sub-sectors, with electronic components at

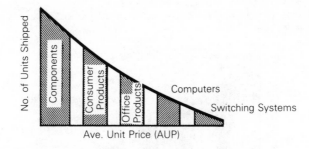

Figure 6.2. The segmented electronics industry of the 1980s.

one end (lots of units shipped at very low average AUPs) and large systems, like big mainframe computers or public telepone exchanges, at the other (few units, very high prices).

But in each sub-sector, diffusive forces were at work. The influence of technology, in general, was to push out the boundaries in both directions, permitting some consumer electronics products (as one example) to perform simpler things at cheaper prices, and others to do much more sophisticated tasks at higher costs. At the same time, the pull of the market reinforced these trends since, as the sweeping capabilities of electronics technology became more evident, users demanded products which were both cheaper *and* more complicated.

The changes which resulted from these technological and market forces are shown schematically in Figure 6.3, illustrating how the once-distinct boundaries have overlapped. Thus the electronics industry of the 1980s is more blurred, or de-segregated, with various products (e.g. personal computers, word-processing systems) impinging on adjacent categories. Moreover it is further complicated, of course, by 'products' such as Prestel (marrying consumer products, computers and telecommunications).

And in the 1990s (Figure 6.4) there will be a true price:volume continuum of products. This means that in certain applications microcircuits will be available with such performance, power and intelligence that they could be thought of as 'systems'. At the other end of the scale, there will be some 'black boxes' (systems) which, despite a relatively high AUP (relative, that is, to a simple IC), will be shipped in large numbers. A posible example is the kind of standardized private-branch switch

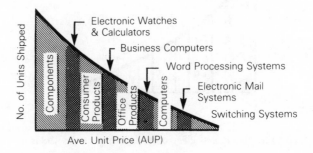

Figure 6.3. The desegregated electronics industry of the 1980s.

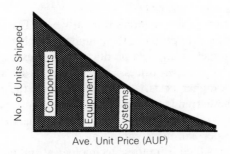

Figure 6.4. The product continuum of the 1990s.

which will be appropriate for the integrated voice-and-data networks now appearing.

It is the product continuum, therefore, which best represents the real meaning of convergence.

TECHNOLOGICAL FUTURES

As in most industrial sectors, it is difficult in the electronics industry to draw sharp demarcation lines between technological, market (demand), economic and strategic forces of change. Nevertheless, for clarification it is desirable that they be compartmentalized by concentrating on the primary nature of each factor.

Microelectronics marches on

In the realm of technology, there can be no doubt that the main life force of electronics over the past 25 years or so has been microelectronics, and so it will remain. Constant improvements in IC technology will be made and there will be an inexorable trend towards smaller on-chip feature sizes stimulated by the advent of new lithographic techniques involving ion beams, X-rays and electron beams. Together with the trend to ever-larger wafer sizes and more sophisticated production equipment (e.g. computer-controlled remote handling), this will result in ever cheaper, better and more complex memory, logic and analogue/linear chips. 'Zero-cost' intelligence and memory will be approached asymptotically.

Integrated circuits at the end of the century will not look markedly different from those of today, except for much finer resolution of the device (e.g. transistor) features and metallic interconnection patterns. Moreover, most ICs will continue to be manufactured from silicon – the most pure, most understood and most perfect material yet known to man.

A relatively new semiconductor material will begin to play a significant role, however. This is the compound gallium arsenide (GaAs), already being used to produce commercial and military ICs, albeit of much lower complexity than contemporary silicon ICs. By 2000, GaAs ICs will become of considerable importance, particularly for high-speed and low-noise applications, and whenever hgh radiation levels may be experienced (e.g. in a 'Space Wars' environment).

Moral fibres

In the communications segment, one important force of change will be its convergence with computing, as previously described. The other will be the rapid substitution, already under way, of optical fibres for copper cables in a wide variety of new communications networks.

Whatever forms these new networks may take (there are two major contenders, of which more later), communications in the next century will consist primarily of broadband digital systems based on optical fibres for essentially all long-haul routes and, more importantly, for many local 'loops'. In remoter areas and in some difficult terrains (for example, in Brazil and Indonesia), microwave links and satellite communications will predominate on trunk routes, and transoceanic traffic will continue to be shared between a judicious mixture of satellites and undersea fibre-optic and conventional cable systems.

The third major technological force of change in this area will be the pervasion of standardized cellular radio networks, coupled with the advent of the cordless, take-anywhere telephone.

Electronics at home

As described in Chapter 3, it took the Japanese to teach its occidental rivals the economic power of harnessing electronics technology to the consumers' discretionary expenditure, with the result that the once-proud but muscle-bound American consumer electronics industry was reduced to a skeleton of its former self – and the European survivors are beginning to cling together for mutual protection guarded by that currently benign Goliath, Philips. *That* was a force of change which was already discernible in the mid-1960s and which, had it been fully recognized and acted upon, could have been used to increase the defences of consumer electronics companies outside Japan.

In the remainder of this century, entertainment electronics will be impacted by at least two major technological forces of change. First will be the widespread use of advanced forms of cable TV, probably delivered over the same broadband communications networks referred to above, and simultaneously capable of providing tele-banking, tele-shopping, tele-games, tele-security, tele-anything. Here, then, will be the perfectly vicarious life, whereby no-one need stray beyond reach of the television set umbilical to see, hear, feel, buy and do almost anything.

Direct broadcast by satellite (DBS) will also be an expanding business. It is unlikely, however, to represent a significant force of change, since it will merely represent one of a number of alternative methods of delivering a video picture, but will suffer some debilitation through being virtually non-interactive (i.e. it will not have a meaningful two-way transmission capability).

What certainly will be important is the trend to high-definition television, coupled with large-screen displays. The pervasion of digital techniques will permit a host of new features which consumers will find attractive, such as enormously enhanced video and audio reproduction, much as the compact disc is now beginning to revolutionize domestic high-fidelity systems.

Workers of the world united

It will probably be the workplace which will experience the most rev-olutionary impact of new technological forces of change. Despite the long-awaited advent of so-called office automation, we are still at the very beginning of learning how to make intelligent use of information for optimizing the performance of our businesses.

For example, although there is also evidence of demand pull, the gradual transition to the paperless office will mainly be technology driven and will be based on major new developments in areas such as new imaging techniques, high-capacity information-storage systems, video phones, and a proliferation of intelligent work stations (e.g. personal computers).

Moreover, much of the work-station equipment, whether in the office or the factory, will attain very high levels of intelligence, one example of which will be that voice- and pattern-recognition techniques will become well established, based on the rapidly developing capabilities and decreasing costs of ICs.

The overriding technological force of change in the workplace, however, will be the development, at last, of efficient methods for interconnecting these proliferating work stations so that they can communicate efficiently with each other, with whatever mainframe computers may be relevant and with the rapidly expanding population of databases.

The means of uniting all of these equipments – of great functional variety, and possibly separated by thousands of metres or miles – will be a plethora of LANs, cables and satellite links. And the great magic glue – the *enabling* force of change – will be immensely sophisticated software which will essentially allow any machine to communicate effectively and efficiently with any other part of the system.

Software core

In short, it will be software which will move up to take parity of importance with microelectronics as a primary force of change.

The advances in the range and capabilities of software since the mid-1970s have been impressive and exciting, even if the claims of the software industry have sometimes run ahead of its ability to deliver – an indictment which could also be levelled against many other segments of the electronics industry. But, relative to microelectronics, the science of software is in its infancy. There will undoubtedly be some critical breakthroughs in software engineering before the end of the century, and this could well be one segment of information technology where defence R & D plays a constructive part, probably through the extraordinary dictates, again, of 'Star Wars' systems.

DEMAND SIDE

User-friendship

The single most important force of change in the area of demand can be categorized as convenience – or, to use the industry jargon, 'user-friendliness'.

It is perhaps helpful to remember that it was the convenience of the transistor, in comparison with the thermionic valve or tube, which really got this industry going, and ease-of-use has been a major factor in the growth of product markets as diverse as calculators and head-up displays, electronic watches and personal computers, video recorders and PABXs.

The nature of the 'friendliness' will, of course, vary from product to product, although saving time and making life easier will always be common themes. Thus remote control is always convenient; so is pushing two buttons instead of ten, 'hands-free' operation, ease of access (e.g. to information), 'no-waiting' response times and so on. In general, therefore, many of the new, user-friendly products will make considerable use of voice recognition and will be endowed with a high degree of artificial intelligence. Many of them will be capable of various kinds of advanced behaviour such as self-training and self-diagnosis.

Efficiency drive

Apart from the added convenience which electronics technology can usually deliver, its frequent ability to increase efficiency will also provide significant boosts to demand. This will mainly comprise straightforward enhancements to factory and office productivity through the ability of electronics to assist homo sapiens to do things more quickly, and with greater accuracy and less effort.

Less certain, but still a distinct possibility (particularly in parts of America and Japan), will be large-scale projects based on improving the efficiency of society at large. One example would be massive traffic automation schemes if it is finally accepted by some governments that electronics-based improvements in the efficient utilization of traffic infrastructures could be cheaper to implement than equivalent additions to the travel network itself.

This drive for increased efficiency will also result in a large growth in expenditure on what might be called electronic 'people-processing'. For example, schemes such as electronic passport control and the automation of the administration of social-security payments involving on-line access to massive data bases. In these sort of applications, the enhanced efficiencies will largely stem from the widespread use of so-called 'expert systems'. These, in the simplest terms, are merely electronic collections of information, or experience, about particular problems (e.g. medical diagnosis) which are stored in the memory of a computer. This is then available for recall by a tyro using a set of reasoned questions controlled by some powerful software.

Workers' playtime

A third, fundamental force of change acting on demand will be the trend to greater leisure – i.e. more time on our hands through higher chronic levels of unemployment, plus reduced working hours, allied to increased discretionary funds (for those still in work) to spend, inter alia, on electronics. Thus there will be a continuation, and probably an acceleration, of the sales growth in audio and video systems, with more television sets serving as intelligent, multi-function domestic terminals for displaying:

- off-air broadcasts;
- cable and DBS services;
- cassette and disc recordings;
- video games;
- still and moving-picture home photography pictures;
- home computing;
- tele-shopping and tele-banking;
- home security information;
- electronic mail; and possibly
- picture-phone images.

There are many other potential demand boosts which are large enough to suggest that future growth rates will be higher than those derived from a straightforward extrapolation of historical trends. There is 'electronic money', for example. This will provide the average man-in-the-street with a growing ability to operate efficiently in a cashless society, carrying out numerous financial transactions using an intelligent 'money' card.

Another example stems from the pervasive growth of personal computers, which is a trend already evident, despite recent hiccups. This will lead to tremendous future growth in the demand for micro-peripherals such as low-cost printers and additional video terminals.

ECONOMIC FORCES

It is economic forces, of course, which underwrite all industrial growth – historical or future, IT or general. Thus the foundations for future growth of the electronics industry rest on the assumption that the world's economy will continue to expand and will remain reasonably free from major catastrophes. It seems legitimate to make the same assumption here.

There are, nevertheless, a few economic forces of change which are specific to the electronics industry and which warrant particular comment. The first of these is the rapidly increasing cost of each generation of systems design. This stems partly from the increasing complexity of ICs themselves, of course, which implies large increases in *their* design costs. But this is exacerbated by the increasing cost of designing-in these state-of-the-art IC products, and changing systems architecture to make optimum use of their improved performance.

The second factor is the increasing expense of silicon-wafer fabrication. Driven by enormous competitive forces, the IC producers have to live with a constant search for smaller feature sizes, more complex designs and higher yields, and all of this adds up to an ever-increasing cost of wafer fab. Unfortunately for the IC business, no alleviation of this crushing cost burden is in sight.

The third economic force is the trend towards communications costs which are essentially independent of distance. Until now, we have been conditioned to think that, like physical methods of transportation, the further an electronic signal has to go the greater is the cost. But it ain't necessarily so. Ever since the virtual elimination of the long-distance operator, telephone costs have increased sub-linearly (i.e. less rapidly the longer the distance). In the 1990s, the cost of a typical 'long-lines' telephone connection in an advanced network will divide up into about 90 per cent for the local loops (including, of course, the public switching centres at either end) and only about 10 per cent for the 'trunk' costs.

Taken together with the trend towards increasing network competition, this clearly implies some drastic changes in telecommunications tariff structures, which will have profound and positive implications for the viability of the host of new services (e.g. 'value-added' services, such as electronic mail) which will be on offer by then.

STRATEGIC INFLUENCES

The problem in this area is that almost any major external event will inevitably have an impact on the electronics industry. For example, a new, abrupt change in energy prices; or the gradual division of the world into inward-looking, defensive economic zones (in Europe, the Pacific Basin, the Americas, etc.); or a significant change in East-West relations; or a drastic tightening of America's constraints on 'high-tech' exports and re-exports; all of these would obviously exert a strong influence on IT.

It is more useful, therefore, to concentrate attention on those strategic forces which will have a *selective* impact on the electronics sector.

Designs in demand

The first strategic factor to take into account is the rapid increase in the demand for a diversity of designs of electronic products of all kinds. It is not just that electronics is expanding in present applications, but new uses are emerging, plus new ways of doing things. Also, very importantly, as advanced knowledge of electronics diffuses through industry, new kinds of demands are coming from end-users.

This qualifies as a strategic rather than a demand factor because the key factor is the *diversity* of the designs which are needed. Since novelties usually begin at the component level – generally with the IC – it is on the component designers that the burden of this demand falls. But, even today, the full-scale design of an integrated circuit is a highly skilled undertaking, and requires a degree of talent and experience which is in short supply worldwide. Nevertheless, these designers, supported by their R & D colleagues and their designer-coupled customers, are constantly devising cleverer, better, cheaper and different things that chips can do – in prototype form, at least. Hence the demand is stimulated for more and more of these new designs – in production quantities and of tested quality.

The strategic implications of all this, of course, are that the flow of new designs may have to be constrained to match the inventive capabilities of the community of designers – unless, that is, a way around the bottleneck can be found (see pages 117–118).

Innovation under control

Secondly, and related to the last point, is the increasing determination by the equipment and systems companies to control their own innovation.

Equipment companies have always been bombarded with innovative products constantly being thrown at them by the leading IC companies. During the mid-to-late 1970s, however, they began to realize that their own *systems* innovation had become critically dependent on what the IC companies were doing, and this is a trend, as explained above, which is continuing.

The problem was what to do about it. By the mid-1970s, most company managements in the US, at least, were aware of the difficulties of getting into this obscure, expensive and technically volatile semiconductor business. They had observed the IC business failures of some of America's corporate giants, such as General Electric and Westinghouse, and were generally loath to risk their own shareholders' shirts on similar ventures.

And yet, this being America, the land of (dehydrated) milk and (freeze-dried) honey, where 'new' is synonomous with 'better', the dilemma grew always bigger: whether to risk letting one's competitors steal an innovatory march, or to plunge into the dangerous waters of chip design and production.

Not all companies made the same decision, of course, but the 'Cause and Effect' section (see page 117) reveals (and explains) which force generally proved to be the stronger.

Open circuit

The third and final strategic factor worth mentioning is the well-known trend towards increased competition in communication networks themselves, the supply of network equipment and systems (from simple telephones to public switching systems) and the provision of network services (of an ever-expanding range).

The disembowelling of AT&T and the privatization of British Telecom are long-established facts of life, and plans are advancing for the privatization of Nippon Telephone and Telegraph (NTT). Several European governments or their PTTs (Postal, Telegraph and Telephone authorities) have either begun to open up their telecommunications equipment markets to non-national suppliers, or have begun to lay plans to do so.

The annual purchase of equipment by the central telecommunications authority (privatized or not) represents a massive amount of (mainly) electronics procurement in all advanced countries. For example, in 1982 the aggregate procurement by the PTTs of the European Community amounted to about $10 billion, or approximately 14 per cent of the total, all-products EEC electronics market.

Clearly, such enormous procurement power concentrated into so few hands must inevitably have distorted the normal rules of supply and demand and this, as we have already seen, has so far been largely to the benefit of the various national champions. The gradual opening up of these markets, coincident with the full tide of 'digitalization' within most of the PTTs, promises to send strong seismic reverberations throughout the global telecommunications industry.

CAUSE AND EFFECT

Having briefly surveyed a number of important forces of change of various kinds it is logical to move on to consider their likely impact on the worldwide electronics industry, particularly its markets and competitive structure.

Naturally,the results can only be qualitative, but the overall effect can be illustrated by means of an example. The one chosen concentrates on the logical results which stem from combining four of the previously discussed forces of change: (A) the control of innovation (cf. page 115), (B) the diversity of designs (cf. page 115), (C) increasing system design costs (cf. page 114), and (D) the increasing cost of wafer fabrication (cf. page 114).

Custom conclusion

First we can look at the effect of combining factors B and C. If there is, as already suggested, an escalating demand for new equipment designs, associated with ever-increasing costs of design, then there are only two logical conclusions: either the growth of the electronics business will slow down to accommodate these constraints; or a way will be found to circumvent the problem.

Fortunately, just such a solution exists in the form of the semi-custom IC (see page 38). This special kind of chip, by combining the massive economies of scale of the wafer-fab process with the 'personalization' of the design requirement, provides an attractive way out of the dilemma. This can be called Primary Effect I.

In seeking factual evidence for the validity of this hypothesis, it soon becomes clear that the postulated growth in the semi-custom IC business is already beginning to happen. The total worldwide market grew very slowly (by the standards of the IC industry) during the 1970s – from c.$1 million in 1971 to c.$200 million in 1980. But by 1985, this had grown to $0.6 billion and authoritative forecasts suggest a figure as high as $3.0 billion by 1990.

To the professional analyst, then, this should bring some comfort. A significant change in the nature of the global IC market is taking place, and this can be shown to have a causal relationship with two identifiable but independent forces of change acting at the economic heart of the electronics industry itself.

Vertical take-off

Looking now at the effect of combining factors B, C and D, it becomes clear that the IC producers will be hard-pressed for investment funds. In short, all three of these factors demand the commitment of much greater resources, the inevitable consequence of which is that the production of complex ICs in high volumes will become the exclusive prerogative of the big battalions.

Another, closely related effect can be seen by coupling factors A and B. Because the equipment companies have a pressing need for an increasing flow of new designs, coupled with their innate desire to control their own innovation, and because a great deal of this innovation must begin at the chip level, many such companies have a clear need to achieve an IC capability of their own, as mentioned earlier.

If, then, the separate needs of the IC and equipment companies are considered simultaneously, it becomes clear that they are neatly and jointly fulfilled through the process of vertical integration (Primary Effect II), and the culmination of this analysis can be illustrated schematically as in Figure 6.5.

In seeking evidence of this postulated trend towards more vertically integrated companies (that is, producing both components and equipments/systems), we can first examine Figure 6.6. This is a table of mainline merchant IC producers between 1972 and 1982. (These are defined as companies which earn more than 50 per cent of their annual revenues from the sale of ICs to the open, merchant market.)

Clearly, since 1977 there has been a strong trend to the point where in 1985 only four substantial companies can be identified which fit this description. Even then, AMD and Intel have large, minority shareholders in the form of Siemens and IBM, respectively; SGS, while appearing to act very independently, is actually a 100 per cent-owned subsidiary of STET, the Italian holding company for the telecommunications sector; and National has for some time been systematically integrating upwards into various equipment businesses, including mainframe computers.

A much clearer picture emerges from Figure 6.7 which represents the trend over 15 years of vertically integrated, open-market IC producers (that is, companies which participate in the merchant IC market but derive a majority of their sales from equipment markets). The evidence for

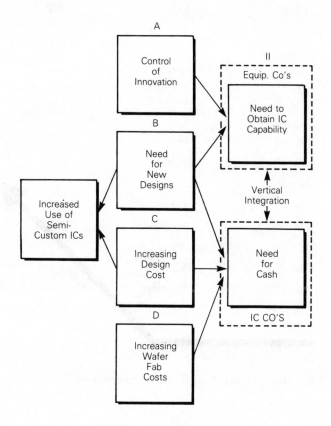

Figure 6.5. The primary effects of four forces of change.

a systematic trend seems overwhelming. From only five such companies in 1970, 16 can be identified in 1976, and over 30 in 1985.

Since, therefore, the theory is backed up by convincing experimental evidence, it seems clear that the trend to vertical integration is real and will be a permanent strategic factor in the evolving structure of the electronics industry unless and until there is a major change in one of the underlying forces of change.

Parenthetically, we may note that, so far as Europe is concerned, this is a helpful trend. All of the sizeable IC producers are effectively within

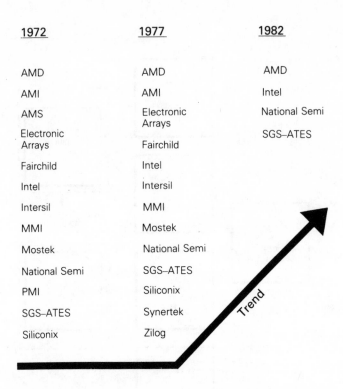

1972	1977	1982
AMD	AMD	AMD
AMI	AMI	Intel
AMS	Electronic Arrays	National Semi
Electronic Arrays	Fairchild	SGS–ATES
Fairchild	Intel	
Intel	Intersil	
Intersil	MMI	
MMI	Mostek	
Mostek	National Semi	
National Semi	SGS–ATES	
PMI	Siliconix	
SGS–ATES	Synertek	
Siliconix	Zilog	

Figure 6.6.   Main-line merchant IC producers (worldwide).

vertically integrated groups already. So, for once, Europe has something going for it – even if more by accident than by design.

Unfortuntely (for the Europeans, and perhaps for the Americans), the same holds true for Japan. Indeed it is now clear that the advantage of being within a major industrial group, as is the case for all of the leading Japanese IC producers, has been a major factor in their growth. The ability of these groups to sustain the heavy and unrelenting financial burden of developing a world-class semiconductor capability, and their steadfastness of purpose through all the cyclical excesses of the IC business, have been shown to be at least as important as entrepreneurial fleetness of foot.

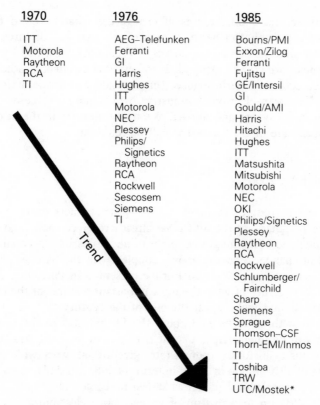

1970	1976	1985
ITT	AEG–Telefunken	Bourns/PMI
Motorola	Ferranti	Exxon/Zilog
Raytheon	GI	Ferranti
RCA	Harris	Fujitsu
TI	Hughes	GE/Intersil
	ITT	GI
	Motorola	Gould/AMI
	NEC	Harris
	Plessey	Hitachi
	Philips/	Hughes
	Signetics	ITT
	Raytheon	Matsushita
	RCA	Mitsubishi
	Rockwell	Motorola
	Sescosem	NEC
	Siemens	OKI
	TI	Philips/Signetics
		Plessey
		Raytheon
		RCA
		Rockwell
		Schlumberger/
		Fairchild
		Sharp
		Siemens
		Sprague
		Thomson–CSF
		Thorn-EMI/Inmos
		TI
		Toshiba
		TRW
		UTC/Mostek*

* At the time of going to print, MOSTEK is being taken over by Thomson, France.

Figure 6.7. Vertically integrated/merchant IC vendors (worldwide).

PLUS ÇA CHANGE

By a similar process of logical analysis, it is possible in principle to identify the main effects on the worldwide electronics industry which will stem from the kind of forces of change previously discussed. In fact, these sort of changes are happening all the time in the IT business. They can be viewed as part of the backdrop of volatility in front of which the companies play out their competitive dramas. They are also part of the lubrication of growth in the sense of providing an anticoagulant: if the industry is constantly undergoing change, so must *your* company – and in the electronics industry, only bigger is better, only 'up' counts as success.

So these and similar forces of change are what have led to all the creative confusion and heady growth of the past two or three decades. They are what lie behind the curves of Figure 5.1, in which Europe's IT deficiencies are cruelly exposed. It follows that to effect a radical change in these projected performances (in particular, to create a significantly better European electronics industry), will require a force of change of extraordinary power and impact. We try to measure in the next chapter the magnitude of the force that will be required.

THE YEAR 2000

With the current plethora of 'futurologists', almost every conceivable high-tech scenario of the future has already received some kind of airing. Anything and everything, one might think, is possible. Nevertheless, the forces of change discussed above, coupled with the baseline sketches of America, Japan and Western Europe presented in Part One, do lead to a coherent picture of what the most important features of the electronics industry should look like at the end of the century.

The first thing to be said about the IT industry in the year 2000 is that it will be much larger than it is today. In fact, the straightforward projections of historical growth rates give a total, worldwide electronics market of $920 billion in 2000, in terms of 1983 US dollar values, broken down by geographical region as shown in Table 5.4.

This adds up to a picture of an enormous electronics industry (the largest manufacturing industry of all time, measured on any scale), based on the most revolutionary technology since the internal combustion engine, and fuelling the growth of very many other manufacturing and services sectors through the impact of the 'Information Era'.

This massive industry will be dominated by broadline, vertically integrated and multinational producers capable of assembling the technological and manpower resources to compete effectively in all of the key product segments and in any significant market place, of whatever colour, creed or constraint. These monster companies will support, and be supported by, a host of smaller niche producers supplying specialist software and hardware products and services where the impact of the quality of what is supplied transcends the quantitative influence of economies of scale.

Finally, in this brief summation, by the year 2000 we shall be well and truly launched into the Information Era. Most of the exciting things which have been talked about for the last 10 years or so will actually be with us – things like tele-shopping, work-at-home and video phones.

If this seems difficult to believe, it is instructive to reflect back on the state of electronics 30 years ago. In particular:

- the transistor was not yet commercially available;
- the recently invented electronic digital computer was a cumbersome hall full of unreliable, power-hungry thermionic tubes just about capable of out-performing today's $5 pocket calculator;
- 'defence' consisted of a 'dumb-bell' mixture of Enfield rifles and atomic bombs;
- colour television was not yet available;
- xerography was in its infancy; and
- to make a telephone call from London to, say, Nice was a full day's work.

Allowing for the fact that the pace of change is accelerating, it seems obvious that the remaining years of this century will see advances in the applications of electronics technology which are no less revolutionary in both economic and social terms.

7 The Economics of Renaissance:

Assessing the costs of catching up

INTRODUCTION

Europe's end-of-century posture in the manufacture and use of electronic products, as projected in Chapter 5, is truly abysmal. If, indeed, that is how the relative strengths of the three continents actually turn out, it will effectively signal Europe's retreat from the high-growth, high-tech industries of the twenty-first century.

Moreover, the analysis of forces of change (Chapter 6) reveals few favourable trends which might decelerate Europe's widening performance gap vis à vis America and Japan. Instead, it suggests that reversal of this divergent trend, so that Europe actually begins to close the gap, will require a new force of change of quite unprecedented magnitude and, therefore, cost.

Whatever the cost may be, however, it must, it really must, be paid. Nevertheless, the 1980s have witnessed a large increase in the political respectability of monetarism and, in many countries, a long overdue revival of governmental fiscal responsibility. The renaissance costs, therefore, must be pared to the irreducible minimum consistent with doing the job properly. For, no matter how many politicians et al. may accept the essential need to stimulate a rehabilitation of the European IT industry, life being what it is, and the demands on the public purse being what they are, any recovery plan will die of malnutrition unless it captures the hearts and minds of governments, *and* can be seen to be affordable.

The main thrust of this chapter, therefore, is to establish a credible method for estimating what these minimum renaissance costs will be.

METHODOLOGY WANTED

We can deduce from numerous government actions over the past ten years or so that the question of quantifying renaissance costs has never seriously been posed. Or if it has – as may have been the case in France in the early 1980s – the calculations were wrong, or were ignored.

In fact, it is by no means an easy problem. In the first place, the answer will obviously depend critically on a number of key assumptions made about the renaissance plan itself. At the most basic level, what are the criteria of success? The allotted timescale will also influence the cost: first, because if there is a minimum, 'critical mass' investment which must be made, the longer it can be spread the lower will be the annual cost. Against that, the performance curves are constantly diverging, as we have seen, so that the later effective action is taken, the greater will be the cost.

In the second place, there is no recognized methodology for estimating these costs. Despite the multitude of IC companies, for example, which have been created, and the countless business plans which have thumped onto the desks of venture capitalists and government officials, there is no simple, infallible formula for calculating investment requirements, cash-flow implications, return-on-investment expectations or anything else. Most ventures of this kind are assessed by that most expert of all expert systems, the experienced industrialist – and his criteria, his methodologies may well be unique to him.

So we must endeavour to create a 'universal' methodology. It will need to be simple, so that it can be widely understood. And it must perforce be approximate because of the need to apply the formula to disparate segments of the overall IT industry.

FIVE FACTORS

At the heart of this analysis lie five foundation assumptions on which any IT renaissance strategy must be built, and its costs assessed.

Economies of scale

In common with many high-tech industries (e.g. aircraft, pharmaceuticals, biotechnology), economies of scale play a very powerful role in the IT industry. All of these sectors must bear the burden of high R & D expenditures, and it is the amortization of these which provides the main ingredient of scale economies. Also of consequence, depending on the sector, are the design costs (obviously higher the more complicated the end-product), the manufacturing process (important where the fixed costs are high, as in IC wafer fabrication) and marketing (when, for example, worldwide distribution centres are mandatory).

There is rarely a critical mass effect, however, in the sense that the benefits of scale only come to be felt once a threshold of production or sales has been reached. It is a graduated process: generally speaking, the more you make, the lower your unit costs.

The prominence of economies of scale in the IT sector cannot be overstated. The degree to which their importance is recognized is, these days, probably the single most critical measurement of management's awareness of the economic realities of the electronics business. If this sounds bizarrely obvious, we shall later be discussing examples of segments of the European IT industry where the current behaviour of some of the participating companies can only be explained on the assumption that they either don't, or don't want to, recognize this basic law of survival.

The essential point, which would bear much repetition, is that economies of scale represent the pre-eminent, unavoidable, uncomfortable fact of life in the IT business. In short, no electronics company can possibly be successful in the long run unless it can achieve at least comparable economies of scale to those of its leading international competitors. By and large, that means achieving similar levels of production, and even producers of niche products must achieve competitive economies of scale appropriate to that niche.

Product interdependence

In Chapter 6 we have discussed the coming of the 'product continuum', whereby the selling price of electronic goods will increase smoothly from the cheapest component to the most expensive system, with no clear demarcation lines between these once-distinct product segments.

Allied to that phenomenon is the well-recognized fact that some segments of the IT sector have a critical relationship with other segments. The most obvious example is the dependence of all equipments on components and software. Through the working of the designer-coupling effect and similar, the development of many kinds of sophisticated equipments depends on access to a state-of-the-art IC company and/or a leading group of software designers. And the other side of that coin is that these component and software suppliers obviously need an active marketplace in which to fashion competitive goods and to hone their marketing skills.

The conclusion, which is of profound importance, is that a successful capability cannot be created in isolated segments of the IT sector. Rather, an IT renaissance strategy, and its concomitant costs, must allow for establishing and sustaining a globally competitive capability in all of the key, interdependent product segments.

These are identified by applying the criterion that a key segment can be of critical importance for either strategic or economic reasons. Thus, while consumer electronics has little strategic significance, its economic importance can be substantial – as an employer, exporter and as a market for indigenous component producers. At the other end of the scale, the semiconductor industry has relatively little economic importance but, for reasons scattered throughout this book, is of great strategic importance.

Table 7.1   The principal IT segments

Product segment	Importance		Key segment
	Strategic	Economic	
Computers	1	1	+
Consumer electronics	0	1	+
Industrial automation (inc. instruments)	1	1	+
Integrated circuits	1	0	+
Medical electronics	0	0	−
Passive components	0	0	−
Office equipment	1	1	+
Telecommunications	1	1	+

0–Relatively unimportant.
1–Essential.

Table 7.1 lists the eight principal segments of the IT sector (each assumed, as before, to embrace its own software content), from which six can be seen to meet the criterion: (1) computers (principally mainframes and minis, and including computer peripherals); (2) consumer electronics; (3) industrial automation and instrumentation (embracing various products from simple process-control instruments to full CIM systems); (4) integrated circuits; (5) office equipment; and (6) telecommunications. The defence segment is not included because, as already discussed (see pages 60–62), its relevance to a revival of Europe's *commercial* IT capabilities is low.

Consequently, when we come to assessing costs, one of the salient assumptions will be that any realistic renaissance plan must be based on the establishment of a world-class capability in each of these six, irreducible, interrelated product segments. No less, and not necessarily any more.

International character of the electronics industry

Almost uniquely in the spectrum of manufacturing industries, the electronics sector is dominated by international forces beyond the control of any single country or region. In the highly unlikely event, for example, that America was to 'lose interest' in electronics, Japan would gladly thrust itself into even more decisive leadership; and if Japan were to falter, its place would be taken, inevitably and gleefully, by any number of up-and-coming nations in SE Asia, notably South Korea.

The pervasiveness of R & D in electronics technology, the accelerating rate of new product development, the swift and efficient dissemination of knowledge about new products, the historical accessibility of most IT markets in advanced countries and, above all, the dominance of economies of scale in this sector, mitigate against attempts to develop an indigenous IT capability in a technological fortress.

In other words, it is not possible to create a viable IT industry in geographical isolation from the world's centres of technological leadership simply by creating barriers to the importation of electronic goods and concentrating indigenous production on supplying just the domestic market. Nevertheless, there might be circumstances in which 'fortress' tactics of this sort, applied for a limited period, could form a useful constituent of an overall strategic package.

Urgency of the problem

The European tortoise waddles slowly down the road to technological nirvana wistfully eyeing the American and Japanese hares accelerating out of sight. The gap is constantly widening, and the more time that elapses before Europe initiates a catch-up spurt, the further the distance that will need to be covered.

From the curves of Figure 5.1, annual IT production is projected to increase in both the US and Japan by about $250 billion between 1983 and 2000, compared with a mere $20 billion or so for Europe. This is an order of magnitude slower, and while its competitors' production is projected to be growing at an arithmetic average of $15 billion per annum, Europe's rate of growth is only a little over $1 billion. Thus the projected gap in IT production is growing each year at the frightening rate of almost $14 billion (in terms of 1983 US dollar values).

The conclusion is stark and unequivocal. A meaningful effort to close this IT gap should have been mounted years ago, and it is already perilously close to being too late to start one now. There is certainly no risk of doing too much, too soon.

Disadvantaged Europe

In the electronics sector as a whole, the European nations have no natural advantages but many intrinsic liabilities. As a case in point, in the three largest EEC nations, current labour costs (taking account of 'social' overheads) are comparable to those in the US and higher than in Japan.

Also – a crippling disadvantage, this – there is no 'common' market for IT products in Europe, whereas Japan and the US enjoy the availability of large national markets, with a considerable degree of import protection, of some form or another, in the case of Japan. In addition, European IT producers wanting to sell into neighbouring markets find themselves having to overcome a tangled web of linguistic, legal and (sometimes) trading barriers which, by and large, make America look like an easier (as well as larger) market to attack.

The conclusion is that any European country, acting alone, would have to do it the hard way: from a small market base, a relatively weak technological position, and without any of the intrinsic advantages (not excluding the power and intelligence of MITI's guiding hand) which are enabling Japan to fight its way towards parity with the US. Even for the European community as a whole, no significant advantages can be discerned except for its *latent* power to act coherently in a marketplace of 300 million or so inhabitants.

THE RENAISSANCE MODEL

The achievement of competitive economies of scale, it has been made clear, is the first essential condition for success in the IT industry. It doesn't guarantee profitability, but long-term viability is impossible without it.

The route to viability

So we can now contemplate the performance of two hypothetical IT companies, both operating in the same product segment, and use their

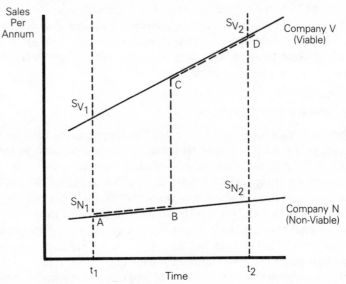

Figure 7.1.   Schematic comparison of sales growth in viable and non-viable IT companies.

sales per annum (equated, for the sake of argument, to production) to compare economies of scale. One company (V for viable) is probably American or Japanese and has a high level of sales which is increasing at the segment norm (5–15 per cent per annum would be typical). The second company (N for non-viable) is probably European, has much lower sales per annum, but these are also increasing at the segment norm. That is, both companies are maintaining market share, but the growth of sales for company N is of course lower in absolute terms.

This is the situation depicted schematically in Figure 7.1, where Company V increases its sales from the level S_{V_1} at time t_1, to S_{V_2} at time t_2, and during the same period Company N increases from S_{N_1} to S_{N_2}.

If company N is non-viable at the beginning, it is in even worse shape at time t_2 since, although the two companies' relative market shares have not changed, the sales of Company V have increased enormously compared with those of Company N, and its economies-of-scale advantages, therefore, are even more overwhelming.

To become a viable producer, company N must somehow, at some time, increase its sales to the level of company V. In the example, this is postulated to occur abruptly about midway through the period. In other words, the sales of Company N progress normally from A

$(=S_{N_1})$ to B, make a quantum leap to the 'viable' level C, halfway through the timescale being considered, and then track the sales of Company V, dollar for dollar, to the point D $(=S_{V_2})$. In short, ABCD is the assumed route to viability.

The catch-up costs

The total catch-up costs in the kind of situation depicted in Figure 7.1 consist of two distinct elements. First there is the cost of maintaining market share (low though it is) as sales increase from A to B. What is first needed, therefore, is a coefficient, C_m, to correlate the ongoing investment needed to produce each additional dollar of sales in a non-viable IT company which is nevertheless maintaining worldwide market share in free-market conditions. If a credible value can be established for C_m it will be a simple matter to calculate the *additional* investment required to achieve each *additional* dollar of sales under these market conditions.

A nominally different element of cost is also concerned with maintaining market share, but at the much higher (viable) level of sales represented by line CD. However, prejudging the results of much background analysis, we shall discover, not too surprisingly, that the same value of coefficient, C_m, can be used. This merely implies that the ratio of additional investment required to produce additional sales is much the same, regardless of the actual sales, once these exceed a non-negligible level.

A different process is working, however, to produce the quantum leap, BC, in sales. The only mechanisms for achieving this sort of instantaneous increase are by acquisition or by bringing totally new ('greenfield') production facilities on stream. In either case, it is convenient to characterize such a large and rapid increase in sales by means of a new coefficient, C_q, correlating the once-off investment required to achieve this quantum increase in sales.

Summarising, then, since points A to D represent the actual sales at the depicted times, the total catch-up cost, C_T (for company N to move from S_{N_1} to S_{V_2}), is:

$$C_T = C_m \ (B\text{--}A) + C_q \ (C\text{--}B) + C_m \ (D\text{--}C).$$

This is the formula which lies at the heart of assessing the renaissance costs, whether for a single country or for an entire region such as the EEC.

The maintain-parity coefficient, C_m

A full derivation of the value of coefficient C_m is given in Appendix C. Here, for the sake of completeness, a brief summary is presented of the salient features of the analysis.

The basic methodology has been to analyse the balance sheets and profit-and-loss accounts, over the most recent five years for which reliable financial data are available, of about 50 companies in the IT sector. From this it is possible to calculate the total increased investment and the overall growth in (IT) sales.

Investment was calculated by adding together shareholders' funds, long- and short-term loans and bank borrowings, and deducting therefrom any short-term investments and bank deposits. Thus, the increase in investment represents the difference between the results of this calculation at the beginning and end of the five-year period considered and, hence, includes retained earnings. It similarly includes additional investment required to fund any trading losses over the period. The increase in sales, quite obviously, was obtained by subtracting annual sales at the start of the same period from the corresponding figure five years later.

Despite some variation among the companies examined, the average ratio emerged as 0.8. To within sufficient accuracy for our present purposes, this means that, for an average IT company, it costs about one dollar of additional investment to achieve each additional dollar of long-term sales. In the later analyses, therefore, a value of unity is assigned to the coefficient. C_m.

The quantum-leap coefficient, C_q

It will be intuitively obvious that calculation of the additional investment required to leap very rapidly from a low level of sales to a substantially higher level is a much more difficult task. In principle, this coefficient could be obtained by examining the case histories of companies which have achieved quantum sales increases by bringing new facilities on stream. In practice, however, in most cases this sort of financial analysis is rendered impossible through the clutter of other effects. There is also the problem with greenfield start-ups of defining when the start-up investment has been completed and when the concomitant sales level has been reached.

A description of the method used to derive a value for coefficient C_q is given in Appendix D. It is based on the assumption that the cost of 'buying' sales by means of acquisition is as reliable a guide as any. After all, companies intent on achieving a quantum increase in sales have the option, at least in theory, of building a (new) factory or making an acquisition, and it is not unreasonable to assume that they make comparisons of the alternative costs. If there was a significant difference, the cheaper method would be vastly more common. There is little evidence of this, however: the balance between acquisitions and greenfield investments seems to be fairly stable.

Accordingly, about 20 relevant IT acquisitions have been analysed, mainly of American companies in a position of technical strength in their product segment(s). The result is that, despite quite a wide variety of individual ratios (investment cost to sales 'purchased'), the average value is about 2.0. This, then, is the value assigned to C_q, and implies that quantum increases in sales bear a cost of about two dollars for every dollar of new sales obtained.

Some corroboration of this figure comes from the rule of thumb, common in the electronics industry, that profitability depends on 'turning over the assets twice a year'. In other words, a $100 million new investment in an IC facility, say, should (rapidly) produce about $200 million per annum in attributable sales.

THE REAL COSTS OF VIABILITY

In order to calculate the actual costs of achieving viability, or global competitiveness, it is now necessary to start using real numbers. The analytical procedure is identical for each of the six key product segments (see page 127), and involves the following steps.

First, the current sales of the principal viable producers, worldwide, must be known. This is a relatively easy matter, given diligent analysis of annual reports and other sources, and the average of these (if averaging is sensible) yields a value equivalent to S_{V_1} in Figure 7.1. Since the analysis cannot, in any case, be done precisely, it will be of little consequence if the companies' sales values do not cover exactly the same 12-month period, provided they are sensibly close in time.

Second, it is necessary to project the sales growth of the viable producers. Since there is no way of foretelling the sales performance of individual companies, it can be assumed for simplicity that market shares will remain stable so that each company (including the non-viable producers) will increase sales at the same rate as the segment as a whole.

The segment growth rates can be obtained by means of a calculation similar to that by which the IT performances of the US, Japan and

Europe were projected to the year 2000 (Chapter 5). Namely, a systematic analysis has to be carried out of the apparent growth rates of markets in the main geographical countries, corrections made for historical inflation rates and exchange-rate variations, and 'global' growth rates then calculated in terms of a specific currency (for consistency, the 1983 US dollar). Projecting these growth rates from the base year gives the anticipated sales of viable segment producers up to about the year 2000. These calculations are detailed in Appendix E.

The third step is to establish the relevant sales, in each segment, of the leading European producers. The same caution, interpretation and approximation is necessary as in the first step, but the result is an approximate value for the point S_{N_1} in Figure 7.1.

All of the data are now available to carry out the calculation of catch-up costs as already explained in outline.

THE COMPUTER SEGMENT

While it is not necessary to go through the entire analysis for each key product segment, there is some purpose in demonstrating the analytical method by reference to one, not untypical segment. The one selected is computers—i.e. that portion of the IT industry concerned with manufacturing electronic data-processing (EDP) equipment.

The computer market, of course, embraces a wide range of individual products, but is adequately defined by the appropriate national product codes – the Standard Industrial Classification (SIC) codes in the UK, the US and the Federal Republic of Germany (FRG); and, elsewhere, by the relevant CCN, SITC (R2) and NACE codes[1]. Word processors, however, are classified here as office equipment, not computers.

The triad[2] EDP market in 1983 was valued at c.$63 billion (Table E.1), and is projected to grow (in the leading countries, i.e. the US and Japan) at the compound annual average growth rate (CAAGR) of 11.6 per cent (Table E.2). This projects to a figure of about $80 billion in 1985, $235 billion in 1995, $410 billion in 2000 and $700 billion in 2005 (Table E.3).

Before going further, however, it is necessary to take note of a unique feature of this segment, which is the astonishing domination of a single

---

[1] Exactly what these codes all mean and imply is of little importance in this book; the specialist will in any case know.

[2] Coined originally by Mr K Ohmae, the word 'triad' is now accepted as shorthand for Japan plus the US plus Western Europe.

company, IBM. Total sales of this megacompany in 1983 were $40.2 billion, of which about 80 per cent (*c.* $32 billion) can be classified as EDP. IBM is undoubtedly viable – uniquely so, indeed – but it would be unrealistic to assume that all other computer manufacturers would have to achieve a similar level of sales to be viable. In short, the approach here is to treat IBM as an aberration and to regard instead the leading second-rank American and Japanese companies as representing typical segment viability in a triad, ex-IBM 1983 market of *c.*$31 billion.

Another complication about this segment, as about many, is that it covers a multitude of different products. In particular, the product range stretches from vast 'number-crunching' super-computers, through mainframes and minicomputers, to the ubiquitous personal computer (PC), and embracing along the way a huge variety of peripheral devices such as memory, storage and input/output devices plus a wide range of terminals.

Because of this fragmentation of EDP products, it is not a simple matter to define the number of companies which are competing for the ex-IBM market. It seems reasonable to exclude manufacture of the very largest machines because, by the specialized nature of their markets (e.g. military, scientific, seismological, weather forecasting), the salient business factors determining success (including economies of scale) are rather different from the rest of the EDP segment. Similarly, the PC business is highly specialized, having many features more in common with consumer electronics than computers, and this is also excluded. It can be concluded, therefore, that a 'typical', viable EDP company, with which a European producer would have to be compared, would have an integrated capability in mainframes, minicomputers and peripherals.[3]

Because of the aggregated nature of their revenues in the published sources, it is difficult to be precise about the EDP sales of most of the Japanese producers. In the US, however, the leading manufacturers had EDP sales in 1983 in the $2–5 billion range, from Digital Equipment Corporation at $4.8 billion, through Burroughs ($4.0 billion), Control Data ($3.5 billion), NCR ($3.3 billion), Sperry ($2.8 billion) to Honeywell at $1.7 billion.[4]

Since several of these companies have recently been exhibiting some signs of non-viability, it can be assumed that the minimum 1983 sales level at which a well-managed, multi-product, leading-edge EDP company would be long-term viable is at least $4 billion. At this level, a European

---

[3] It would also be possible, of course, to carry out this analysis separately for each of these product sub-segments, but the result would be approximately the same as collating them together in the manner being explained.

[4] Most of these data are sourced from the magazine Datamation, 1 June 1984.

producer would possess the necessary international sales and distribution network and should enjoy the same economies of scale, R & D expenditure and return on investment as its hypothetical multi-product, leading-edge US competitor – excluding IBM, of course, whose 1983 EDP sales were roughly eight times higher.

There is the interesting corollary that, excluding IBM, the global market can sustain only about eight variable, broadline EDP companies (or their disaggregated equivalents). Since there are currently at least 20 substantial American or Japanese companies fighting for EDP market share, there is unlikely to be much room for many European aspirants.

On the assumption that IBM's market share does not change in the future, and that the 'viability' sales level increases in line with segment market growth, the annual sales of this hypothetical, multi-product, American EDP company will increase from $4 billion in 1983, to about $5 billion in 1985, $15 billion in 1995, $26 billion in 2000, and $45 billion in 2005, which can be regarded as the course of line S_{V_1} to S_{V_2} in Figure 7.1.

Turning now to Europe, the four leading European-owned producers (all of whom currently tend to cover the mainframe/mini/peripherals ground quite sparsely) had 1983 EDP sales as follows:[5]

Bull	:	$1.38 billion
ICL	:	$1.02 billion
Olivetti	:	$1.30 billion
Siemens	:	$1.38 billion

the average of which is $1.27 billion. However, there may be some exaggeration of the figure for Olivetti due to the inclusion of some products which do not properly belong in the EDP category.

In addition, another ten or so EEC-based EDP computer producers (mostly of special-purpose machines) had 1983 sales in the range $100 – 900 million, with an approximate average of $300 million.

In the language of practical politics, it must be assumed at this point that any European computer renaissance plan – whether based on the EEC, a single member state, or something in between – would necessarily start with some degree of merging of the indigenous producers. In other words, governments would almost certainly try to persuade their EDP companies (perhaps as a *quid pro quo* for massive new funding) to consolidate, probably by merging with the relevant national champion. The real costs of such mergers would be modest; that is, the additional sales,

---

[5] *Datamation*, 1 August 1984.

and some associated improvement in economies of scale, could be obtained without significant new investment.

For this reason, the hypothetical, non-viable, European EDP producer, on which any renaissance plan would be focussed, starts from a 1983 sales level somewhat higher than the average ($1.27 billion) of the four current leaders, derived above. While details of the postulated merger process cannot be predicted, an assumed, consolidated sales level of about $2 billion must be near enough for our purposes, albeit rather optimistic, perhaps. Thus, assuming that the mergers had already taken place, this would become the postulated value for S_{N_1}.

By simply maintaining 'parity' (i.e. market share), this 'enlarged' company would achieve a rate of sales increase equal to the segment as a whole (11.6 per cent per annum), taking it to about $2.5 billion in 1985, $7.5 billion in 1995, $13 billion in 2000 and $22.4 billion in 2005 – all in terms, it will be remembered, of 1983 US dollar values.

In calculating the renaissance costs, whatever the segment, two other assumptions must be made: first, about the duration of the renaissance process (i.e. $(t_2 - t_1)$ in Figure 7.1); and second, the timing of the quantum sales leap.

The assumed duration of the overall process of catching up is not difficult to work out. A lower limit can be set by the straightforward inertia of current policies. In other words, even in the best of circumstances, there would be a significant delay before enactment of the major policy decisions which this book advocates in Part Three. A further constraint is that the shorter the renaissance period, the higher the per annum financial burden (whoever it may fall upon).

The upper limit must be influenced strongly by the rate of divergence between Europe's IT capabilities and those of the US and Japan. Clearly, the longer the process takes, the greater the final bill. Moreover, the indirect price that Europe is paying for its technological failure continues to mount year by year – for example, the heavy cost of a substantial degree of 'unnecessary' unemployment, the cost of attracting high-tech inward investors, the restrained level of business efficiency through the continued use of obsolescent information-processing techniques, and the large and growing trade deficits.

Taking all such factors into consideration, ten years is clearly too short a time, and 30 is too long. Hardly surprisingly, the renaissance period assumed in this analysis is therefore 20 years. To be more precise, the hypothesis employed here is that the 20-year process of revitalizing the European IT industry (or, at least, the six key product segments) actually began in earnest in 1985. It obviously didn't, but it does have the virtue of illustrating what could be done, and at what cost, without stretching the projected solution to Europe's IT problems too far into the twenty-first century.

As to the timing of the quantum jump in sales, it is safest to assume that this takes place midway through the renaissance period (i.e. in 1995) since this will give the most probable estimate of the overall costs.

For the computer segment, then, the sales progress of the hypothetical model European EDP company is as depicted in Figure 7.2.[6] Starting at $2.5 billion in 1985 (point A), it progresses up the non-viable track until it achieves sales of $7.5 billion in 1995 (B). It then jumps to a viable size (of $15 billion in sales per annum), point C, and continues to grow

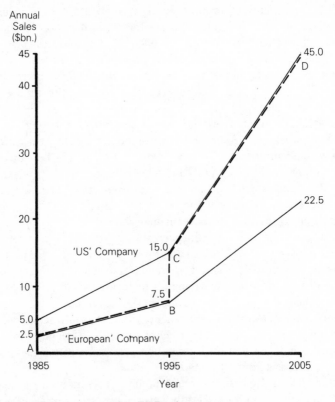

Figure 7.2. The route to viable EDP sales.

---

[6] Although the sales growth has been assumed to be at a constant CAAGR (i.e. percentage), and is therefore obviously non-linear, for schematic simplicity Figure 7.2 represents sales as growing in straight lines between 1985 and 1995, and 1995 and 2005.

thereafter at the segment rate, taking it to annual sales of $45 billion by 2005 (D).

By applying the coefficients and formula previously derived, we can now calculate the total amount of new investment funds required, viz.:

$$\text{Total cost} = C_m \ (B–A) + C_q \ (C–B) + C_m \ (D–C)$$
$$= 1.0 \ (7.5 - 2.5) + 2.0 \ (15 - 7.5) + 1.0 \ (45 - 15)$$
$$= \$50 \ billion.$$

This neat, well-rounded figure is accidental, but it does serve to illustrate the point that this is a neat, well-rounded calculation. No claims are being made for great accuracy, although there is a considerable weight of argument, as already presented, to suggest that this is undoubtedly the kind of bill which will have to be paid to create a European company with a long-term viable level of EDP sales.

In fact, it may be useful to reflect on what this large sum of money actually represents. According to the conservative assumptions and approximations carefully spelled out above, this is the total amount of new investment (wherever it may come from) required to lift a leading European EDP company of 1985, plus some merged activities, to a size where its sales and economies of scale in 2005 would be sufficiently high for it to be able to compete effectively, and over the long haul, against the best and biggest of its foreign competitors – except IBM. In short, it is the 20-year cost of creating *one* world-scale EDP company in Europe.

In case it is felt that this cost has been exaggerated, it is salutary to reflect on the recent financial performances of IBM, with which the European computer 'phoenix' would obviously have to compete in the free market. For example, IBM is reported to have invested, between 1977 and 1982, more than $10 billion merely to re-equip its many manufacturing plants, and is continuing to invest in enhanced production facilities at the rate of about $2 billion per annum. In 1983, IBM invested more than $2 billion on R & D alone. If it maintains its market share, the projections suggest that by 2005 IBM will reach total triad EDP sales of about $400 billion, compared with the prospective revitalized European EDP company of $45 billion. And finally, despite all of IBM's information-processing strengths, it has recently had to pay c. $1.5 billion in order to acquire Rolm and obtain access to its leading-edge telecommunications (PABX) technology.

It is a recurring theme throughout this book that Europe – its companies, governments and financial institutions – have always underestimated the electronics business: underestimated its importance, pervasiveness and potential – and, most of all, underestimated the cost of keeping up with the technological rat race. But the time has now come when neglected bills must be paid. If they seem unduly large it is merely a legacy of past neglect.

THE OTHER FIVE SEGMENTS

The kind of detailed analysis given above obviously need not be presented here for each key product segment. Nevertheless, it is desirable to provide an outline of each analysis if the overall treatment is to be convincing. This section therefore contains a rather daunting parade of numbers and names although, for the non-specialist, it will be the final figures for renaissance costs in each segment which will be of principal interest.

Consumer electronics

In this segment, no single company dominates as IBM does the EDP market. In fact, the 12 leading companies had 1983 consumer electronics sales covering the range *c*.$8.2 billion to *c*.$1.2 billion, with Matsushita at the top and Grundig at the bottom of that select list.

Since Matsushita is bigger by a factor of about two than its nearest rivals, Philips, Hitachi and Sony (with 1983 segment sales in the approximate range $3–4 billion), it is realistic to regard these three companies as representing the minimum size of consumer electronics company which should be capable of remaining long-term viable across the appropriate range of products, which includes VCRs, television and audio as the principal constituents. The average 1983 sales of a viable, all-products consumer electronics company has therefore been assumed to be $3.5 billion.

The historical, corrected growth rate in this segment is about 2.0 per cent (Table E.2), from which the sales of these viable companies project to $3.65 billion in 1985, $4.45 billion in 1995, $4.9 billion in 2000 and $5.4 billion in 2005.

By comparison, the leading consumer electronics companies in France, Germany (FRG) and the UK (i.e. excluding Philips and all of its subsidiaries) had 1983 average sales of approximately $1.1 billion, which projects to $1.15 billion, $1.4 billion, $1.55 billion and $1.7 billion in the same sequence of years (i.e. 1985–2005).

By carrying out an analysis similar to that spelled out in the previous section, the total cost, over the period 1985–2005, of establishing a single, fully competitive, technologically advanced consumer electronics company (in France, FRG or the UK) works out to be $7.3 billion.

At projected sales in 2005 of *c*.$5.4 billion, this company would have captured a global market share of about 8.5 per cent. This would almost certainly be sufficient for it to be long-term viable even in an industrial segment which is likely, by then, to be in much greater technological and strategic turmoil than today.

If it may again seem that the cost has been exaggerated it is helpful to remember that, even at this size, the postulated revitalized company's worldwide market share would be lower than that of Philips today (*c.* ten per cent), and few would argue that Philips is not having a considerable struggle to maintain its technological and market lead in many areas of the consumer electronics product spectrum.

Industrial automation

This is a segment richly (and confusingly) endowed with a great variety of products. At one end of the scale are relatively simple electronic instruments; at the other are the systems used for controlling industrial manufacturing processes, including robots; and in between lie expensive testing and analytical equipments such as high-performance oscilloscopes. What they all have in common is a (varying) degree of electronics intelligence and applications in the control, measurement and testing of industrial processes and products.

Although this diversity of products means that the segment is populated by a myriad of small, niche producers, there has been a growing tendency over many years for more and more market share to be concentrated in fewer and fewer hands. This natural consequence of industrial maturity has been reinforced, as in most things electronic, by increasing technical sophistication, with its premium on R & D and economies of scale, and this process will accelerate with the application of artificial intelligence (AI) over a wide range of industrial automation systems.

The result is that in most industrialized countries major companies have emerged which dominate the segment. In almost all cases, these producers are divisions (sometimes several divisions) of large industrial corporations which have developed systems for use in their own manufacturing plants and have gone on to sell the control instruments and equipments on the open market. Thus the structure of the segment also confuses the analyst, the product heterogeneity being further confounded by the obscurity of the data provided in the published accounts of most industrial giants.

This being said, we can still apply the methodology, albeit with more reservations than in the other key product segments. In the US and Japan, the top fifteen segment producers whose sales can be estimated with reasonable accuracy are, in alphabetical order, Cincinnati Milacron,

Computervision, Eaton, Fanuc, Foxboro, General Signal, Gould, Hewlett-Packard, Hitachi, Honeywell, Johnson Controls, Mitsubishi, Omron Tateisi, Perkin-Elmer and Westinghouse (Unimation).[7] Their 1983 sales ranged from about $1.7 billion down to $0.5 billion, with a weighted average of $0.85 billion. However, with some of the smaller producers (e.g. Computervision) having recently suffered worrying losses, the 1983 viable sales level has been assumed to be about $1.0 billion. At the segment growth rate of 5.7 per cent, this would increase to $1.12 billion, $1.95 billion and $3.4 billion in 1985, 1995 and 2005, respectively.

In Europe, the top five producers were probably ASEA, Brown Boveri, GEC, Siemens and Thomson. Their average 1983 sales in this segment were about $500 million and, at the same growth rate, this increases to $560 million, $970 million and $1.7 billion in the period 1985 – 2005. Using the same methodology, therefore, the theoretical renaissance cost in this segment adds up to $3.8 billion.

Now it should be clear from what has gone before that the general approach to estimating renaissance costs is as conservative as possible. The sums are in any case large and the methodology is inevitably somewhat imprecise, so the calculation should err, if at all, on the low side. In this segment, however, the methodology has almost certainly yielded a total-cost figure which is significantly understated.

The main problem is that this segment has only a short history in its current high-tech form, so the postulated growth rate may be too low. With the recent surge in the use of design automation techniques and computer-integrated manufacture (CIM), plus the forthcoming impact of many new aspects of AI, it is highly likely that the actual growth rate will be significantly higher in the future.

For this reason, the cost of force-feeding one of the European industrial automation companies to become a large, fully viable competitor, on a par with the best of America and Japan, will probably be well above the cost of about $4 billion which emerges from use of this simple but systematic analysis.

Integrated circuits

Microelectronics, as stated many times, must be the technological keystone of any renaissance policy in the IT sector, and it is expensive to

---

[7] Fuji Electric, General Electric, IBM and Toshiba are excluded due to the absence of reliable data, and Schlumberger is omitted because of ambivalence about its nationality (nominally a European company, but run from the USA).

resource. For example, a recent authoritative report[8] has estimated that the Japanese government and companies together invested a total of $4–5 billion in the semiconductor segment between the years 1978 and 1982. The result, however, has been the creation of a Japanese semiconductor industry which, from small beginnings, achieved 1983 sales of about $6.5 billion, and five or six very successful Japanese IC companies are now beginning to broaden out from their initial narrow concentration on semiconductor memory.

In most analyses (this being one of the most analysed industrial segments of all time, as the American domination has increasingly been challenged by Japanese companies), the semiconductor segment is usually treated as an entity. This is because of the technological and production synergy which exists between ICs and discrete devices such as transistors – which still account for about 25 per cent by value of worldwide semiconductor production. Nevertheless, because it is primarily ICs which represent state-of-the-art semiconductor technology, and because this is where Europe is fast losing ground, this present analysis is focussed entirely on the IC segment. However, no distinctions need be drawn between the relatively few sub-categories such as MOS/bipolar and memory/logic.

Triad sales of ICs (excluding purely in-house, 'captive' markets) were about $13.7 billion in 1983 (Table E.1) with an historical segment CAAGR of 13.3 per cent. If maintained, this projects to around $17.6 billion in 1985, $61 billion in 1995, $115 billion in 2000 and $215 billion in 2005 (Table E.3).

There are about ten IC companies worldwide which can be regarded as being at the leading edge of technology and large enough, in principle, to enjoy significant economies of scale. These range from TI in first place (1983 IC sales of c.$1.5 billion) to Philips in tenth (c.$500 million), with AMD, Fujitsu, Hitachi, Intel, Motorola, National, NEC and Toshiba lying between. Because some of these companies were only marginally profitable at that time (profits are difficult to come by in the IC business), it seems appropriate to use the average sales of only the top eight ($c$$1.0 billion) as the minimum 'viability' level for 1983. This then projects to levels of $1.3 billion, $4.5 billion and $15.5 billion in 1985, 1995 and 2005, respectively.

So far as Europe is concerned, neglecting Philips (included in the above list and a majority of whose sales, in any event, emanate from its US subsidiary, Signetics), the average level of 1983 sales of the top five

---

[8] *The Effect of Government Targetting on World Semiconductor Competition – A Case History of Japanese Industrial Strategy and its Costs for America* by the American Semiconductor Industry Association, 1983.

producers (e.g. Plessey) was significantly below $100 million. In fact, the average is somewhat unrepresentative since it includes the (relatively) dominant Siemens. That is, the leading European IC producers had 1983 sales in the range of $40 million to $150 million, and it is the average of their sales, strictly speaking, which should be used in the renaissance cost calculations. Nevertheless, maintaining a conservative approach, the calculations assume average European IC sales rounded up to $100 million.

This figure, uplifted by the segment growth rate of 13.3 per cent, increases to $130 million, $450 million and $1.55 billion in 1985, 1995 and 2005, respectively, from which use of the usual formula yields the total cost of creating a fully competitive IC company in Europe as $19.4 billion.

This, it must be stressed, is very much a minimum cost figure. For one thing, it would be about 25% higher had the analysis included discrete devices. And for another, as discussed in Chapter 6, the IC business is becoming inexorably more expensive and this is likely to be manifest by higher than average values for the two coefficients C_m and C_q. In other words, the IC segment, relative to the other segments, is likely to require more investment per unit of increased sales – whether to maintain market share or to grow abruptly.

Overall, therefore, the estimated total renaissance cost of $20 billion (1983 dollars), spread over the next 20 years, to create a single, successful, European IC company can be regarded as conservative.

Office equipment

As in other cases, the office-equipment segment presents the analyst with several difficulties. The first concerns word processors and work stations, since these can often perform both text-processing and computing functions, and are variously located in official statistics. The second problem arises from the importance of plain-paper copiers in this category. While these are clearly and properly classified as office equipment, their electronics content (as a percentage of the sales price) is low, although increasing. And thirdly, many office-equipment companies derive a significant portion of their total revenues from rentals, thus blurring assessment of the actual sales value of the equipment.

Briefly, the approach taken here is first, to classify all word processors and work stations as office, not EDP, equipment; second, to include all copiers in this segment; and third, to aggregate revenues from equipment rentals and outright sales (but not services and office supplies) on the grounds that, since most companies have adopted similar marketing policies, comparisons will still be in order.

The triad market for office equipment was c.$15.8 billion in 1983, with the high CAAGR in Japan and the US (and, coincidentally, in Western Europe also) of about 14 per cent (cf. Appendix E). This projects to values of $20.6 billion in 1985, $77 billion in 1995 and $290 billion in 2005 (all values, let it be remembered, in terms of the 1983 US dollar).

A word of caution, however. The 1983 market figure, as in most other cases in this book, is based on 'apparent consumption' – that is, 'market' equals production plus import minus exports (cf. EIAJ data). But the official statistics underlying this calculation regard any equipment produced for rental as an outright sale in the year of production. Direct comparisons between the market figure and the aggregated revenues of office-equipment companies (i.e. including a significant rental constituent) are not very meaningful, therefore.

Bearing this in mind, and including (wherever possible) only revenues derived from outright sales and rentals, the leading ten non-European office-equipment suppliers are probably, in alphabetical order, Canon, IBM, 3M Company, Minolta, Nashua, NCR, Ricoh, Toshiba, Wang and Xerox. Average 1983 office-equipment revenues of these companies were about $2.6 billion, which is heavily weighted by the two heavyweights of this contest, IBM (at c.$80 billion) and Xerox (at c.$7.3 billion).

A counter balance to these two behemoths exists in Europe, however, in the form of Rank Xerox, which had 1983 revenues (at c.$1.9 billion) more than twice its nearest rival, Olivetti. These two, together with L. M. Ericsson, Olympia/AEG and Philips, dominate European production, and the five producers had average 1983 office equipment revenues of c.$800 million.

Assuming, in the usual way, that the typical, viable, non-European company and the typical, non-viable European producer both maintain market share (i.e. grow at the segment CAAGR of 14.5 per cent), their relative sales levels in 1985, 1995 and 2005 become $3.4 billion, $12.7 billion and $47.3 billion compared to $1.05 billion, $3.9 billion and $14.6 billion. Applying the usual formula then gives the total 20-year renaissance cost in this segment as $55 billion.

Telecommunications

Relative to some of the other key product segments, telecommunications seems well defined, and the market and production statistics should be reasonably accessible and credible. Unfortunately, they are not. Many companies (not just in Europe) are secretive about their own sales/ production data and, despite the easy segmentation into a relatively small number of well-defined sub-categories (such as public switching systems, data communications, subscriber equipment, PABXs, etc.), there is considerable variation from company to company in what is included under the heading 'telecommunications'.

The approach taken here has been to collect data from a variety of sources and make an intelligent judgement about the specific value of each parameter. Fortunately, the variations in the numbers are not enormous and do not invalidate use of the standard methodology.

Two key characteristics of this segment have already been commented on. The first is the fact that the telecommunications industry is now embarking on a massive technological change-over from analogue to digital systems, with a concomitant major effect on practically every aspect of a PTT's operations and organization. The driving force is the increasing reliability and cost-effectiveness of digital techniques, coupled with the growing demand for data (and, soon, combined voice-and-data) networks.

The second characteristic is the fact that in some important countries, the telecommunications market is now being opened up (deregulated) to suppliers other than those national champions which have historically enjoyed a comfortable and close relationship with their national PTT customers. Both of these events imply that some restructuring of the industry can be expected, especially in Europe, even without the stimulus of the analyses presented here.

The triad telecommunications equipment market in 1983 was $26.7 billion. The historical growth rate of this market has been 1.8 per cent per annum although, as mentioned in Appendix E, this probably understates the stimulus to future growth afforded by the rapid growth of private communications networks based on digital switching techniques, and the convergence with office equipment and computers. The latter phenomenon, however, merely implies that the renaissance costs for office equipment may be overstated and those for the telecommunications segment understated.

In any event, using this factually correct CAAGR of 1.8 per cent means that the triad telecommunications market would grow to $27.6 billion, $33 billion and $40 billion in 1985, 1995 and 2005, respectively.

In North America and Japan there is a total of six major telecommunications companies[9] – ATT Technologies (the sometime Western Electric), Northern Telecom, NEC, GTE, Motorola and IBM/Rohm – serving a total 1983 market of about $14.5 billion. Their average sales, therefore, were $2.4 billion. In Western Europe, on the other hand,

---

[9] ITT is omitted since, despite being controlled from the US, a majority of its telecommunications sales are in Europe.

a total of about ten, largely national, telecommunications equipment companies (e.g. Alcatel, Italtel and Plessey) had total sales of approximately $12 billion, giving average sales of $1.2 billion – i.e. half the level of their non-European rivals.

On the usual assumption of maintained market share, the non-European, viable company will increase its sales to $2.5 billion in 1985, $3.0 billion in 1995 and $3.6 billion in 2005; the comparable figures for the 'non-viable' European producer are $1.25 billion, $1.5 billion and $1.8 billion. Using the standard methodology, the total cost of building up one European company, over 20 years, to join the vanguard companies in this segment works out at *c*.$3.9 billion.

There is, however, another important wrinkle, related to the size of the national markets for telecommunications equipment. To achieve the 'viable' sales level of $3.6 billion in 2005, a European company would need to have 100 per cent of its own national market *and* be exporting about half of its total production. Apart from L. M. Ericsson, no European telecommunications company has so far achieved anything like this large amount of exportation (in equivalent mid-1980s terms).

RENAISSANCE COSTS REVISITED

This chapter holds the crucial, quantitative key to unlocking the chains which are dragging down the European IT industry. Total costs have been calculated for revitalizing, over a 20-year period, the six salient segments. They are certainly not modest numbers, particularly when compared with recent investments in high-tech renaissance by both European governments and companies. But they warrant a little further examination.

Table 7.2 summarizes the results of the calculations outlined in the preceding pages. In particular, it shows that the total 20-year investment required to establish one successful European company in each of the six key product segments is approximately $140 billion, and that, by the year 2005, these six companies would have achieved combined sales of $120 billion.

Although there are inevitable uncertainties about the basic methodology and the accuracy of the renaissance costs for each segment, the main potential errors tend to be self-cancelling, as pointed out in the text (e.g. the cost of the office equipment segment is probably exaggerated and counterbalances an understated cost for the telecommunications segment). Indeed, it is a cause for comfort that, despite the various and independent assumptions made in each segment analysis, the ratio of total required

Table 7.2   The costs of viability

Segments	Non-viable sales levels		Viable sales level in 1995	Cost to achieve viability	Sales level in 2005	Investment total to 2005
	1985	1995				
Computers	2.5	7.5	15	20	45	50
Consumer electronics	1.15	1.4	4.45	6.3	5.4	7.3
Industrial automation	0.56	0.97	1.95	2.4	3.4	3.8
Integrated circuits	0.13	0.45	4.5	8.4	15.5	19.4
Office equipment	1.05	3.9	12.7	20.4	47.3	55
Telecommunications	1.25	1.5	3.0	3.2	3.6	3.8
Totals (rounded)	6.6	16	42	60	120	140

All figures in terms of 1983 US dollars (billions).

investment to sales in the year 2005 covers the narrow range of 1.05 (telecommunications) to 1.35 (consumer electronics).

Overall, therefore, the total renaissance cost is believed to be highly credible. The proposition that, on average, it takes a long-term investment of about $1.20 to produce each dollar of viable (i.e. long-term) sales is supported by much empirical evidence from the electronics sector, including the example, cited in the preceding Section, that it took $4–5 billion of investment for the Japanese semiconductor industry to achieve sales of $6.5 billion.

As discussed in the following chapter, it is also noteworthy that the total investment required initially to reach the viable sales level for the aggregation of six companies is about $60 billion – assuming that all of the necessary quantum leaps in segment sales occur simultaneously in 1995.

In summary, there is now a considerable weight of evidence that the methodology is sufficiently credible, and the data sufficiently precise, that this investment sum – or a sum very much like it – will simply have to be found if this essential IT renaissance is to have any chance of happening. Because, while money isn't everything (cf. Part One), it is certainly one of the critical resources without which the prospects for success are negligible.

In the following chapter, we shall take a look at what these renaissance costs would mean to a single nation – i.e. one attempting to go it entirely alone – and to an aggregation of states, of which the present ten-nation European Economic Community will serve as an important, existing model.

8 United We Stand – A Chance:

The economic case for a multination European IT renaissance policy

THE BACKGROUND

Japan has been a single nation for about 1200 years, welded firmly together by a common language, common law and a common government; America has been a confederation of united states since the end of the Civil War, in 1865, held together by a common language, common (federal) laws and a common federal government. Both have large populations and large cohesive markets; both have achieved enormous economic success through the commercial exploitation of electronics technology.

Western Europe had hardly begun to think seriously about possible forms of economic co-operation until 1945, since when the irresistible logic of political union has been opposed by the immovable objects of nationalism, diverse languages, uncommon laws and uncommonly disparate governments. As already noted, the EEC is currently held together by the Common Agricultural Policy, which so dominates Europe's energies and finances that little of either is left over to grapple with other forms of co-operation. Meanwhile, with a population substantially larger than either America or Japan, but crippled by a fragmented market, Europe is sinking perceptibly into technological incompetence.

But, while the tenor of this book is unequivocally pan-European, the case has yet to be proven that two or more European countries acting together could do the job better than one – the job being, of course, the creation somewhere within Europe of a competitive IT capability.

The advocacy starts here.

THE LONESOME ROAD

To make the case for multination co-operation it is first necessary to examine the feasibility (and cost) of a single nation trying to achieve IT renaissance on its own. The basic model, then, is a single, sovereign state, typically one of Europe's 'Big Three', embarking upon a policy of IT renaissance, acting entirely alone and without assistance or co-operation from any of its European neighbours. The key questions are: can it be done; and what would it cost?

The composite state

The disparity in performance and capabilities in the information-technology (IT) sector between the principal European nations on the one hand, and Japan and the US on the other, is so great that the relatively small economic and technological differences between these EEC nations themselves will have no significant impact. In other words, the main economic parameters for the Federal Republic of Germany (FRG), France and the UK are comfortably close in comparison with the very substantial gaps which exist between them and their international competitor nations in the IT sector. We can therefore envisage that this go-it-alone policy is being attempted by a composite EEC nation representing an approximate average of these three countries.

Criteria for success

The first realistic criterion for defining success by this lone seeker of the high-tech high ground is that its own industry (i.e. that part which is not majority-owned by foreign investors) must contain at least the six interdependent product segments identified above (see page 127). Their interdependence has been proven, after all, and the absence of any one implies the risk that the remainder will collapse like a house of cards. The single nation, therefore, must contain at least one company in each of the six segments.

The second (and final) criterion is that each of these IT companies must expand to reach a world-scale size (giving the prospect of competitive economies of scale) and achieve comparable profitability with the world leaders (giving the prospect of long-term viability). By definition, its R & D budget, return-on-investment and growth rate must also be on the same scale as its major international rivals.

It is implicit that this quality of success can only be achieved by competing successfully with leading-edge IT products. At any point in time the single-nation IT industry, as in any other country, will be producing a mix of leading-edge and older products, but the success will be transitory unless there is a constant injection of new products at a rate comparable to that of the most aggressive and innovative competitors.

What should *not* be a criterion of success for the single nation is the achievement of a positive balance of trade in IT products since this is not directly linked with the establishment of business viability in each key product segment. It is conceivable, for example, that a relatively small nation could achieve a positive balance of trade in IT products by a number of different routes (e.g. heavy emphasis on inward investment) without even coming close to establishing a long-term viable IT industry.

On the other hand, it may be possible (although very unlikely) that a relatively large nation, such as we are considering here, could successfully create a fully viable, profitable, multi-segment IT industry under 'national' ownership without at the same time achieving a positive balance of trade in the IT sector overall.

Moreover, trade balance is strongly influenced by the (foreign-controlled) flow of products within large multinational enterprises (MNEs) and these, by definition, do not form part of an indigenous, nationally owned IT industry. In fact, in the EEC about half of the production capacity in the IT sector is currently foreign-owned.

In summary, the analysis must be based on establishing, in each of the key segments, a national capability which is sufficient to achieve a large enough share of the worldwide free market to result in economies of scale on a par with the leading producers in each segment. The profitability thus implied presupposes both a quality of management and a speed of decision-making adequate to meet the rapidly changing challenges which are so characteristic of the IT sector.

The 20-year plan

Since we are talking in terms of a composite European nation, and since the calculations in Chapter 7 were based on the average performance of the current EEC leading companies in each segment, those estimates of renaissance costs can be applied directly to the case of the single nation.

Thus, over the 20 years 1985–2005, this nation will need to find new investment funds as follows (rounded-off figures from Table 7.2):

Computers	$50 bn	($45 bn)
Consumer electronics	$7 bn	($5 bn)
Industrial automation	$4 bn	($3 bn)

Integrated circuits	$20 bn	($16 bn)
Office equipment	$55 bn	($47 bn)
Telecommunications	$4 bn	($4 bn)

giving a total cost of $140 billion. The sales generated by these segment investments are shown in parentheses and total $120 billion in 2005.

While a very large amount of detailed planning of the overall programme would be necessary in a real-life situation, for the present purposes it is sufficient to assume that the various individual segment plans would be intelligently phased so that the financial burden (and manpower burden, see Chapter 12) was spread fairly evenly over the full 20-year renaissance period. This means that some of the segments will enjoy their quantum leap in sales early in the period, whereas one of them will go through this metamorphosis only at the very end.

The requirement for new investment funds averages $7 billion per annum, and it will intuitively be obvious that the bulk of these monies will need to come from the public purse. Not all, however, according to the following reasoning.

In the first phase of renaissance, the country's main constituent companies within each segment would be consolidated into a single 'chosen champion', as briefly described above (p. 136) and as actually happened in France to a large extent during the restructuring of its electronics industry in the early 1980s. The costs of banging these industrial heads together have been ignored in these calculations, although substantial long-term loans had to be made to the French companies to cover the upset costs of absorbing and disposing of various industrial activities.

What these companies could not afford, however, is the investment required to maintain their market share, low as it is, during this early phase. The track record of European IT companies shows that this has in any event been the case for very many years because, collectively, their worldwide market share has been declining, and at a slowly accelerating rate. Indeed, were this not so, there would be no crisis in the European IT industry, no call for a renaissance strategy and no need for this book.

The assumption, therefore, is that government funds would be needed to finance the whole of the early maintain-parity investments as each key segment consolidates into chosen champions and gears up for the all-important quantum jump.

These second-phase sales leaps will also require total funding from the exchequer. Although the relevant cost coefficient, C_q, was derived from analysis of acquisition costs (see p. 132), and although there may well be some acquisitions of high-tech companies outside the single nation (e.g. in the US), the vast majority of the investment will be associated with creating new greenfield production and research facilities within the country's own borders. After all (although it was glossed over in the derivation of C_q), there would be very little point in basing most of the country's revitalized IT industry in some other nation's back yard. This would amount to being a large outward investor (inward investment is discussed in Part Three), and little benefit would accrue to the single nation, whether in the form of increased economic activity (of which employment would be a crucial element) or enhanced designer coupling.

Phase Two, then, would involve huge programmes of construction, training, acquisition of technology and the creation of essential elements of logistical and technical infrastructure. Neither the corporate coffers, nor the investing institutions could be expected to bear any part of this cost.

The picture changes in the final phase, however. By the time a company has been injected into a viable orbit, to the point where its sales, economies of scale, R & D investment and worldwide marketing organisation are on a par with its leading international competitors, it should be profitable enough to be able to invest in maintaining worldwide market share through retained earnings. Moreover, the company's business prospects should now be mouth-watering enough for the financial institutions to provide any required long-term funding. This portion of the renaissance costs, therefore, would not be a charge on the public purse.

The actual cost to the exchequer will obviously depend on the timing of each 'leap to viability'. If this occurs on average at the mid-point (i.e. 1995) of the postulated 20-year renaissance plan (in accordance with the assumptions underlying the analyses in Chapter 7) then, as shown in Table 7.2, the bill comes to $c.\$60$ billion.

However, it is useful to note parenthetically that the total cost to the taxpayers would be reduced if the more expensive segments (i.e. computers, ICs and office equipment) were tackled earlier rather than later.

On the other hand, in practice there is bound to be a considerable period of preparation (covering matters such as planning, industrial restructuring, gearing up education and training, and constructing infrastructure and greenfield factories) before any renaissance plan could be implemented, so that the first segment to be revitalized might be in year 5, with the remaining five segments going through the metamorphosis at three-yearly intervals thereafter. Depending on the segment sequences, it can easily be shown that this sort of delay would increase the public cost to somewhere between $70 billion and $100 billion.

Taking these considerations into account, it is assumed from now on that the overall 20-year cost to the exchequer of the six-company renaissance plan would be $80 billion, or an average of $4 billion per annum. Total sales generated in the year 2005 would remain, of course, at $120 billion (all values being in terms of the 1983 US dollar).

Footing the bill

The next question concerns the feasibility of this postulated composite nation being able and willing to initiate, and sustain over 20 years, a national IT renaissance plan of this magnitude.

A starting point is to put the prospective financial burden in context with the other demands on the public purse. According to *International Financial Statistics*,[1] the 1983 GDP values in the FRG, France and the UK were, respectively, DM 1667 billion ($654 billion), FF 3935 billion ($516 billion) and £301 billion ($456 billion), using average 1983 exchange rates against the dollar. Their average (composite) GDP in 1983 was thus $540 billion.

Now it is necessary to project this GDP value to the mid-renaissance year, 1995, to ensure that we continue to compare averages with averages. The view of the Organization for Economic Co-operation and Development (OECD) is that average GDP growth in the 1980s will be somewhat less than the 2.8 per cent per annum experienced by the principal European countries in the 1970s. In fact, an average rate of GDP increase of about two per cent per annum seems as likely as any, which would give a projected 1995 GDP for the composite nation of $685 billion. This assumes, of course, that future inflation rates and changes in the exchange rates will be insignificant, which is entirely in line with the assumptions made throughout this book.

On average the public exchequer in the principal EEC member states presently controls and disburses about 42 per cent of GDP. Depending on the political complexion of intervening governments, some changes in social priorities, defence commitments and similar influences may act to alter this percentage 'take'. However, since it is difficult to see any dominating force of change, up or down, the only sensible approach is to assume no significant change. By 1995, therefore, the composite nation will disburse total government revenues of about $290 billion, being 42 per cent of $685 billion – all in terms of 1983 dollar values.

---

[1] 1985 edition, published by the IMF.

Table 8.1   Breakdown of projected 1995 composite-nation
government expenditure

Sector	Percentage	Amount ($ bn*)
Health, social security and welfare services	49.4	143.3
Education	12.9	37.4
Economic services	12.1	35.1
General public services	9.5	27.5
Defence	8.9	25.8
Housing, community amenities and other collective services	7.2	20.9
Total	100.0	290

* 1983 US dollar values.

A broad historical breakdown of government expenditures[2] shows that, taking an average of the three principal European countries, about half goes on health, social security and welfare services, with the other half spread between education, defence, economic services and other categories. In fact, using the averages obtained from the Eurostat Review,[2] and applying them to the projected composite government expenditure figure of $290 billion, gives a national budget as shown in Table 8.1.

This shows that if the composite country were to effect an IT renaissance plan of the magnitude and urgency here propounded, in 1995 it would amount to about 1.4 per cent of the total governmental budget. For comparison, it would represent 16 per cent of the defence budget and 11 per cent of the exchequer cost of education. And, on the basis of a composite 1995 population of 60 million, it would be equivalent to an annual per capita cost of $67.

While this can obviously only be guesswork, it is difficult to envisage (in any European country) an explicit national concensus agreement to make a sustained IT investment of this magnitude by foregoing expenditure in other sectors. It is equally unlikely, given the current political/economic climate in Europe, that the composite nation's prevailing government would be prepared to raise taxes significantly to pay for the renaissance plan, especially since the public (which means the voters) would not see any significant return for this national sacrifice for many

---

[2] *Eurostat: Basic Statistics of the Community*, 1984 edition, published by the Statistical Office of the European Communities.

years. Moreover, by the very nature of politics, it is unlikely that 'the Opposition', if elected to office during the renaissance period, would exhibit the same level of commitment to the plan.

Overall, while annual public expenditure of $4 billion for such a vital cause would be entirely justified by the eventual economic returns, it is undoubtedly a massive sum by any standards. Given the many conflicting claims on the public purse, the powerful monetary, social and political constraints now acting on European governments, coupled in most cases with increasing commitments to defence budgets, it would be unrealistic to believe that any single nation would be willing and able to sustain such a heavy investment in just one area of industrial activity.

Demand constraint

There is, however, a markedly more serious barrier to IT renaissance which the lone nation would bang up against. It is concerned with supply and demand, and is amenable to broad quantification.

Although the six segments have historically represented about two-thirds of the IT/electronics sector as a whole (Appendix E), it is anticipated that this will increase to about 90 per cent by the early years of the twenty-first century. This will come about because of the exceptionally high growth rates in the six segments allied to increasing impact of the convergence effect. Since the one-nation, six-segment sales (post-renaissance) would reach $120 billion by 2005 (Table 7.2), total IT production from the composite single nation would therefore become approximately $130 billion. (Parenthetically, at this level it would represent about 25 per cent of the projected IT production levels in both Japan and the US at that time.)

This can be compared with the nation's own home market by assuming that its per-capita IT consumption would lie somewhere between the minimum and maximum figures given in Appendix A – i.e. $440 for Western Europe and $2400 for the US. The composite nation would have a population of about 62 million by 2005 so that, as shown in Table 8.2, the national market would lie somewhere between $30 billion and $150 billion. In fact, a more likely figure would be $80 billion, assuming that the single nation's per-capita expenditure on electronic goods had by then caught up with that of Japan.

At this median level of domestic demand, the country's IT trade balance would be $50 billion positive. Put another way, it would need to be exporting about 40 per cent of its total, nationally owned IT production, taking no account of imports or the indigenous sales of the

Table 8.2   Projected range of one-nation IT market and trade
surplus in 2005

	W. Europe	Japan	US
Projected per-capita spend (S)	440	1300	2400
National IT market ($ bn)	30	80	150
Projected post-renaissance production over whole IT sector ($ bn)	130	130	130
Projected sector trade balance ($ bn)	100	50	(20)

All figures in terms of 1983 US dollars.

foreign-owned MNEs, both of which will take domestic market share away from the revitalized national industry.

This, it should be clear, is simply not a credible scenario. Of the major countries in the industrialized world, only Japan has achieved – very recently – this sort of high-tech export ratio, despite the vigour of its national commitment to the electronics sector going back to about 1960. Indeed, it is not projected to achieve an overall 60 per cent export level, international political tensions permitting, until about 1995, despite its modest level of imports and the relatively sparse number of Japan-based IT multinationals.

Given the progressively worsening export performance of European IT companies over the past 20 years, it is extremely difficult to believe that any nation could even come close to achieving such exceptional export success in high-technology products.

There would therefore arise within the composite nation a gross imbalance between supply and demand. If the production-based IT renaissance plan worked as depicted in this book, the country's national IT companies would be producing about $130 billion of electronic products of all kinds, of which substantially less than $80 billion would be sold in the home market (allowing for some imports and indigenous production by foreign-owned MNEs), and desperately trying to export the remaining $50–90 billion worth – to a world which would be in no condition (consumption too low) or mood (trade deficit too high) to buy them.

Ergo, total collapse of stout effort. Massive (exchequer) costs would arise, either for stockpiling the excess products (which would rapidly become obsolete) or for winding down the production (to non-viable levels) and associated employment.

Dixi! Magna est veritas et praevalet.[3]

THE PAN-COMMUNITY ROUTE

The multi-state model

The other extreme from the single, go-it-alone nation is Western Europe as a whole. This, however, is ill-defined and has even less political and economic cohesion than the European Economic Community – which is, therefore, the chosen alternative model for which the financial costs of an IT renaissance are now calculated.

It should be stressed, however, that use of the EEC as the multi-state model does not imply that this is the only grouping of European nations which could collectively embark on a programme of IT renaissance. While the EEC has many things going for it, there are some aspects of its Byzantine workings which make it less than ideal as a vehicle for trans-frontier high-tech co-operation. One is the afore-maligned Common Agricultural Policy – enormously beneficial to the 7.7 per cent of the EEC's working population who produce food, but massively detrimental to the much larger number of EEC industrial, office and services workers (92.3 per cent) whose current and future prosperity depends critically on Europe's ability to compete successfully in the production and use of IT products. Another EEC drawback is the principle of unanimity which applies in matters involving national interests. It will be difficult enough, Heaven knows, to get three or four European countries to agree to sink or swim together in the IT sector; the mind boggles at the prospect of achieving a unanimity of view from Athens to Copenhagen, Paris to Dublin and London to Rome.

So, despite using the recent ten-nation (now 12) EEC as the model, it needs to be borne in mind that other alliances – perhaps two big plus two smaller European countries – are also possible, and could be more practical.

---

[3] Be assured! Great is the truth and it prevails.

Success redefined

For the single nation, the criteria of success boiled down to the need for its own IT industry to contain at least one fully viable, world-scale company in each of the six interdependent key product segments.

For the EEC as a whole, however, the criteria need to be reassessed. In the first place, just one producer in each segment would raise insuperable problems. For example, who would control it? where would its head-quarters be located? and what would be its working language?

It is, of course, clear that in a world entirely populated by wholly rational men and women, untainted by greed, envy or nationalism, these issues could all readily be solved. But Europeans, regrettably, are no more altruistic than the rest.

Besides, it seems an unlikely way of restoring Europe to its proper place at the high-tech high table: *the* European computer company in France, say; ICs in the FRG; office equipment in the UK; industrial automation in Italy; consumer electronics in the Netherlands; and tele-communications in . . . ?! Hardly a recipe for harmony; surely a deterrant to designer coupling.

If ten or 12 sovereign nations are to commit themselves jointly to an IT renaissance plan, something grander is required. Something which can be measured, progress towards which can be monitored, and in which Europeans as a whole can take some pride.

The concept of 'fair share' seems appropriate in this context. In 1983, the combined GDP of the EEC member states totalled $2260 billion, representing about 25 per cent of the free-world GDP of $8690 billion. Since 1983 was not an exceptional year for Europe or the rest of the world, it can be regarded as representative. Thus, in any sector where the EEC is not achieving 25 per cent of world trade, it is doing less well than average. And in the IT sector, above all, Europe (the EEC) must achieve at least this level if it is to counterbalance the gradual shift to the Third World of the older, 'smokestack' industries.

By way of comparison, IT production (including that of the MNEs) in the EEC was only about 19 per cent of the free-world total in 1983 and, according to the projections of Chapter 5, will fall to about eight per cent by the end of the century unless something drastic is done to reverse the decline.

The key criterion, then, is that at the end of a 20-year IT renaissance programme, the EEC should have achieved no less than about 25 per cent of free-world trade in electronic goods. A second, related criterion is that it should be producing more than it consumes. In other words, and especially in light of the dismal projections of Chapter 5, it should be one of the objectives of any IT renaissance plan to achieve a positive trade balance in this sector by the year 2005.

The EEC renaissance model

In a revitalized European IT industry, the American/Japanese segment growth rates of Table E.2 would apply, giving a triad, six-segment market in 2005 of $1370 billion (Table E.3). Assuming, as in the previous section, that the six segments will then represent about 90 per cent of the IT sector as a whole, that the RoW markets will constitute about 20 per cent of the free-world total by 2005, and that – post renaissance – the rest of Europe (RoE) market will be about ten per cent of Western Europe as a whole, the market values can be calculated, as shown in Table 8.3.

Table 8.3   Post-renaissance electronics markets in 2005

	Six-segment	Other segments	All IT
Triad	1370	150	1520
RoW	330	40	370
Free World	1700	190	1890
EEC (25% of Free World)	425	50	475

All figures in 1983 US dollars (billions).

This indicates an all-IT EEC market in 2005 of $475 billion which, on the basis of a population of 290 million, implies a per-capita expenditure by then of about $1650. This is larger than the projected figure (Appendix A) for Japan ($1300) but significantly less than the figure for the US ($2400). This, it must be said, sounds wholly reasonable if the renaissance is successful.

Indeed, due to the worldwide market stimulation caused by a revanchist Europe, there is likely to be some stimulation of the domestic IT markets even in Japan and the US, so that a not improbable rough breakdown of the free-world IT markets in 2005 could be as shown in Table 8.4. In this event, per-capita expenditure in Japan and the US would increase to about $1500 and $2900, respectively. (All of these figures, needless to

Table 8.4   Approximate geographical breakdown of post-renaissance IT markets in 2005

Geographical area	Market value	Percentage
US	800	42
Japan	200	10.5
EEC	500	26.5
RoE	50	2.5
RoW	350	18.5
Totals	1900	100

All figures in 1983 dollars (billions).

say, should be regarded as broad estimates, mainly because they stem from a number of approximate – albeit credible – assumptions.)

In any event, this analysis indicates an EEC six-segment market in 2005 of $425 billion and, because of the assumption of a positive trade balance, this would also be the minimum level of production.

It almost goes without saying that a subsidiary criterion for success is that the EEC should not only contain at least one world-scale producer in each of the six key product segments, but should also achieve a 25 per cent free-world market share in each segment – approximately, at least.

It is now a simple matter to calculate the investment costs of creating a viable EEC-owned capability in each of the six key product segments, in accordance with the above criteria.

Column 1 of Table 8.5 shows the approximate free-world markets in each segment in the year 2005 (being the triad numbers of Table E.3 uplifted by 20 per cent for the RoW); column 2 is the assumed EEC share (25 per cent); column 3 is the minimum viable sales level in 2005 of a producer in each segment (from Table 7.2); column 4 shows the number of viable producers required to achieve those sales (by dividing column 3 into column 2); column 5 shows (from Table 7.2) the investment cost, per producer, to reach the initial viable sales level (in 1995, on average); and in column 6, the (exchequer) investment required in each segment is obtained simply by multiplying columns 4 and 5.

Paying up for Europe

The total investment cost emerges as *c.*$220 billion. Making the same kind of allowances as in the previous section (for intelligent phasing of

Table 8.5 Public cost of EEC six-segment renaissance

Segment	(1) Free-world market in 2005	(2) EEC share (25%)	(3) Viable sales level (per co.) in 2005	(4) No. of companies required	(5) Investment (per co.) to viability	(6) Total cost to exchequer
Computers	860	215	45	4.8	20	96
Consumer electronics	60	15	5.4	2.8	6.3	18
Industrial automation	100	25	3.4	7.35	2.4	18
Integrated circuits	270	67.5	15.5	4.35	8.4	37
Office equipment	360	90	47.3	1.9	20.4	39
Telecommunications	50	12.5	3.6	3.5	3.2	11
Totals	1700	425	—	c.25	—	c.220

All figures in 1983 US dollars (billions).

segment revival and for the inevitable gestation period before implementation), raises the exchequer cost to nearly $300 billion, or $15 billion
per annum on average. On the basis of a ten-nation EEC population by
then of 290 million, this represents a per-annum, per-capita cost of around
$50 – 25 per cent less than in the single-nation case, but still a significant,
long-term financial burden.

In order to make direct comparisons with the one-nation case, this cost
translates into just over one per cent (i.e. $3 billion per annum) of the
total government revenues of the average (composite) big European country (*c*.1.4 per cent in the one-nation case), 12 per cent of the defence
budget (16 per cent) and 8.3 per cent of the exchequer cost of education
(11 per cent).

Again, these very large sums of money will be extremely difficult to
raise in a Community composed of diverse, nationally minded governments of widely varied political philosophies. In relation to the go-it-
alone case, however, it has several potential advantages.

First, there is the significant reduction in per-capita cost – which is
bound to be important in an era when government departments usually
have to battle against their exchequer authorities for every million of
budget allocation. In fact, at a level of only 12 per cent of the typical,
large-nation defence budget, IT renaisssance should be regarded as an
irresistible 'best buy'. Military defence against potential foes is obviously
essential, although the necessary level of spending is always uncertain,
depending on which combination of threats is believed to be most
probable. What is *not* uncertain, however, is that Europe's ability to
maintain any meaningful defences depends critically on its economic well-
being – and that, come the next century, will depend in turn on its ability
to re-create a fully competitive, world-scale IT industry.

Second, if a long-term multination (e.g. EEC) IT renaissance project
was formally adopted, it would reduce the risk that a change of a national
government would diminish that country's commitment to the plan.

Third, and of great significance, is that the problem of distributing the
investment would be dramatically reduced. With a total of about 25
successful high-tech companies to be created (Table 8.5), there should
be enough goodies to spread around, and taxpayers of individual member
states would have tangible evidence – in the fullness of time – of the
resurgent electronics industry. Moreover, while each company would
necessarily have its headquarters located in one country, its total R & D,
design and production facilities could be spread more widely within the
Community, consistent with ensuring competitive economies of scale, in
order to distribute the economic benefits in an equitable manner.

But the single most important advantage of carrying out this essential revitalization programme on a pan-Community scale is that, unlike the single-nation plan, it would not be damned by impossible demand constraints – as we shall now see.

Supply side

It was shown above (page 158) that if, as a result of a national IT renaissance, the single nation raised its per-capita IT consumption to the level projected for Japan in 2005, its home market would become *c*.$80 billion. But, to achieve viability, its own IT companies would need to be producing at least $130 billion, despite the fact that at least some part of the home market would necessarily be served by imports and foreign-owned MNEs. The lone nation would therefore have to be exporting, by 2005, at least 40 per cent of its own production – and more likely 70–80 per cent if imports and the MNEs are taken into account. This, it is argued, is simply untenable.

In principle there is no such problem in the case of the EEC. According to the preceding calculations, IT production (equated, for simplicity, to sales) from *EEC-owned* companies in post-renaissance 2005 will total $425 billion for the six key segments and $475 billion for the entire IT sector. And this size *market* is equivalent to per-capita IT consumption only marginally above that projected for Japan.

The picture, however, is complicated by the inevitable existence of imports (even if these are modest, in 2005, in the six segments) and the continuing presence within the EEC of foreign-owned MNEs (which, being largely independent of governments, import, add value and export as they think fit).

Production from the EEC facilities of non-European MNEs was about $35 billion in 1983 and, lacking the stimulation of government support, can reasonably be expected to continue expanding at the historical rate. This is somewhat higher than the corrected historical CAAGR of 1.3 per cent (Table A.6) since that figure effectively represents a balance between the static or declining European companies and the expanding inward investors. As well as it can be assessed, production from the IT MNEs has been growing at a real rate of 3.5 per cent, which would take their output to a level of $75 billion by 2005.

Imports, of course, are quite impossible to forecast. Nevertheless, even in the post-renaissance EEC they will not be insignificant, and a level of ten per cent of the total IT market (i.e. *c*.$50 billion) seems a reasonable assumption.

The overall IT trading position in the EEC, post renaissance, could

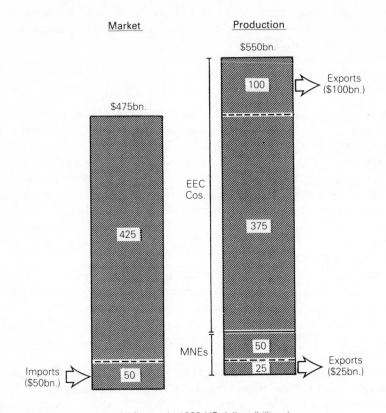

All figures in 1983 US dollars (billions)

Figure 8.1. Schematic of possible post-renaissance EEC trade in IT products.

therefore look roughly as depicted in Figure 8.1. The total market of $475 billion would be served by $50 billion of imports, $50 billion of production from the MNEs, and $375 billion of production from the revitalized, EEC-owned producers. On the basis of their hard-won international competitiveness, these companies should also be capable of exporting around 20 per cent of their total prodution (i.e. *c*.$100 billion), to which it is assumed that the MNEs would add another $25 billion (i.e. 3 per cent of *their* production). Total production would therefore be around $550 billion, giving a positive trade balance of $75 billion.

It may be noted that, at this level of production, the EEC would actually have captured about 29 per cent, not 25 per cent, of the estimated free-world IT trade in 2005 of $1900 billion. This, of course, is entirely possible given the tremendous momentum the EEC IT industry would have generated by then. On the other hand, if the lower level of $475 billion is reached the overall trade picture will be marginally different from that shown in Table 8.1. It is the more optimistic (and more difficult) outcome which is assumed in what follows.

THE DEMAND GAP

On the basis that the EEC represents about 77 per cent of Western Europe, use of Table A.7 shows that the EEC IT market as a whole was about $65 billion in 1983 and, on historical trends, will grow to merely $125 billion in 2005.

But, as argued above, an IT renaissance in the EEC depends on the development of a market in 2005 totalling at least $475 billion. There is therefore a demand gap of $350 billion, the filling of which is a major preoccupation in Part Three of this book. For without this level of demand, production will be too low, economies of scale will be uncompetitive and the postulated $300 billion of taxpayers' investment will go down the drain.

It is in its concentration on trying to quantify demand, and seeking means to create it, that this book is believed to offer a different and more realistic formula for success than some other nostrums. Europe's main problem, in short, is not a lack of R & D, nor technology, but straightforward demand. If a way can be found of creating, by 2005, an *additional* EEC market for electronic goods of about $350 billion per annum, *and* the concomitant exchequer burden of $15 billion per annum of renaissance investment for 20 years can be afforded, the Community electronics industry will become on a par with the world's best, and Europe's economic prosperity in the twenty-first century will have been asssured.

We have discussed the problem of bearing the costs of renaissance investment; now we must try to identify a feasible way of closing this forbidding gap in IT demand.

PART THREE
Trying the Measures

Choosing each stone, and poising every weight,
Trying the measures of the breadth and height;
Here pulling down, and there erecting new,
Founding a firm state by proportions true.

The First Anniversary of the Government
under Oliver Cromwell, A. Marvell

9 The Lure of Easy Options:

A review of two losing policy options

THE STORY SO FAR

In Part One of this book, the historical roots of America's early domination of the electronics/IT sector have been described, together with some of the foundation strengths on which Japan has been building up its competitive capability in high technology. These early chapters also document the slow but steady deterioration in the competitiveness and relative size of Europe's IT industry and describe some of the causes of this decline.

It is, by now, a well-known and oft-repeated story of technological decay, which is given a quantitative dimension in the calculations of Part Two. These analyses, of course, have been heavy on numbers – probably heavy reading, to boot. Apologies, however, are not in order. The problem which Europe faces is huge, and finding a solution to it (if there is one) will unavoidably be hugely expensive.

In other words, because so much taxpayers' cash has already been spent on national IT support programmes, to very little apparent effect, it is obviously essential to try to establish whether yet more money will do the trick – and, if so, how much. Moreover, since this sort of calculation has never been done before, so far as is known, there is a pressing need to develop methodologies which would give at least a rough guide to the total investment required to lift the European IT industry from where it is today – in technological purgatory – to where it would like to be in 20 years' time – large, competitive and profitable.

This quantification has been the aim of Part Two. Achieving it has necessitated tossing about a lot of tiresome numbers, but it is contended that the effort has been eminently worthwhile. For the resultant figures for renaissance costs exude an air of authenticity – big, but believable.

So big, indeed, for a single, large European nation as to be out of reach, in all probability. Even if done on a multination or pan-Community basis, the estimated per-capita cost is exceedingly heavy.

For this reason, before looking for ways in which the demand gap of some $350 billion per annum could be filled by 2005, and how this theoretical, massive 20-year investment of about $300 billion might be made in a practical, effective way, it is appropriate to consider whether there could be easier, cheaper alternative routes to achieving the same objective. There are only two possible options: one is to rely on inward investors to inject the essential ingredients of technology, jobs and exports; the second would be to base a European IT renaissance on trade linkages (e.g. joint ventures, product licences, technology transfer agreements) with companies in Europe's transoceanic competitor nations, the US and Japan.

THE SIREN SONG OF INWARD INVESTMENT

By way of definition, inward investment is a term generally used to describe an investment by a foreign company in physical assets implanted within a host country's sovereign territory and manufacturing economy. So far as the IT sector is concerned, the most important sources of foreign investments are, of course, the US and Japan, and the physical assets usually take the form of sales and distribution networks, production facilities and equipment, and – rarely – R & D laboratories.

Although foreign-owned, the operations of such an implanted company are obviously subject to the jurisdiction of the host country, and local employment regulations, for example, are strictly enforced. In many cases, however, favourable tax rules and other financial encouragements apply specifically to inward investors and provide an important incentive for the investment.

The promotion of inward investment has been used by a number of countries throughout the world, including Europe, as the main ingredient of their industrial strategy in the IT sector. This is for the highly visible reasons that such investments are perceived to provide employment, improve the balance of trade and inject advanced technology. The primary European exponent of this strategy has probably been the Republic of Ireland, but Austria, Belgium, France and the UK are often keen competitors for whatever inward investments might be going.

Investor Motives

Consideration of inward investment obviously occurs when, and only when, the foreign company can see intrinsic advantages to locating in a particular geographical area. Such natural advantages are often enhanced, however, by national authorities who, through a package of attractive fiscal incentives, can sometimes make a marginal investment seem well nigh irresistible. Indeed, so fierce has the competition become in Europe to attract such companies that the cost to the 'successful' taxpayers, as we shall see, can become very substantial.

Foreign companies which have established manufacturing facilities in Europe believe themselves to have derived certain clear advantages thereby. Probably the most significant is the avoidance of import duties on products manufactured and sold within the EEC, although production in the European Free Trade Area (EFTA) usually confers similar benefits. Secondly, there is the important factor, particularly in high-tech industries, that a European facility can improve the relationships with customers in what is, after all, a very substantial marketplace. Moreover, if the inward investment includes a major design and/or R & D component, the designer-coupling effect can begin to come into play, with a long-term beneficial effect on sales.

Another important factor, especially for Japanese consumer electronic companies, is that the creation of local employment often works to dilute the resentment which is sometimes generated by foreign companies which are simply too successful in the local marketplace.

An increasingly potent factor in a talent-limited world is that the investment will give the foreign company immediate access to the pool of technically trained scientists, engineers and technicians in the host country. This is particularly effective if the area selected for the facilities possesses the kind of amenities attractive to graduate personnel – such things as climate, scenery, sports facilities and easy access to academic and cultural institutions.

Last but not least, a foreign investment can often result in production costs which are lower than in the parent company's homeland. This is obviously so in 'low-cost' European countries such as Greece, Portugal and Spain. But even in higher-cost nations, the combination of financial incentives, good management, a dedicated work force and a favourable exchange rate can produce meaningful cost savings. This is not generally the case, however, in countries where the 'social' cost of labour is particularly high.

In summary, investment in Europe by American and Japanese electronics companies is frequently, but not invariably, a good thing for them. But our preoccupation here, of course, is whether it is good for Europe.

Host of benefits

All host countries are seeking the same principal benefits from their IT inward investors. Above all, more jobs; very much in second place, a contribution to improving the general level of technology and the technological infrastructure; and thirdly, an improvement in the high-tech trade balance.

So far as job creation is concerned, the strategy has apparently been successful. As a crude estimate, something like half of the present *c*.1.8 million IT jobs in Western Europe must be in foreign-owned multinational enterprises (MNEs) since they account for about half of the IT production output (and their productivity is unlikely to be vastly superior to that of the indigenous companies). It gives pause for thought to contemplate what Europe's high-tech employment levels might have been like had it not welcomed these enterprises to its shores.

But it isn't that simple. Many of these MNEs are in Europe for wholly selfish reasons. That is, the advantages to them of establishing local facilities are so strong that no incentives are necessary – indeed, in many cases none are paid since a large number of MNEs have located in non-subsidized regions (see Chapter 4). Moreover, in the cases where financial incentives have been used, there is the important question of the cost per job created. This is discussed below in more detail, but cannot be ignored in light of possible alternative uses of such monies.

The type of facility established by the foreign IT company is clearly of great importance to the success of a national strategy based on inward investment. A satellite assembly-only facility rarely implies a substantial investment and can be particularly vulnerable to contraction and even closure consequent upon decisions made thousands of miles away in the company's headquarters. In fact, the higher the level of technology transferred, the more effective the investment will be in promoting advances in knowledge and techniques likely to be of lasting benefit to the host country. However, for the investment to result in a total business, which is not common in the IT sector, it is necessary to incorporate all of the basic elements such as general management, marketing, product and process development, purchasing, production control and planning, as well as manufacture. Even then, the business can become vulnerable unless its activities are kept up to date through the efficient and continuing transfer of technology.

For the sake of the long-term interests of the IT industry in the host country, emphasis is frequently (and rightly) placed on encouraging R & D and technology transfer into the implanted facility by means of additional R & D grants and the encouragement of joint ventures and licensing agreements. The R & D grants vary from country to country in Europe but are usually substantial, ranging from $33\frac{1}{3}$ to 50 per cent in the UK (with upper limits to the total grant) to 80 per cent in Belgium (in the form of interest-free repayable loans).

Returning to the question of the cost of job creation, investment grants and subsidies form the most tangible component of public expenditure involved in financing an inward investment. These generally embrace a direct investment incentive, a subsidy related to the number of jobs created, training grants and, in some cases, an 'infrastructure' grant. Tax concessions of various kinds are also a significant, if less visible, cost factor. These usually comprise an investment allowance, a favourable rate of corporation tax and an accelerated depreciation allowance.

The jobs created are both direct and indirect. In the case of the Republic of Ireland, for instance, it has been estimated that about $4.6 billion was spent on financing its industrial policy over the period 1973–80, which gave rise to 33,000 directly created jobs. Due to the multiplier effect, an additional 39,000 jobs were created indirectly, although the value of its multiplier will inevitably vary between nations, and between regions within those nations.

In any event, that yields an average cost per job created – of both types – of about $67,000. Although comparisons in this area are fraught with difficulty, it is of interest that in Austria and France the costs, ostensibly calculated on roughly the same basis as in Ireland, have been estimated as $35,000 (1981) and $27,000 (1982), respectively. These costs, however, include only the major subsidies and should be regarded as minimum figures.

A question must also be raised about the longevity of the jobs created. This is not yet much of a problem in the IT sector, which has obviously enjoyed almost uninterrupted growth for at least 30 years. But in the older industries a considerable net loss of jobs has occurred in Scotland over the past decade[1] (see Table 9.1), and there is no reason to suppose

---

[1] A detailed study of the retreat of MNEs from Scotland has been carried out by N. Hood and S. Young of the University of Strathclyde, from which the figures in Table 9.1 have been obtained.

Table 9.1   Multinationals in retreat

| Company | Peak employment | | Closed | Latest employment |
	Value	Year		
Chrysler*	7300	1979	1981	—
Goodyear	c.830	1978	1980	—
Honeywell	c.6000	c.1979	—	1870
Hoover	5400	1973	—	c.2000
NCR	6500	1971	—	c.1000
Singer	16000	1960	1980	—
	42,230			4570

* Sold to Peugeot–Citroen in 1978–80.
Source: N. Hood & S. Young, *Multinationals in Retreat, The Scottish Experience*, Edinburgh, 1982.

that the same thing hasn't happened elsewhere and that the same process will not occur in particular segments of the IT industry as they mature. Indeed, although the particular Scottish facilities affected were not exactly state-of-the-art high technology, the presence of Honeywell and NCR in Table 9.1 is possibly symptomatic of the ease with which companies, controlled from far-off foreign cities, can decimate 'offshore' satellite operations – particularly when, as in these cases, a radical technological change has to be absorbed.

The injection of leading-edge technology is a clear example, it seems, of the host nation benefitting from inward investment, although it is not a common event. It can be a double-edged sword, however. Such imported technologies are likely to be in advance of those being used locally, and although this could result in some spin-off benefits, it may swamp local competitors. There is also the problem, already referred to, of competition for scarce technical talent.

Two other potential benefits justify brief comment, the first being an uplift in the quality of management. Most of the inward-investing companies are, by definition, expanding and successful. In general, therefore, they will be well managed, and the skills thus implanted in the local management (i.e. when they are nationals of the host country) will tend to diffuse in time into the local industry. Thus the influence of those early and successful high-tech inward investors, IBM and Texas Instruments, can be seen everywhere in Europe as their alumni fill top jobs and inject new management techniques into the indigenous IT companies by whom they are so eagerly hired.

Finally, there are the possible benefits of local purchase – i.e. the stimulus of serving a demanding, leading-edge, foreign company that can be given to host-country subcontractors and suppliers of components and sub-systems. Although this undoubtedly happens, it is less prevalent than might be expected or desired, particularly when the build-up of a local supply infrastructure within the host country has not occurred.

The balance sheet of inward investment

A balance sheet for inward investment is shown in Table 9.2, under three main headings. Most of the sub-categories will have a net positive or negative effect, depending on circumstances.

Employment can rise or fall, depending mainly on the status of the technology used in the implanted facility. The higher it is, given the generally backward state of the European IT industry, the more likely it is to create wholly new jobs; the lower it is, the greater the likelihood of displacing jobs in local companies. In addition, jobs are usually created in downstream activities such as the supply of materials, components and sub-systems. Overall, however, the net effect of inward investment on local employment is invariably short-term positive, although this may not be the case in the long term. And there are some inevitable side effects.

The most critical of these is the extra demand which the foreign companies create for IT graduates and technicians. The whole topic of graduate supply and demand is dealt with later in some detail (see pages 241–244), but there can be no doubt that, even today, there is an acute shortage of real talent throughout the worldwide IT industry, including Europe. Inward investors always exacerbate this shortage, although some of the more enlightened foreign companies have played a useful role in encouraging the creation of more, and better, educational courses and facilities in electronics generally. The effect of inward investment in this particular area is emphatically negative, although there is undoubtedly a net positive impact on employment generally.

On the question of job durability, the verdict is negative. Every IT company worthy of a place in the technological vanguard locates its technical masterpieces on a site close to home. So their facilities abroad

Table 9.2   Balance sheet for inward investment

Factors	Assets	Liabilities
Employment		
Job creation	Gain for high-tech jobs	Loss for low-tech jobs
Skill shortages	—	Seriously exacerbated
Job durability	—	Long-term insecurities
Management skills	Local skills improved	Management cream hived off
Labour relations	Generally good effect	—
Technological		
Technology up-grading	—	State-of-art technology rare
Technical infrastructure	—	Local demand usually too small
Financial		
Local procurement	Modest, but positive	Continued reliance on parent's suppliers
Cost of job creation	Probably worthwhile	Money might be better used
Trade balance	Important contribution	—

are never a critical survival factor, and when things get tough these are generally the first to go. Out of site, one might say, out of mind.

The verdict on management skills is favourable, on balance, to the inward investors. This is despite the fact that the US companies, in particular, tend to recruit a substantial proportion of young Turks and managerial high flyers in the host nation, and that a dispiritingly high proportion of the most successful of these recruits eventually move to jobs in the US. But there is convincing evidence, as mentioned, that the insistence such companies place on highly disciplined reporting and decision-making procedures is percolating through to several European IT companies – particularly those of medium size – to their benefit.

Whether inward investment improves or worsens labour relations depends very strongly on the management style and expertise of the incoming company. Several European subsidiaries of Japanese electronics companies, for instance, have shown that very good labour relations can be created when working with trades unions which have been emancipated from their nineteenth century preoccupations. It remains to be seen, though, whether this excellent atmosphere will survive any decisions taken to cut employment when times become difficult. Many American IT companies, on the other hand, have effectively banned trades unions and operate – quite contentedly in most cases – through local management/worker liaison committees.

All of which seems to have had a generally beneficial effect on the national IT industries in Europe. With only a few exceptions, the relevant trades unions have moved with the times, and management attitudes to workers are slowly becoming less autocratic. This is one area, in short, where the inward investors get full marks.

However, on neither of the technological factors is it possible to say much in their favour. Because the implantation process usually begins with a sales office, and/or a factory for assembly of the final product, it takes a very long time – plus, usually, a confidence-building period of uninterrupted growth – for a foreign high-tech company to invest significantly in European design, development and research – at least to the extent that its amputation would be acutely painful to the parent. IBM is the exception, of course, having reached the size and stability to be aware of local political sensitivities, and it has created several prestigious R & D centres in Europe (inter alia). As for other IT companies which have made similar state-of-the-art commitments to Europe, at the present time there are very few Americans and no Japanese.

The same is generally true of the technical infrastructure. Other than ICs, only a few American or Japanese suppliers of components, subsystems and services have deemed it worthwhile to make a significant investment in Europe. While this might be thought to provide an opportunity for local suppliers, the truth is that, in general, they are not initially competent to meet the incoming companies' requirements. They rarely get a chance to, moreover, because the procurement of critical supplies and services tends to remain with foreign suppliers to the parent company. In fact there are very few cases in Europe where inward investors have had a significant impact on the development of technical infrastructure, and in the Republic of Ireland, relying heavily on job creation in foreign-owned, high-tech companies, it has hardly happened at all.

This also influences the verdict on the value of local procurement, as we turn to consider the financial factors. Clearly, this must represent a positive component of the balance sheet since *any* new venture must create local jobs. For reasons stated above, however, the effect is often muted by the incoming company's continuing commitment to its foreign suppliers.

On the cost of each job created (roughly $30,000 – 60,000), it is difficult to judge how good a bargain this is. If the net value to the national exchequer, in unemployment benefits saved and (new) taxes collected, is in the region, say, of $4000 – 5000 per annum per job created, it could be regarded as a worthwhile investment. On the other hand, in a period of increasing monetary constraints in most countries, as discussed in Chapter 8, it is certainly possible that the cash going into foreign hands could be put to better use. Indeed, this forms a not insignificant part of the overall renaissance policy which this book advocates (Chapter 12).

And finally, there is the matter of trade balance, which is undoubtedly an important plus factor for the inward investors (who produce more than 50 per cent of the EEC's IT production). If they were not present, *and* if their places had not been taken by European-owned companies, the West European IT/electronics balance of trade would obviously be much worse than it is.

In conclusion, inward investment in Europe is fragmentary and unsuitable in itself to form the basis for a renaissance of the European IT industry. It can bring improved styles of management and labour relations which may be of some benefit to the host nation, and it can improve the national standard of electronics technology – but only if the implanted facilities operate at the leading edge of technology. As a national policy it can improve the trade balance and create jobs, but only at the expense of increasing the shortage of IT talent and at a cost per job created which could more productively be spent in other ways. In brief, inward investment is at best a short-term palliative whereas the European IT industry is screaming for a root-and-branch cure.

TRANSOCEANIC LINKAGES ASSESSED

Transoceanic linkages are collaborative ventures between individual companies in any two of the three triad 'countries'. In the IT sector, the linkages usually involve some aspect of product know-how. Thus acquisitions, joint ventures, manufacturing licences and technology transfer agreements all lie within this orbit.

Because it is the plight of Europe which is our main concern, this discussion is entirely concentrated on linkages between European IT companies on the one hand and American or Japanese companies on the other. In fact, this is in accordance with reality since trans-Pacific linkages (i.e. between American and Japanese companies) are rare by comparison.

The European perception

Research into the motivations of European companies who have made agreements with US or Japanese companies, or have bought shareholdings in them, shows conclusively that their primary objective was the acquisition of a specific technology and/or product. In many cases, European companies have come to recognize that a particular technology or product was vital to their business, but their own R & D efforts were either not up to scratch, or were directed at other targets. In this event, the normal perception is that it is easiest, quickest and cheapest to acquire the know-how by some form of association with a transoceanic firm.

One characteristic of these deals is that the European firm invariably wants to stay in control of its business. It is also clear that in a majority of these linkages, the European partner is a powerful company with the financial resources to buy itself a piece of the overseas high-tech action. Taking these two factors together, it is hardly surprising to find that the transoceanic partner – particularly in the US – is often a relatively small company which has established a leading position in some technological niche. For this reason, such agreements sometimes include acquisition by the European company of shares in its technology-rich American partner.

There are, however, relatively few small-to-medium entrepreneurial IT companies in Japan, so these linkages tend to be between two large corporations – e.g. Siemens and Toshiba in memory ICs, Philips and Sony in laser-disc technology and GEC and Hitachi in television manufacture.

Another prominent objective of the European companies, particularly in the case of acquisitions or partnerships in the US, is the desire to establish a presence in the transoceanic market. One reason is that, as in other countries, the public-sector portion of the market will only buy goods with a considerable local content. And, especially in the wide open markets of the US, the general buyer of electronic goods has a remarkably broad choice, and is not likely to buy, in competition with 'national' products, European products which have not been especially tailored to suit his needs.

A third and important motivation which has been declared publicly by several European companies, is their need to have a significant US presence as an aid to keeping up with the rapid advances in American technology, and applications of IT. Some of the more sophisticated companies which have followed this strategy have also recognized the constructive challenge which comes from trying to compete head-on with their leading competitors in what is, in most respects, the world's most sophisticated and demanding high-tech marketplace.

And finally, some companies have been driven to forge transoceanic linkages through despair at finding suitable European partners. Recognizing their need for technology, or new markets, or symbiotic partnerships, while still preserving their independence, they have not found a rich vein of prospects in Europe. For one thing, the population of small, high-tech firms in Europe has been miniscule in comparison with the US, so most prospective European partners tend to be of similar size. Unless the agreement is on a narrow front, this can presage eventual domination of one by the other.

Moreover, other European companies are either seen as competitors or are believed not to be in the vanguard of technological advances. And even when suitable partners can be identified, the fragmentation of the European market usually means that, to achieve satisfying pan-European sales, deals would have to be made with acceptable partners in several different countries.

On the whole, it is clear that many European companies adopt the transoceanic strategy (predominantly, it should be said, transatlantic) because it seems the natural thing to do, whereas the disadvantages are contingent. They are more likely, they believe, to find what they want without uncomfortable 'strings' ; it is perceived to be a low-risk strategy in that it provides access to leading-edge technology with minimum commitment; they will obtain, they hope, easy entry into a large market; and they do not risk losing their own identity or control of their business destiny.

European reality

That, it should be stressed, is what European firms *think* they can get out of transoceanic linkages. The reality is rather different.

For instance, analysis shows that the penetration of the US market by European firms on the basis of acquisitions or joint ventures is not great when viewed against their aspirations announced at the time of the original deal. The other side of that coin, however, is that low though their US market share may be, it is generally higher than that of European companies which have not ventured into the shark-infested waters of North American business.

Another feature of transoceanic links, particularly with Japanese companies, is that a part of the 'payment' for access to technology often requires the European licensee to market Japanese products in Europe. The licensees themselves rarely object to this sort of proposition, mainly because the selected products are never in direct competition with their own, but also because they can readily see the profits to be gained from selling Japanese products (anybody's products) through their own, often highly efficient distribution channels.

It is clear, nevertheless, that in a broader context, the effect of such Trojan-horse agreements can only be detrimental in the long run to the interests of the European electronics industry as a whole. Japanese companies are astonishingly adept at devising innovative tactics for the defeat of their commercial rivals, and this particular ploy has already yielded many Japanese successes – simply by pandering to short-term (European) corporate greed. It must provide considerable food for thought, for example, that a significant factor in the Japanese capture of the Europen VCR markets has been the acquiescence of several major European consumer electronics companies to this sort of marketing deal – sometimes on an 'own-label' basis.

A much larger drawback of these technology transfer agreements is that the technology transferred is often of dubious quality. More particularly, it is rarely state-of-the-art. In the case of US companies there is invariably full disclosure of information (within the boundaries of the legal agreement) from both large licensors and smaller acquisitions, whereas in the case of Japanese companies it seems that the European firm must rely much more on what the licensor decides to tell him (although European firms generally feel confident that they have been told the truth – and sufficient of it).

Nevertheless, in essentially all cases the know-how which is being transferred is, by definition, at least one step on the way to obsolescence. On the one hand, most small American high-tech companies – the kind which are occasionally wholly or partially acquired by European firms – have usually got where they are on the back of a very small number of good ideas or products – usually one. They become candidates for acquisition, more often than not, either because they have run out of money and cannot raise more from the US capital markets, or because they have recognized a (low) ceiling to their growth ambitions and hope for a more contented future in the loving arms of some large, comfortable European corporation. In either case, it is rare for the acquired company to have maintained the necessary high expenditure on R & D and intense commitment to product innovation.

On the other hand, with know-how agreements involving large donor corporations (of any nationality), the technology being transferred has inevitably already reached a mature state, is extensively practised and well documented. Indeed, it is precisely these attributes which make the technology a good candidate for licensing and of dubious value to the recipient. For it is almost always the case that the donor firm has something better up its sleeve – back in the labs, or even ripe to move into full production status. So the licensee will not infrequently find himself trying to compete, inter alia, with his licensor but equipped with inferior products or technology.

In fact, given that the limitations of technology licences are common knowledge in the electronics industry, it is surprising that they are still so much in vogue. The reason can only be that each recipient company sees this as a short-term amelioration of some product deficiency, perhaps hoping to build up its future strength on the foundation of the imported know-how. In theory, this should be feasible; in practice, it rarely happens.

The reason is not difficult to find, because the energy and resources soaked up by the complicated importation of a sophisticated technology – process or product – cannot simultaneously be applied to thrusting the licensee into market leadership on the more solid foundation of home-brewed technology. In short, unless carried out with a clear perception that this can be only one small piece in the long-term strategic jigsaw, the licensing of technology implies the perpetuation of obsolescence.

NO CHEAP CHOICES

The overall conclusion to be drawn from the foregoing is that neither inward investment nor transoceanic linkages can provide the central core of a national or European strategy for revitalization of the IT industry.

The case against inward investment can be reinforced by postulating a future in which the impending, huge high-tech trade deficit, and its concomitant problems of chronic unemployment, has at least been neutralized by a large influx of subsidiaries of foreign electronics companies into Europe. This would, of course, be extremely expensive since, as already stated, such companies only establish satellite operations outside their own borders if it is commercially sensible to do so. To increase the rate of inward investment into Europe from its present 'natural' level to that required to achieve trade balance (for example) would require financial inducements on a massive scale – probably necessitating the injection of public funds (into 'foreign' balance sheets) comparable to the costs of the prospective demand-led renaissance strategy outlined in Chapter 8. To be more precise, the enhancement of production by the $c.\$60$ billion required simply to close the projected European IT trade gap in the year 2005, based on the productivity figures of Table 5.5 and an assumed cost per job created of about \$100,000, would be roughly \$100 billion.

Moreover, such a policy would tend to be divisive, rather than cohesive, in a European context, since it is difficult to believe that national governments, whose political survival will constantly be threatened by escalating unemployment, could resist the temptation to outbid one another in attracting the bigger prospects.

And finally – *reductio ad absurdum* – the end result would be a 'European' IT industry dominated by non-European owners, the future growth and prosperity of which was dictated by alien managements for whom the economic well-being of Europe would (quite properly) rank far below the narrower business interests of their own companies.

Transoceanic linkages can similarly be dismissed with some ease. The principal grounds, put succinctly, are that a persistent European IT renaissance can only be founded on avant-garde products, not the kind of technological hand-me-downs which are the (rotting) fruits of such technology transfer agreements.

To close this chapter on a more positive note, it is not being argued that these policy options are worthless. It seems clear that a coherent strategy for European renaissance in high technology could beneficially include a modest programme for the controlled acquisition of certain key technologies by means of carefully considered technology transfer deals – either by acquisition or licensing. Moreover, the more powerful the European company, the more immune it would become to being fobbed off with yesterday's know-how.

And inward investment, while of no significant influence in moving Europe towards technical parity with the US and Japan, is at least relatively unharmful.

10 A Song for Europe:

Searching for a European IT renaissance project

THE LIBRETTO

So there is no easy option. If the European IT industry is to be saved – from the crushing power of its competitors, from some hidebound governments and uninformed politicians, and from itself – some feasible way must be found of creating $350 billion of additional demand by about 2005. Moreover, some delicate mechanism will need to be set in motion whereby the bulk of this enhanced demand is selectively channelled to the European-owned electronics companies, since the European cause would be ill served if such a colossal project merely increased the sales, production volumes and economies of scale of its foreign competitors.

The challenge, then, is to identify something akin to the American Apollo project of the 1960s which, by an unprecedented peacetime focussing of national effort (on the task of getting a man on the moon by the end of that decade), achieved the well-nigh impossible goals publicly set by President J. F. Kennedy. As we all know, it was hugely expensive. It was also magnificently successful in restoring America to the vanguard of space technology, resuscitating national pride and creating countless new American jobs engaged in the pursuit of a key technology of the future.

A SEXTET OF CRITERIA

Before attempting to compose a European melody as enchanting as Apollo, it is as well to establish what must be its key characteristics. That way, we lessen the risk of being seduced by a pretty little tune, while increasing our ability to recognize perfect harmony when we hear it.

Technical feasibility

In the first place, the project will have to be technically feasible and focussed on leading-edge technologies and concepts which are already recognized and accepted. We are talking, after all, about a project which must get off the ground rapidly, and there would be little point, therefore, in directing it at some ill-defined, far-off target – especially one which might turn out to be a mirage.

It is certainly vital to eschew the fatuous sort of 'leap-frog' strategies which were pursued by some European electronics companies during the 1960s and 1970s, who seemed to believe that, by means of some God-given technological foresight, they could outwit and outrun their competitors to achieve a global lead based on some half-baked notion gleaming in the eyes of a few unworldly scientists. Electronics technology generally advances by small, evolutionary steps, one evidential example of which is that today's micro-chips are very similar in appearance to those of the 1960s, despite the dramatically greater precision and packing density of their topology.

Such is the overwhelming importance of this enormous, one-chance renaissance project that it must be launched from a firm technical base, and its trajectory must be planned with great care so that it intercepts the constantly advancing US/Japanese technical capability at a given time.

For these reasons, long-range R & D of the kind being encouraged and financially supported by the European Commission's ESPRIT[1] programme will not make much of a contribution at the beginning of the renaissance 'window', although it will obviously become of increasing importance as time goes on. Parenthetically, ESPRIT (and similar Commission initiatives) is in any event fully justified by the stimulation it provides to trans-frontier co-operation between European electronics research laboratories and establishments. For the first time, such organizations are learning to work together towards a common, multination objective, and this can hopefully act as a pathfinder for the larger, commercial linkages which will be an essential ingredient of any realistic renaissance plan.

---

[1] European Strategic Programme for Research in Information Technology.

Speed of implementation

The essential characteristic of any such project is that it must be agreed, planned and implemented with great urgency.

The analyses of Part Two have adequately documented the diverging capabilities of Europe *versus* the US and Japan, and each year of indecision will inevitably increase the final bill. Roughly speaking, a delay of five years in starting the overall 20-year renaissance programme would increase the total pan-Community exchequer cost from $300 billion to $400 billion. Ten years later and Europe will be so far behind that any hopes of future IT-based economic property will have been irretrievably dashed.

Critical mass

Thirdly, as will be clear from the earlier calculations, this is not a job that can be done on the cheap. Chapter 7 outlines the only known method of estimating the costs of expanding various kinds of IT producers to achieve 'critical mass' – or globally competitive economies of scale – and Europe is going to need about 25 interacting, designer-coupled, well-managed versions of these to gain its rightful place in the high-tech sunshine.

While no claims are being made for the precision of these calculations, every effort has been made not to overstate them. Indeed, there is inevitably some danger that obscure but significant costs have been overlooked. Nonetheless, the sums required are roughly what could be expected, given the magnitude of the problem and various empirical rules of thumb.

Prior levels of IT support from European governments have been timorous or prudent, depending on one's point of view. But they have incontestably been too small, and directed too much at R & D, to have much effect. There is no excuse now, however. This book not only spells out what is needed, but also the dire consequences of not meeting that need. Governments which now fail to act with appropriate vigour cannot claim that they were not warned.

Political acceptability

Following on from the above, the renaissance project must also be politically realistic. Whether it is adopted on a pan-Community or (lesser) multination scale, it will need to be duly sensitive to the widely different national capabilities of the participating states, and to their various national aspirations.

Fortunately, the sheer variety of economic structure and size of the EEC's member states could become an important asset. Provided that there is Community agreement on the overall objectives, timing and financing of the project, it should not be difficult to devise formulae – probably based loosely on the principle of *juste retour* – whereby each nation benefits not only generally but specifically according to its own special requirements.

Selective procurement

As mentioned briefly at the beginning of this chapter, an essential feature of this project is that it must firmly grasp the nettle of preferred procurement from EEC-owned IT companies. This will certainly (and understandably) be a sore point with the importers and MNEs, and all hell can be expected to break loose. However, without it the proposed demand-led renaissance will merely provide handsome handouts to Europe's most successful and well-heeled competitors.

How to do it, consistent with conforming to anti-monopoly legislation and free-trade agreements is, of course, one of the key questions. The contributions of MNEs (IBM being a prime example) who have made proportionate investments in Europe must obviously be taken fully into account, particularly where they have had the courage and commitment to implant leading-edge technologies. And the inward investors and joint-venture enterprises will also have to be fitted into an equitable scheme.

It may sound a tall order, but there is good reason to believe that this particular circle can be squared, as will be seen.

Economic viability

Whatever the candidate for providing the central core of the renaissance project, in the long term it must be economically viable in its own right. While this may seem blindingly obvious, some additional comment may be useful.

It has been postulated that the full renaissance period will last for 20 years, during which it is envisaged that a number of the usual rules of the (commercial) game in a free-market society will have to be temporarily modified or suspended (e.g. 'open' procurement). If all goes according to plan, this will lift the European electronics companies (albeit, reduced in numbers) to world-scale production levels, mainly to supply the demand stimulated by the core project.

But, at the end of the 20 years, it is obviously essential that the project itself will have reached a self-sustaining momentum – i.e. will be economically viable in its own right. If this is not the case, then either the European taxpayers will need to go on pumping in large sums of money (into what will have become recognized to be a white elephant) so that it can continue to provide the base demand levels for the newly viable European IT companies, or the termination of the core project will result in a severe reduction of the domestic (i.e. European) markets for which these companies had become geared up.

Given the considerable political difficulties which will have to be surmounted before embarking on a 20-year, end-in-sight project, it seems neither possible nor desirable that there should be any prospect whatsoever of open-ended public investment. All ingredients of the plan, therefore, must be capable of standing on their own unprotected, unsubsidized, free-enterprise feet come the end of the 20 years.

THE CHORUS OF CHOICES

In searching for the central core of a demand-led renaissance strategy in information technology, it is necessary to examine a host of possibilities. Even some of the policies which have been used in the past need to be dusted off and looked at again, in case, with the postulated prospect of a born-again European electronics industry, they might at last provide the necessary degree of uplift.

But there are, in fact, few real contenders...

Microelectronics

The integrated circuit has featured strongly in this book, and microelectronics is undoubtedly the primary enabling technology which powers the growth in performance and cost of a vast variety of electronic equipments. It has been recognized as such by a number of governments in Europe (and, crucially, by MITI in Japan), and to the UK government of the day (1967) goes the credit of having mounted the first significant (c. £1.5 million) programme of non-military development support for this segment. Nevertheless, as previously documented, these government ministrations have singularly failed to reverse the slide in Europe's share of the free-world IC market.

More seriously, in the present context, the IC industry simply cannot provide the market stimulation which is needed. In short, microelectronics can supply the technology push, but not the demand pull. It is therefore not a candidate for the central role of a renaissance plan, although it must remain high on the list of segments requiring large restorative public investment if a feasible and economically viable project can be identified on the coat-tails of which it could ride to success.

Computers

The whole area of electronic data processing is another segment which has enjoyed considerable government support over many years. In Europe and Japan, this has been both direct (e.g. product-development subsidies) and indirect (e.g. preferred public-sector procurement); in the US it has been primarily direct support, with the Department of Defence acting as the main conduit.

The computer segment also has the advantage of size. At a 1983 European market value of $19.2 billion (Table E.3), it is the largest key segment and enjoys a high (11.6 per cent) projected growth rate. Moreover, it has been clear for many years that mainframe, mini- and microcomputers will be (are) the 'intelligence engines' for a wide variety of electronic equipments and systems.

Unfortunately, the segment has several characteristics which mitigate against it playing *the* key role in any European renaissance plan. Probably the major factor is the very diversity of applications – from video games to industrial automation systems – which make this such a large industry. And further dispersion comes from the enormous diversity of equipments contained within the segment – dramatically (but not uniquely) exemplified by the spectrum containing portable (lap) computers at one end and number-crunching supercomputers at the other. There is, therefore, no single area (or even cluster of areas) where computer procurement could be used to power a European IT renaissance.

Another debilitating factor is that the bulk of the EDP market is in the private sector, and it is not easy to see how the normal computer buyer – who has a strong predilection for independent choice – could be persuaded to submerge his idiosyncratic needs into a stylized mould for the greater good of Europe. Moreover, the existing installed base of machines represents a very big user investment, particularly when account is taken of the associated software (much of it specific to each customer), and many buyers are therefore reluctant to change system suppliers. This market inertia is exacerbated, of course, by the dominant position of IBM, with something like 70 per cent of the present European-installed base.

For these reasons, it is difficult in the extreme to envisage a single Apollo-like project centred on the computer segment. In particular, it fails hopelessly on the fifth criterion above, selective procurement. Nevertheless, whatever the project may turn out to be, it will need to take account of, and benefit from, the projected $215 billion EDP market in the post-renaissance European Community.

Software

Like microelectronics, software is an enabling technology. It lies at the heart of the whole business of information processing and is of gathering importance. Indeed, it is these two aspects of software which justify its inclusion in this select list.

For reasons already stated, software has not been treated in this book as a segment in its own right, but account has been taken, wherever possible, of the integral software costs in each hardware segment. Nevertheless, taking software and computer services together,[2] the free-world market in 1983 was about $40 billion and will grow (in terms of constant 1983 US dollars) to approximately $600 billion by 2005 – i.e. around 70 per cent of the then free-world total EDP market. However, about a quarter of the total software business currently resides with the hardware manufacturers themselves and, as software costs increase inexorably, this will probably rise to at least 50 per cent. Thus the 'independent' software/computer services market in a post-renaissance EEC is likely to be around $75 billion.

Like microelectronics, its sister enabling technology, software *per se* therefore cannot provide sufficient economic driving power. It is, however, a portion of the IT industry which is rapidly increasing in importance and will need to be taken care of in the overall renaissance plan.

Defence

Defence electronics is big business indeed – not only in the US, but also in France, Italy and the UK. So big is it that much energy has been expanded in trying to find ways of spinning off commercial products from the very substantial government-backed defence R & D programmes.

Unfortunately, only in the US have such spin-off benefits ever been observed and enjoyed to any significant extent. This has been due to a number of special circumstances pertaining in the US, particularly the

---

[2] Comprising packaged software, customized software, independent management of EDP facilities, computer-training and data-processing services (local batch, remote batch and remote auto-transaction).

intimacy of the military–industrial establishment and, more important yet, the sheer size of the effort. However, it has decreased in relative importance as the non-military markets for electronic goods have grown at a much faster pace.

In modern times, as detailed in chapter 3, the technology used in defence systems which are actually in production is often quite elderly, despite the avant-garde nature of much of the R & D. Therefore, whatever success might be achieved from a search for commercial exploitation of defence technology, it is clear that this segment cannot possibly provide the magnitude of demand for leading-edge products which must lie at the heart of any renaissance programme.

Miscellanea

There is little point in going systematically through all of the other potential candidates because the ground rules are now clear enough. Office equipment, industrial automation, consumer electronics, satellite communications, mobile communications (e.g. cellular car radio systems), etc. – all of these segments fail to meet one or more of the salient criteria. In particular, if they are of sufficient economic weight they are not susceptible to the kind of procurement constraints briefly described (e.g. consumer electronics); and where selective procurement might be possible (e.g. mobile communications) the projected demand levels are simply not high enough.

So there is only one remaining candidate . . .

TELECOMMUNICATIONS IN TUNE

Power of the PTTs

Total telecommunications revenues of the PTTs in the ten-nation EEC were approximately $41 billion in calendar year 1983. That, clearly, is a big number, being more than twice the size of the largest (i.e. computer) key segment – although we are actually comparing chalk (telecommunications services) with cheese (hardware manufacture).

More to the point is that in 1983 these ten PTTs invested approximately $17 billion on new telecommunications facilities of all kinds and, with the accelerating digitalization of their networks and switching centres, are expected to increase this level of investment at the rate of about six per cent per annum in real terms. If this is what really happens, the ten PTTs will be investing something like $60 billion per annum collectively by 2005.[3] So this segment obviously packs a reasonably powerful economic punch.

Also encouraging is the fact that, until the advent of deregulation around 1983/4, all of the PTTs in the major industrialized countries (AT&T in the US) obtained the bulk of their equipment needs from a select group of (mainly national) suppliers – and most of them still do. So the principle of preferred procurement is, in fact, hallowed practice in this segment. But the tide is turning. Already, in the US, the operating networks have been totally divorced from their sometime captive supplier, Western Electric, and the probable dire consequences of this for the remnants of the original AT&T have been spelled out in chapter 3. In the UK also, the 1984 privatization of the PTT is leading to an opening up of British Telecom's range of equipment suppliers.

Whether, in Europe, this process could be encouraged to embrace all qualified European suppliers, but discouraged to the point of excluding those of non-European parentage, is clearly moot. But it is worth re-emphasizing that, other than the defence area, telecommunications is the only segment which combines large size with a well-established preference for buying from national champions.

Another advantage, already lightly touched upon, is the huge change-over now underway from analogue to digital systems. Tele-communications is currently embarking on its most difficult and expensive technological transmutation since the invention of the telephone switch-board, about a century ago. This change has so far been taking place mostly on a national basis, with many of the large manufacturers around the world having developed electronic (i.e. digital) public switching systems (analogous to the older telephone exchanges). Thus, in the UK there is System X (GEC and Plessey), France (CIT-Alcatel) has its M10, FRG (Siemens) has EWSD, and so on. However, strenuous efforts are now being made to agree (whatever the detailed functioning of the 'national' switching systems) on standard international procedures (protocols) and services which would be provided on a harmonized basis. This has been labelled the Integrated Services Digital Network.

The point, of course, is that this technological sea-change is in any event requiring the PTTs to gear up for very large investments in totally new digital systems, and to re-organize themselvs to handle this changing and expanding business. The time could be ripe, therefore, to try to

---

[3] The discrepancy between this figure and those of Table 8.5 can be explained – once again – on the assumed convergence by then of the telecommunications, computer and office-equipment segments. The PTT investments also include expenditure on various items (e.g. buildings) which have not been included in the analyses of Part Two.

harness this powerful engine of change to the weakened, stuck-in-the-mud European IT industry.

Terminal velocity

But there is yet another encouraging facet of the telecommunications segment – one which shines brightly enough to put the others in the shade. Whatever form the network digitalization may take, there is no doubt that it will lead to a significant increase in the services available (e.g. text-plus-data-plus-voice; low-speed facsimile transmission) and this, in turn, will result in a rapid expansion in the demand for tele-communications terminals. In the past, there have been only three main categories of such 'terminals' – defining these to be equipments which are attached to the user end of a telephone line or lines. There is the ordinary telephone handset, of course; the modem (modulator: demodulator) which allows data to be carried over the classical voice network; and private automatic branch exchanges (PABXs), which can range from a tiny switchboard suitable for an office of just two or three persons, up to very large, sophisticated systems capable of serving thousands of extensions, connected to hundreds of individual telephone 'lines' and vying in complexity with some of the smaller public switches.

With the advent of local area networks (LANs) capable of inter-connecting all work stations in an office block or factory full of telephones, computers and word processors, plus the ever-increasing pervasiveness of the personal computer (PC), plus the availability of a universal networking software system to allow all such terminals to be able to communicate with all others, wherever located, there is bound to be a significant expansion in the number and use of such terminals. It is this postulated increase in the variety and number of such terminals which may hold the key to the enhanced demand on which any renaissance plan must be based.

Communication gap

In case there is some scepticism about the magnitude of the *potential* demand, the following simple analysis can provide some elucidation.

Table 10.1 shows comparitive 1983 data for total telecommunications revenues in the US and the EEC, plus data for GDPs and populations. From this it can be seen that the per-capita revenues are currently more than a factor of two greater in the US than in the EEC. Moreover, per-capita telecom revenues in the US have recently been growing at the rate

Table 10.1 Comparison of expenditure on telecommunications services in the US and Europe (1983)

	US	EEC
GDP	$3130 bn	$2260 bn
Population	230 m	270 m
Telecomms revenues	$76.3 bn	$40.8 bn
– Per-capita	$330	$150
– As % of GDP	2.45%	1.8%

All monetary values in terms of the 1983 US dollar.

of about five per cent per annum in real terms which, if maintained, would take the figure to about $960 by 2005.

If it is now assumed that in a revitalized Europe, the *use* of the tools of the Information Era would also have been stimulated, it is quite possible to believe that per-capita telecom revenues would have accelerated to the point where they matched those in the US. In that event, EEC telecom revenues in 2005 would become (on the projected population of 290 million) approximately $280 billion.

Finally, it can be assumed that some portion of these PTT revenues would be invested in new and expanding facilities, networks and services, yielding an extra stimulus to the Community IT industry. Moreover, as already pointed out, to use these new services efficiently, and to become fully paid-up members of the Information Society, the users would need very many more terminals of all kinds to connect to the much-enhanced network, thus providing further demand uplift.

CRITERIA SCRUTINIZED

Overall, it will now be apparent that the telecommunications segment comes closest to meeting the criteria cited earlier.

- The feasibility of essentially all of the switching and signal transmission techniques is already well established – although this is not to argue that further evolutionary developments will not happen.
- The speed of implementation is questionable. Although all of the European PTTs are fully aware of the widespread changes which they

must now adopt and adapt to, these organizations are very large and often imbued with a dispiriting inertia stemming both from sheer size and from decades of operating in a technically static, slow-growth, monopolistic marketplace. If these PTTs are to be the engine of change, there will need to be some revving up.

- Critical mass is also still an open question. Telecommunications services of the kind discussed so far, while offering the prospect of a considerable uplift in IT demand, may still fall far short of the $350 billion (per annum) increase which will be necessary.
- Political acceptability cannot be judged as yet. This will obviously depend on who are the politicians (et al.) and what they are being asked to accept. As already said, increased public investment is often viewed bleakly by monetarist minds, so it will be necessary to show that not only is such an investment essential if Europe is to have any chance of maintaining its economic standing in the twenty-first century (cf. Part Two), but that a reasonable return on the investment can be envisaged.
- Selective procurement – the most difficult criterion to meet in most segments – is, as stated, a relatively conventional way of life in the telecommunications industry. But many difficulties still lie in the way of devising a scheme which could work on a multination basis and which would apply the rules fairly to the many different types of players.
- Economic viability is an unknown quantity at this stage, and cannot be assessed until the impeccable Apollo project emerges from these musings.

Following on from this reasoning, the core of the proposed Europen IT renaissance strategy must inevitably lie in the general territory covered by telecommunications. It is described in some detail in the next chapter.

11 Eurogrid:

A new communications network for Europe

INFORMATION HUNGER

Information is a precious commodity. In the running of businesses or governments, its availability in the right place, at the right time, and of the right quality and quantity provides the bedrock of knowledge on which meaningful analyses and good decisions can be built. Certainly there is little future in making decisions based on ignorance.

If that sounds trite, the fact is that in terms of the availability and use of information, Europe is currently in the Dark Ages. This is particularly so in comparison with the US, where the working environment is already information-rich, as evidenced in part by the high per-capita expenditure on telecommunications services (see page 196). That is just the beginning, however. Now permeating the consciousness of American managements, especially in the more mature sectors of the economy, is the realization that it is only through the efficient use of information that they can parry the thrust of competition from their own domestic rivals and from the low-cost countries – particularly the newly industrialized countries (NICs).

Thus General Motors, as one example, has embarked on a huge campaign (the Manfacturing Automation Protocol program) to tie together its 100 or so large mainframe computers, to standardize communication protocols, software and terminals so that, as one benefit, the linkage between an individual customer's needs and what the factories produce becomes ever closer and more efficient. But that is just the tip of the iceberg. Dozens of other American examples could be quoted, of industrial companies, financial institutions and government departments which are gearing up to collect, communicate, analyse and use information, with an intensity of commitment almost unheard of in Europe at the present time.

In Japan, also, there is a burgeoning desire to effect a radical improvement in the communication and use of information. Apart from voice messages and purely numerical data, this ambition has been thwarted until recently by the ideographic written language, which is not conducive to transmission by classical telephony systems. This is clear from the statistics, which show Japanese per-capita expenditure on telecommunications services only slightly higher ($165 in 1983) than in Europe.

This is now changing in two significant ways. The most immediate impact is coming from the development by several Japanese companies of low-cost, high-efficiency facsimile machines, in which product area Japan is threatening to achieve worldwide domination. These machines allow the electronic transmission of full-page images (of, for example, Kanji characters) at relatively high speed and low cost, and effectively bypass Western systems for text communication.

The second, longer-term influence will stem from the accelerating use of a new national communications grid, the Integrated Network System (INS). As described in Chapter 3, this is basically a broadband network (i.e. possessing the capacity to carry a wide band of frequencies) capable of providing a much greater variety of services than the classical telephone system. The INS will dramatically improve the cost and range of electronics-based communications within Japan, and will bring to the Japanese executive information 'power' on a par with that of his American counterpart. It is currently expected to be installed during the second half of the 1980s and the early part of the 1990s, and to be nationally operational by the year 2000.

By comparison, Europe has yet to embark seriously on the difficult and costly journey from the Computer Age to the Era of Information. With only a fw exceptions, industry, commerce and government in Europe still function on the basis of voice communications, data processing and paper records. It is slow, expensive and inefficient. And what makes matters worse is that in some countries, a subconscious cultural antipathy towards technology extends insidiously to the powerful decision-making tools which it can place at the executive's right hand.

Those organizations in Europe which have made progress in the efficient use of information include many banks and some airlines. It is rather surprising that the former, generally endowed with a staid and cautious image, have made such impressive progress – not merely in electronic funds transfer (EFT), but also in electronic funds transfer at the point of sale (EFTPOS). And France is a world leader in the manufacture and use of the 'smart' card. In appearance, this is a conventional plastic 'credit' card but it carries an in-built microprocessor and memory sufficient to permit a wide variety of on-the-spot transactions, including the instantaneous crediting and debiting of vendors' and purchasers' accounts.

In the case of the larger European airlines, blessed with taxpayers' money and cursed by operating inefficiencies and complicated short-haul scheduling problems, the computer and its information-processing capabilities came as the answer to a maiden's prayer. Once the capabilities were recognized, some of the airlines moved swiftly and decisively to develop and instal information systems of considerable power.

Nevertheless, by the pace-setting standards of the US, Europe remains relatively uninformed – which is both a contributory cause and a partial effect of its poor IT performance. That is, the comparatively low importance afforded to information leads to a small market for the products of the IT industry, which implies an under-informed business community, which presages a wider economic decline, which exacerbates the problem of financing Europe's IT renaissance.

ADVENT OF THE WIRED SOCIETY

With information of all kinds now playing a vital role in the normal conduct of business and governments (plus defence), becoming increasingly important in public services such as security, education and health, and also of growing relevance to 'entertainment' services, the question naturally arises as to how it can best be conveyed. By what medium? In what form? At what cost?

Delivery options

There are, of course, many alternatives. The most familiar electronic media are the present telephone and telex networks (which are two-way, or 'interactive') and radio and television broadcasts (which are one-way). The format of the information can be voice, text (including numbers) and pictures (moving, as in TV programmes, or still, as in facsimile transmissions). And the cost per person per 'bit' of information conveyed can either be negligible, as in radio broadcasts, or prohibitively high, as in the early attempts by AT&T to provide a videophone (or picturephone) service to the American public over the existing telephone network.

All of this has been recognized and written about for some years. It is also widely understood that although some applications (e.g. entertainment) require information to be conveyed in one direction only, almost all of the expanding future uses of information flow will demand two-way facilities, frequently on an interactive, point-to-point (e.g. person-to-person) basis.

However, radio communications cannot easily and cheaply provide point-to-point interactive communication links, being more suited to the non-selective broadcasting of information. The only practical method is by wiring up all of the points and enabling them to be connected together via a system of switches, as in the present-day telephone network. This, then, is the basic concept of the 'wired society', which has been with us for many decades.

The present telephone network, which was progressively installed in most industrialized countries during the first half of this century, unfortunately has only a limited bandwidth – meaning that it can normally carry only relatively low frequencies. In terms of digital transmission, this so-called 'twisted-pair' network (the twin wires being twisted together to reduce cross-talk and noise) can be persuaded to carry informtion at the rate of two million (i.e. mega) bits per second although, perhaps more realistically, ISDN (Integrated Services Digital Network) will operate initially at 64,000 bits per second (64 kbit/s), possibly shifting up a gear to 144 kbit per second in a few years' time.

Bandwidth constraints

This bandwidth is perfectly satisfactory for present telecommunications services, including those which will become available with ISDN. They comprise four main types of information – voice, data, text and still-image – although the transmission of the last three types over this slow network has to be at speeds which are very much less than those of which the respective terminals (data, text etc.) are capable. Thus, even when clever things are done to speed it up a bit, the present twisted-pair network can never allow non-voice users to benefit from the extremely high speeds (with concomitant low costs) which advanced electronics technology confers. It is roughly comparable to restricting a Formula One racing car to an eternal 50 kilometres-per-hour speed limit.

Moreover, there is a considerable number of additional services which could be provided, and which information users would probably pay for and benefit from, if the communications network had a very much wider bandwidth. In particular, many of these prospective services are based on good-quality still and moving images, of the standard of a typical domestic television set. They include electronic shopping, distance (interactive) learning systems, remote video surveillance and the video phone itself – as well as, of course, straightforward video (television) programmes.

Demand prospects

Naturally enough, there are great uncertainties about the prospective level of demand for such broadband services. Not *whether* there will be a demand, mind you, but what level it would reach and how much users would pay for each service. But there hasn't been much research done since, apart from cable TV, there is little prospect of the services being offered in the near term. And it is always difficult to try to forecast demand for a product or service which does not yet exist.

Nevertheless, as is well known, the industrialized world did not appreciate how badly it needed paper tissues (and portable calculators, sticky tape, plain-paper copiers, instant coffee, paper clips and frozen food, etc.) until someone invented them, and it is not difficult to believe that users would enthusiastically take up the vast prospective range of broadband services if, but only if, these could be offered at sufficiently low tariffs.

Cable TV is a case in point. While it has been quite successful, especially in America, where it can provide different (and usually more interesting) programme material than could be obtained 'off-air', and where (as in densely built-up areas like city centres) it can provide better quality images, the public has generally been unwilling (as in the UK) to pay a large financial premium for its extra goodies. And most of the present cable-TV networks have been constructed on what are known as 'tree-and-branch' connection systems, which are essentially one-way, or non-interactive, whereas the more modern, two-way 'switched-star' networks (i.e working on the basis of switching by subscribers to specific services, as in the present telephone network) have so far been constrained by some (relatively minor) technical problems and (relatively major) economic problems.

The fibre-optic revolution

A major new factor influencing the viability of broadband networks has been the recent emergence of optical fibres as a practical and economic means of carrying electronic traffic. These are long, thin strands of very high-quality material which allow light to travel along them, over large distances, with only a slight loss of intensity. Thus it is now possible to convert conventional electronic signals (travelling in a wire) into coded optical signals, and to transmit these (in a fibre-optic cable) to a distant point where they can then be reconstructed into a facsimile of the original electronic stream of digits.

Such has been the rate of progress of fibre-optic technology that its use in long-haul ('trunk') cables, whether underground or undersea, is now almost *de rigueur*. More interesting yet, the rapidly growing demand for low-loss, high-quality material suitable for trunk routes has, through the effect of economies of scale, brought down the costs of all types of optical fibres, to the point where it is realistic to consider their use in local connections (i.e. direct to the home, office or whatever) where low cost is essential.

What all of this adds up to is of considerable relevance to our problem:

- First, compared with the US (and, to a lesser extent, Japan), Europe is deficient in the intelligent use of information for the effective conduct of business and government.
- Second, a revolution in the availability and cost of a wide variety of information services could come about if the bandwidth limitations of the ancient, twisted-pair telephony system could be overcome.
- Third, at this crossroads in Europe's history, when the paths it may choose lead either to an economic twilight or to a technological sunrise, a radically new communications medium – optical fibres – has matured to the point where it offers precisely the bandwidth breakthrough which is the key to essentially limitless growth of the Information Society.

It would be strange indeed (and stupid) if these key, distilled facts were not taken fully into account in the construction of a strategy for the renaissance of the European IT industry.

THE CONCEPT OF EUROGRID

Connection miasma

To benefit from the growing possibilities of accessing, manipulating, storing and transmitting the vast range of information and entertainment already available, a home, office or other place of work is currently faced with a daunting proliferation of antennae and network connections. Figure 11.1, for example, depicts an American home of the 1980s which is taking full advantage of all the services currently available.[1] It has seven different input points – eight if it uses two separate telephone lines (which is not uncommon in the US).

---

[1] C. Truxal, 'The Very Hi-Tech Home', *Spectrum*, **22**, p. 64, 1983.

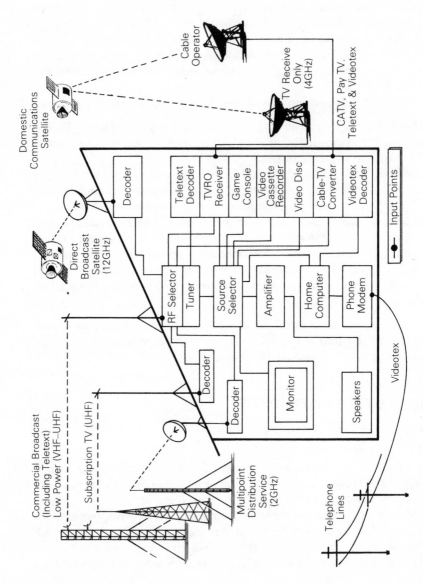

Figure 11.1. The information home of today.

One telephone connection is partially used for the videotex connection to a distant computer and its associated databases (e.g. the Prestel services in the UK), via a modem, and usually feeding a home (personal) computer. The other line then allows incoming and outgoing calls while the videotex service is being used. There is the normal commercial broadcast television antenna feeding any number of TV sets (monitors) and incorporating off-air teletext information services (e.g. Ceefax and Oracle in the UK). Another antenna would be needed to receive subscription TV services (fed to the monitors via an appropriate decoder – which is necessary to restrict the signal to bona-fide subscribers only).

Two separate dish aerials are also shown mounted on or near to the home, one to receive multi-point distribution services and one for programmes via direct-broadcast satellites (DBS); while a more remote TV-receive-only (TVRO) antenna may be used to pick up broadcasts targetted at cable operators, who provide a separate (scrambled) service of pay-TV, etc. In this hypothetical model, the bandwidth requirements of the input points (and their linkages to the in-house decoders, modems and converters) range from about 4 kilohertz (KHz) – or 4000 cycles per second as was – to 12 gigahertz (i.e. 12,000 megahertz).

Two things will immediately be apparent. The first is that there can be no possibility whatsoever that the ordinary telephone (twisted-pair) connection could carry such high frequencies. And secondly, there are substantial inefficiencies and extra costs involved in providing such a multiplicity of antennae, input points and decoders, etc. Moreover, this same general communications syndrome also affects, albeit to a lesser degree, the whole range of work establishments – offices, schools, hospitals, factories and many more besides.

Homogeneous broadband

There must be a better way, one might think – and indeed there is. If Europe is to be put into a position where it can ultimately gain maximum benefit (industrially, commercially and socially) from the information revolution, then each home, school and place of work should have access to a broadband communications network, able to convey all forms of information on a two-way, point-to-point basis. In addition, the network would need to be standardized on at least a European (if not wider) scale, with common protocols, data rates and terminal connections, inter alia. That, in a nutshell, is Eurogrid.

The great advantage of such a broadband network, of course, is that a single connection could simultaneously carry an enormous range of signals and frequencies simply by using conventional electronic means of separation (typically the so-called frequency-division multiplexing of different 'channels', or frequency bands). The Eurogrid home of tomorrow might therefore look roughly as depicted in Figure 11.2.

All of the confused, unsightly and expensive antennae and input points have been replaced by one simple connection to the broadband Eurogrid network – which, at this local level, could be either a low-cost fibre-optic cable or a conventional (broadband) coaxial cable. Through a (standardized) decoder unit, and conveyed around the home by a 'domestic network', the various services would be fed from the Eurogrid network to as many different items of electronic equipment as the consumer might want. They would all be able to function simultaneously, independently and/or interactively.

In a similar way, Eurogrid would become the information conduit for the office (Figure 11.3), the factory (Figure 11.4) and for all the other considerable variety of locations where there is a need for information and/or entertainment services. It is clearly not possible to predict at this stage the full range of Eurogrid users, but it would obviously include educational establishments, hospitals and doctors' surgeries, shops, banks and travel agents. It is also possible to envisage many less obvious users. One example might be the low-cost distribution of information on the expected arrival times of public transport (e.g. buses) at specific locations (e.g. bus stops), as part of a comprehensive traffic automation scheme.

Services rendered

In fact, the range of network services which Eurogrid could offer can be segregated into 16 main categories, clustered into five principal groups (Figure 11.5). The first is voice communications, which can be either two-way (as in normal telephone conversations) or simply one-way (for the delivery and storage of voice messages, as on today's telephone-answering machines).

The second is high-quality audio. This breaks down into two-way switched (i.e. metered) high-fidelity telephony (for remote dictation and conference calls, for example), one-way switched audio services (e.g. selective listening to special-interest events such as a local council meeting) and high-fidelity audio broadcasts (e.g. of concerts).

Third, there are the five distinct forms of video services (i.e. involving moving images). The first two of these are straightforward television broadcasts, one of conventional quality (albeit free from off-air interference and noise, being delivered over an interference-free network) and one of high-definition images to suit the more demanding viewer. Then

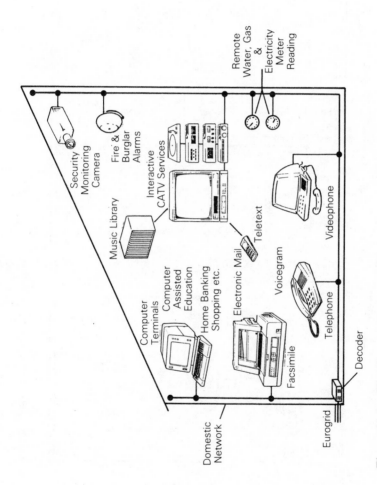

Figure 11.2. The Eurogrid home

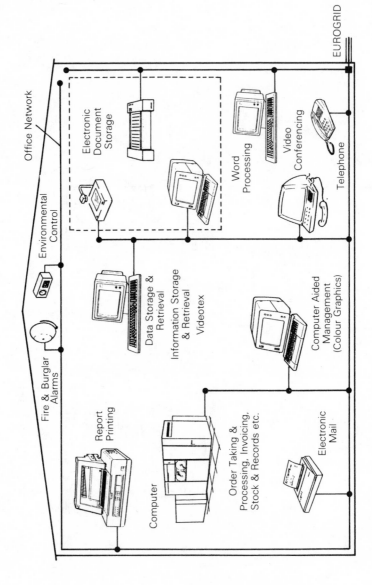

Figure 11.3. Eurogrid and the office

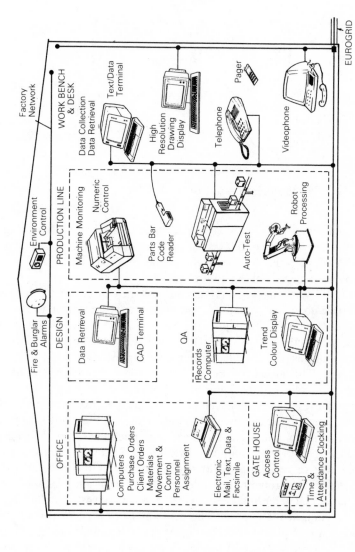

Figure 11.4. Eurogrid and the factory

Figure 11.5. Principal network service possibilities.

there is one-way switched video (e.g. pay-TV), one-way switched high-definition video (the same, but better) and two-way switched video (allowing, for example, the prospectively pervasive videophone and video-conferencing systems linking several remote sites).

The fourth, very important group concerns the delivery of still images. These break down into standard, low-speed services, similar to today's facsimile communications; high-performance image transmission (e.g. for assessing production quality and for security surveillance); and high-definition still images (suitable, perhaps, for publishing directly in newspapers, etc.). This group would also include the vast range of still-image applications involved in the interrogation of remote databases, electronic document files, libraries, financial accounts, mailing lists, remote word-processing systems, educational material, home banking and shopping, electronic mail, computer-aided design, personnel records, and so forth.

And fifth, there is the group of services associated with the transfer of text and data, segregated according to speed. At the low end (up to 64 kbit/s), it would be roughly equivalent to the conventional telex service, where the actual teleprinters (of which there is a vast installed base) cannot function at high speed. The medium-speed services (up to, say, 512 kbit/s) would provide for the higher-speed terminals now becoming available; and the high-speed service (2 Mbit/s or more) would be fully capable of matching the speed and efficiency of the advanced text-and-data terminals of the future and would be well suited to the requirements of the growing population of large organizations which need to transfer huge quantities of information, at minimum cost, throughout their various establishments.

Elements of Eurogrid

Eurogrid, then, is envisaged as a pervasive multination (or pan-Community or pan-European) broadband communications network capable of carrying a comprehensive range of point-to-point services for business, domestic and government users of all kinds. It would be based primarily on fibre-optic cables and would be installed and implemented over a concentrated timescale – ideally the middle ten years or so of the 20-year renaissance period – in parallel with existing networks (including ISDN) but rapidly subsuming their individual roles. The bandwidth capacity of Eurogrid would be at least 50 Mbit/s to each subscriber, so that it could handle several 8 Mbit/s channels, each of which would be capable of carrying all forms of information and entertainment.

It is important to emphasize that Eurogrid would have to be fully compatible with all existing and planned telecommunications networks and services. Thus Eurogrid subscribers would have access to existing networks via 'black-box' adaptors, where necessary, and the network characteristics of Eurogrid would be compatible with those being planned for ISDN. In this way, communications between Eurogrid premises and subscribers restricted to narrowband networks would be entirely painless, albeit constrained to the lower quality, number and speed of the services available to the non-Eurogrid connection.

To ensure maximum penetration, and hence accelerated use of its services, it is essential that Eurogrid be connected without charge to essentially all homes and places of work. Nevertheless, the installation programme would obviously need to be phased, with important centres of government, commerce and industry taking first priority. Were it to be left to each potential subscriber to wait until he felt it was timely to be connected to the new network, as is currently the case with cable TV, the take-up rate would be too slow to achieve the overall objectives of the programme, which are to accelerate the purchase of Eurogrid terminals to the ultimate benefit of both their makers and users.

Everything about Eurogrid would be standardized from the word go. In particular, each connection to the network would terminate on a standardized connection point and decoder. This would mean that any item of terminal equipment – whether for entertainment, educational, business or other purposes – could be connected to the grid and would work efficiently wherever it was plugged in (i.e. in any home or work-place, etc., in any nation which had installed Eurogrid). Once the necessary Eurogrid standards were established, it would be inevitable that compatible networks would be implemented internationally, and this would raise substantial export possibilities for the European manufacturers of Eurogrid-related equipment.

The boost to demand occasioned by Eurogrid is discussed in some detail in the following section. But it is beyond doubt that the widespread availability of the 16 generic services previously listed would result in a significant uplift in the demand for equipment to use them. Fibre-optic trunk systems and high-speed switching centres will be needed, to link up with an intricate, efficient and low-cost distribution network; local-area and domestic networks for homes, schools, offices and factories will be in great demand, as will be the office terminals, monitors, personal computers, security systems and entertainment systems, etc., which they will feed; and a wide variety of materials and components (including the most advanced ICs) will be needed for the decoders, terminals and switching centres.

Even when Eurogrid is fully in place, normal television and radio broadcasting would continue to serve the needs of the mobile audience (e.g. car drivers and joggers). But an inherent aspect of the Eurogrid concept is that the network would simultaneously provide high-fidelity versions of these programmes plus a wide range of extra programme material, particularly television-based entertainment similar to that now carried to certain regions by cable TV. It is important for this new network to carry these services in order to avoid a proliferation of cable networks and the dispersion of investment funds.

While it is neither possible nor desirable to make it mandatory for individual nations to 'join' Eurogrid, there is good reason to believe that the attractions of being within this charmed circle would outweigh all but the most extreme manifestations of nationalism.

For instance, once it is properly launched as the core of an overt renaissance plan (Chapter 12), Eurogrid would become the *de facto* communication standard for the 'joiner' nations and, in time, for other parts of the world. So the spur to that part of the European IT industry which had the advantage of serving the Eurogrid market would soon be manifest, making it increasingly difficult for the 'non-joiners' to stand aside from those industrial and economic benefits. Moreover, the enhanced business efficiencies of European nations endowed with an efficient, cheap and universal network should provide, in time, an attractive feasibility proof to any nations which chose not to join Eurogrid *ab initio*.

The final key element of the Eurogrid concept is that, because of the great intrinsic power of the European telecommunications authorities (PTTs), they must be the organizations through which Eurogrid is established and operated. After all, they already own the existing networks and provide the existing services (other than cable TV, usually); they have the technical skills and economic weight; and, above all, only they have the experience and organizational strength to cope with a project of this size.

Although it is clear that each member nation will decide what specific services its own PTT should provide, there are strong arguments for restricting the PTT's role to running the network itself and to provision of the basic telecommunications services – i.e. those concerned with the straightforward transport of information. The substantial business opportunities which will arise for 'value-added' entertainment and information-oriented services carried on Eurogrid would better be left to private-enterprise companies which could move swiftly to supply a perceived service need and to take the associated business risks.

THE ECONOMIC IMPLICATIONS OF EUROGRID

Means and ends

The critical, interrelated questions governing the economics of Eurogrid itself are the level of demand for the proffered services, the tariffs charged for them and the costs of providing them. But given the size and complexity of the Eurogrid concept, plus the multiplicity of implementation options, finding realistic answers to these questions is clearly not a simple matter.

At this stage, it is appropriate to remind ourselves that Eurogrid is being proposed as a means to an end – namely, the revitalization of the European IT industry. To achieve this, the demand must be maximized for Eurogrid-related equipments and components of all kinds, plus any products which can ride on their coat-tails, and designed to fully harmonized specifications throughout.

The demand for Eurogrid terminals, etc., will obviously be higher the lower the tariffs charged for using them. What must be sought, therefore, is a believable scenario which represents maximum demand for 'terminals' (using this as a generic label for the variety of equipments which would be used in conjunction with Eurogrid) consistent with a satisfactory financial outcome for the network providers – i.e. the European PTTs.

As it happens, a substantial amount of research has already been carried out on this topic,[2] including the extensive use of computer modelling. While it is unnecessary to reproduce this work in any detail, a synopsis of the main elements is provided in Appendix F. Here we can simply concentrate on the main findings.

Network economics

The principal underlying assumption is that this broadband network, based primarily on optical fibres and a switched-star topology, would be installed as an overlay on existing networks throughout the present ten-nation European Community.

Forecasts of the traffic which the network would carry, at tariff levels conservatively assumed to be substantially lower than today's (where the service is directly comparable, as in straightforward telephony), result in predicted network revenues (to the Community PTTs) of between $350 billion and $400 billion[3] in the year 2005. Discounting the forecast entertainment (e.g. cable TV) constituent, this would then represent a per-capita, per-annum expenditure on telecommunication services of about $1150 in the EEC (mainly, of course, from businesses), compared with a projected figure in the US of about $1000 (see page 196) – but without the assumed stimulus of an American version of Eurogrid.

Considering the massive investment which would have gone into installing the network, plus the postulated public investment in the revitalization of the IT companies (Chapter 8), it would be expected that, by the end of the renaissance period in 2005, Europe would at least have caught up with the US in the sophisticated transportation and use of information. That is precisely what these per-capita expenditure comparisons suggest, and thus lend some credence to the predicted Eurogrid revenues.

The total costs of designing, planning and installing Eurogrid can be calculated with a relatively high degree of confidence. This is because there is already much information on the various constituent costs. The subscriber connection costs, for example, are well known from current telephone installation and cable-TV costs. Similarly, the local switching units, trunk and junction network costs, etc., can be estimated – and forecast – with a reasonable degree of precision.

From such considerations, cumulative installation costs over the 15

---

[2] This work was carried out by Mackintosh International on behalf of the Commission of the European Communities (CEC), to whom acknowledgements and thanks are due for permission to summarize them here.

[3] All figures, as usual, in 1983 US dollar values.

years 1990–2005 have been estimated (Appendix F) as about $400 billion. Of this, approximately half is absorbed by the physical process of instal- ling the subscriber connections, which is of significance when we come to consider the employment implications.

Taking due account of network operating costs and depreciation, among many other PTT cost elements, the research has predicted an internal rate of return to the PTTs somewhere in the range 25–40 per cent (assuming a ten-year straight-line depreciation rate), and a pay-back period of between six and 11 years, both figures depending critically on the assumed tariff structure. However, the new network services are not expected to be particularly price-sensitive and, in any case, the PTT's financial performance will necessarily be adversely affected by the low traffic levels generated while they are absorbing the heavy costs of instal- ling the network.

What this probably implies is that some underwriting of PTT invest- ments in the Eurogrid infrastructure will have to be provided by govern- ments or EEC financial institutions during the peak years of network installation. These sums cannot be calculated with reasonable accuracy at this stage but, since they should represent gilt-edged investment oppor- tunities, are unlikely to be a significant drain on national exchequers.

In short, as a stand-alone investment possibility, and based on what are believed to be conservative assumptions, Eurogrid looks like an attractive long-term prospect to the PTTs, providing them in due course with vastly expanded revenues and full control over the all-important information highways of Europe.

Information-technology (IT) demand implications

But, as already stated, the key question for the European IT industry is whether Eurogrid can provide the necessary degree of demand stimulus to give the electronics companies a chance of achieving international levels of production and economies of scale.

There are three elements to the IT demand which will be generated by Eurogrid. The first is the use of *direct* terminals – i.e. the wide range of equipments which will necessarily work in conjunction with, and as a consequence of, the new broadband network. Examples of these are given in Appendix F (videophones, high-speed text-and-data terminals, high- definition television monitors, etc.), and have been estimated to amount to a market in 2005 of about £130 billion.

The second element comprises the *indirect* terminals – namely, those which have a stand-alone capability but will still need to be compatible with Eurogrid in order to enhance their utilization. Examples in the business sector include items such as on-site telephone systems, stored-voice databases and a range of office products (such as copiers) which can function in isolation but which also need an inter-establishment communication facility. And in the domestic sector, there are equipments such as 'home' computers and word-processing systems, TV monitors and high-fidelity audio systems which, while being capable of stand-alone operation, will be of enhanced value if they are also capable of accessing the range of Eurogrid services.

The total EEC demand for these 'indirect' terminals has been estimated to amount to about $155 billion by the year 2005.

Thirdly, there is the demand for IT products which will stem directly from installation of Eurogrid itself. A crude estimate of this can be made by assuming on the basis of historical precedent, that this will amount to around ten per cent of the total PTT revenues, which would represent an additional demand of *c.* $40 billion in 2005.

The full-scale implementation of a Community-wide Eurogrid network is therefore predicted to provide a demand for IT products by 2005 amounting to approximately $325 billion. This is later compared (Chapter 12) with the need to find a means for the European IT companies to be producing, by 2005, a total of $475 billion of electronic goods in order to achieve world-scale levels of competitiveness (Chapter 8).

EUROGRID REVISITED

There is nothing very new or radical about the basic concept of Eurogrid. Broadband networks of this kind have been widely discussed for many years. It is also recognized by some observers that countries which want to make effective progress into the Era of Information – thereby bolstering their hopes of future international competitiveness and economic growth – will make the necessary investments to provide government and businesses with the efficient, low-cost communication facilities which such information highways provide.

Indeed, it is of great significance that Japan, on whose strategic planning much praise has been lavished in this book, is in the vanguard of developing and implementing a national, broadband network – the Integrated Network System (INS). While there are still uncertainties about some details of this vast scheme, it is simply not conceivable that the Japanese authorities would have embarked on it at all without their usual thorough attention to matters such as technical feasibility, demand, costs and profitability.

In Europe, also, embryonic broadband projects have already begun to appear. A significant (local) pilot network has been established in Biarritz by the French telecommunications authorities (Direction Générale des Télécommunications), and British Telecom has a small pilot scheme operating in Milton Keynes. The German Bundepost has also announced impressive plans to install a national broadband network in the 1990s.

Typically, however, these European projects are largely unco-ordinated. Each nation is blithely contemplating its own technical navel and taking a blinkered view of the perceived special needs of its own national subscribers, just as if there were no such thing as the Common Market.

What *is* new about the Eurogrid concept, therefore, is the plea to harmonize Europe's gathering commitment to broadband networks and, of transcendent importance, to co-ordinate and accelerate these invest-ments so that they can provide the kiss of life to the European IT industry.

The principal characteristics of Eurogrid, as proposed here, can be summarized as follows:

1 a wholly new, fibre-optic-based, broadband, interactive network cover-ing a number, if not all, of the European countries;
2 standardized in all aspects of its design and performance within the participating nations;
3 installed and implemented over a concentrated ten-year period (1990–2000), in parallel with existing networks but rapidly subsuming their original roles;
4 connected, free of charge, to essentially all homes and places of work;
5 with a bandwidth of at least 50 Mbit/s to each subscriber so that it can provide all conceivable information and entertainment services;
6 operated and controlled by the national telecommunications authorities, but with most entertainment and value-added services provided by the private sector;
7 financed mainly by the PTTs themselves, partly by borrowing against future revenues, and underwritten where necessary by national govern-ments; and
8 with the overt intention of channelling demand so far as possible to the collective IT industry within the participating nations.

It will be clear that this last point warrants more careful consideration – which it gets in Chapter 12. Moreover, the analysis of the economic implications of Eurogrid, while believed to be conservative, has necess-arily been carried out with a broad brush, and much more detailed attention will need to be paid to network costs, revenues and profitability as an integral part of the planning phase which would obviously precede the start of cable installation.

The question of Eurogrid *versus* ISDN seems to be dead and buried. Because, while an internationally harmonized ISDN will be a definite advance on the confusion of communications standards which exists today, it will represent only the lesser of the two giant steps which the world of telecommunications must now take. The first, smaller step is full conversion to digital switching and transmission techniques, and is basically taken care of by ISDN. But the second giant step – the urgent provision of the kind of broadband services essential to further growth of the information society – is not. Moreover, although ISDN is a much less revolutionary concept – technically and financially – for the PTTs to have to cope with, and therefore better suited to the gradualist mentalities with which they have been until recently imbued, this limited extension of network services cannot possibly provide anything like the kind of demand stimulus for lack of which the European IT industry is dying on its feet.

In the last analysis, there can be no question that the communications networks in the advanced countries of the world will eventually go broadband. But all the ingredients are already available. In particular, fibre-optic *technology* has opportunely come of age right on cue; namely, as the *demand* for low-cost distribution of mass information is becoming increasingly insistent in the most advanced industrial societies.

Given its postulated benefits to the hard-pressed European IT industry, it is impossible to resist the conclusion that Eurogrid's time has come.

12 Project Theseus:
A strategic plan for European IT renaissance

THE LABYRINTH

Not so long ago, Europe seemed permanently set on a course of rising prosperity, full employment and political stability. Inspired by the West German phoenix emerging from the ashes of Berlin, Europe's once-warring states began to recast their swords into plough-shares and rebuild their devastated factories and cities. The long journey in search of economic fusion started in earnest with the signing of the Treaty of Rome. And many European countries enthusiastically embraced some form of socialism in the confident, civilized belief that the flip side of increasing affluence was social legislation to ensure decent minimum standards of housing, health, education and protection for the under-privileged.

But these exemplary ambitions are now turning sour, and perplexity reigns where confidence once was king. The energetic post-war rebuilding of industries has led not to a socialist Utopia but to the free-enterprise mugging of Europe's businesses in their own 'free' marketplace – to the point where, in many nations, the economy can no longer bear the full burden of a welfare state. The dispiriting facts of economic decline now contrast starkly with the awful statistics of increasing crime, unemployment, civil unrest and urban violence.

Governments in Europe, dimly perceiving these trends, sought to spur national economic growth by a variety of incentives, generally modest in scope and naturally centred on the classical industrial sectors which most politicians understood best: industries such as steel, ship-building, machine tools and textiles, where European employment had been high and competition from the Pacific Basin was most ferocious.

But the diagnosis was wrong. The real threat to Europe was coming not from far Eastern dragons dragging smokestack industries into their low-cost, disciplined lairs but from a new monster lurking overseas. This high-tech Minotaur began by exacting tribute in legendary human form. Not merely seven virgins and seven young men, but the cream of Europe's numerate intelligentsia. Then the toll increased as the brain drain was augmented by the dollar drain.

Meanwhile, the industrial dilemma became ever more puzzling to those who govern. With no MITI compass to guide them, new blind alleys and higher walls made the dark labyrinth of high technology seemingly impossible to escape from. Neither (inward investment) bribery, nor (technological) leap-frogging nor digging new (transoceanic) tunnels led to the clear light of sunrise.

Moreover, when the chips were down, the nations of Europe were still divided, one against the other. France and Germany battled to impose competing television designs on their fellow Europeans (inter alia); the British and Germans could find no common ground in the development of computer systems; and France and Britain became locked in a bitter struggle to conquer export markets for defence electronics.

Thus, while European co-ordination and harmony is slowly taking hold in the nineteenth-century industries of coal and steel (where it matters little), all is disunity in the twenty-first-century industry of information technology (where it is a matter of economic survival).

Europe's salvation therefore depends on identifying a means of slaying the Minotaur, uniting the fractious states and discovering an exit from the high-tech labyrinth. The candidate here proposed is Project Theseus.

THE PROCRUSTEAN GAP

One of Theseus' more notable adventures was his meeting with Procrustes. As is well known, this giant's hobby was to invite passing strangers to rest on his iron bed. If they were too long for it, however, he cut them down to size; while, if they were too short, he stretched them to an appropriate degree. Theseus sorted out Procrustes by applying the same treatment, which will now be used to close the significant IT demand gap which appears to exist in the EEC in 2005.

The analyses in Part Two have shown that if, by 2005, the IT industry in the ten-nation EEC is producing $475 billion of electronic goods, give or take a few billions, it should be capable of competing successfully against all comers in all (free) markets. If the total EEC market for IT products reaches this level, then Figure 8.1 gives a feasible picture of what the total trade in IT products will look like in 2005, making reasonable allowance for imports, exports and the size by then of the MNEs.

In Chapter 10 it has been argued that no segment other than telecommunications can provide anything like this kind of demand uplift, and the calculations of Chapter 11 show that the postulated installation of Eurogrid will give rise to a total demand for IT products of $325 billion by 2005. Of this, about $40 billion represents the anticipated extra demand for telecommunications products needed specifically for the new broadband network, $130 billion is for terminals which could only be used in conjunction with it, and $155 billion would be for 'indirect' terminals – i.e. terminals which also possess the capability of functionng usefully on a stand-alone basis.

It is probably not far off the mark to assume that about half ($75 billion, say) of these indirect terminals would have been bought anyway, so that the total, direct uplift in demand attributable specifically to the installation and use of Eurogrid becomes about $250 billion.

But Chapter 8 points out that, using the real but very low historical growth rates for the West European IT market as a whole (Appendix A), the EEC market would in any event have reached *c*. £125 billion by 2005 – most of which, by definition, would be wholly independent of Eurogrid. Together, then, these represent a total demand of $375 billion.

If the critical-mass figure of $475 billion is regarded as sacrosanct, these elements of IT demand still fall short of what is needed by about $100 billion. The question which must then be asked is whether this is a reasonable value to assume for the EEC market in 2005 for IT products which have not already been accounted for.

It is clear that the bulk of the consumer-electronics, integrated-circuit, office-electronics and telecommunications segments have been taken into account in the sense that they will be integrally associated with the use of Eurogrid. Of the six key segments, therefore, this leaves only computers and industrial automation from which the demand gap might be filled.

While most computer and industrial automation equipments will obviously possess a communications facility in the Eurogrid era, many of these, especially the larger systems, cannot be (and have not been) classified as terminals.

The projected triad market for these two segments combined will be *c*.$780 billion in 2005 (Table E.3), from which a free-world market value *c*.$970 billion is obtained. On the consistent assumption that the EEC, post-renaissance, would represent about a quarter of the free-world IT market, its projected demand for computers and industrial automation systems in 2005 will be c.$240 billion. Thus, making appropriate allowance for the weight of these two segments in the no-renaissance market figure of $125 billion, even if only about half of this computer/industrial automation demand is unrelated to Eurogrid, the gap will have been closed. Moreover, there are many other IT segments (e.g. medical electronics, defence electronics, navigational aids) which have so far been ignored but for which the aggregate demand by 2005 will be substantial.

Given the necessarily approximate nature of these various calculations, it is reasonable to conclude, therefore, that the economic impact of Eurogrid, and the stimulus it will provide for the enhanced use of the tools of information technology, will indeed be sufficient to lift the EEC market to the required level in 2005. And, even then, it is useful to remember that per-capita IT expenditure, at $1650 (Chapter 8), will still be significantly below that projected for the US ($2400) even when based on current trends.

So much for the demand problem. The challenge now is to find a feasible mechanism for channelling a sufficiently large portion of this business to the European-owned IT producers so that their production levels are raised, in accordance with the estimates of Chapter 8, to world-scale proportions.

LE PLAN PHÈDRE

Channels of demand

It has already been said, emphatically and repeatedly, that the European electronics industry is dying for lack of sales. It follows that no renaissance strategy will succeed unless at its heart is an organ big enough to pump a rich flow of demand through the arteries of the anaemic European IT producers. And Eurogrid, plus its knock-on benefits, will meet this need nicely.

Although that huge project can overcome the biggest difficulty, it still leaves the critical problem of how to direct the demand to the companies which really need it. As things stand at present, the Eurogrid market would be open to all, and it would inevitably be served in the main by non-European IT producers. That, needless to say, would be anathema to the European taxpayers who were funding the expansion of Europe's IT production facilities.

Moreover, it is not just a question of demand, pure and simple. The products will have to be skillfully designed to meet the sophisticated requirements of Eurogrid and its users, in terms of costs, quality and

performance. And even that implies a moving target, since the irre-
pressible advances in electronics technology will necessitate a continuing
programme of research and development to ensure that these components,
equipments and systems remain state-of-the-art and comparable to the
best that can be produced anywhere.

The other salient constituent of a European renaissance strategy, therefore, must be a mechanism for harmoniously but selectively sharing out
both demand and research funds primarily to the European electronics
companies. Since Phaedra, wife of Theseus, is known to have distributed
her favours, albeit selectively and solely to Europeans, we might choose
to name this plan PHEDRE (Programme pour l'Harmonisation Euro-
péenne de la Demande et de la Recherche en Electronique) in her honour.

Preference predicaments

Any such plan is bound to run into a host of difficulties, of course. One
is the General Agreement on Tariffs and Trade (GATT), which includes
a requirement that imported goods should be treated the same as goods
of national origin regarding laws and regulations affecting their internal
sale. In addition, there is a GATT agreement which requires liberalization
of government purchases of specific products once the order exceeds a
stated threshold value.

In practice, however, this would probably not turn out to be too
much of a hurdle. For one thing, most telecommunications products are
excluded from GATT. And for another, there are many precedents for
the evasion or disregard of GATT regulations, ranging from complicated
bureaucratic constraints which Japan is alleged to have used for many
years to deter would-be importers of various goods, to the short-term
action by France in 1981 to throttle back the importation of Japanese
VCRs by funnelling them all through one small Customs post at Poitiers.

Moreover, retribution from its major trading partners for Europe's
flouting of GATT provisions would be highly unlikely if, as argued later,
the defensive actions were to ease a well-publicized balance-of-trade
problem, were applied over a limited period of time and were confined
to a specific class of goods.

There is also the Treaty of Rome, Article 85 of which prohibits the
sharing of markets between firms. Although the basic objectives of Plan
Phèdre appear to contravene Article 85, there is an exception from the
rules for agreements which improve production and promote technical
and economic progress while allowing consumers a fair share of the
benefits.

Article 86 also prohibits abuse of a dominant position by, among other things, limiting production or technical development to the prejudice of consumers. But since anything that is done to promote an IT renaissance must operate to the ultimate benefit of the European consumer, this Article is unlikely to present insuperable difficulties.

Love us or leave us

More intractable will be the problem of the large number of high-tech MNEs which have made investments in Europe. If these are mainly of an opportunistic nature (e.g. simple 'kit' assembly), there should be little to restrain European authorities from treating such companies as not much more than straightforward importers.

On the other hand, however selfish may have been their motives, foreign-owned electronics companies which have implanted major high-technology facilities in Europe's industrial landscape, especially where there is a strong R & D component, clearly deserve something substantially better. It seems difficult in the extreme to reconcile official commitments which will have been made to such firms, and commitments which they may have made to their European customers, with excluding them entirely from the large and potentially lucrative orders which will emanate from a European IT renaissance programme. Phèdre will need to have her wits about her to resolve this dilemma.

At its most basic level, the solution must lie in allowing 'qualified' MNEs (i.e. those which have made irreversible high-technology investments in Europe) to participate in the renaissance activities, but only under conditions where their contribution to Europe's technical revitalization is unequivocal.

What is proposed, then, in the overall framework of the Plan Phèdre is a scheme by means of which research, development, design and production of Eurogrid-related products is parcelled out equitably among qualified IT companies, the bulk of which are likely to be controlled from countries which are participating in Project Theseus.

Research collaboration

Beginning with research, this is already on the right road, at least as regards long-term, non-competitive and multination research is concerned, through the ESPRIT programme (see page 187). However, using the well-established rule of thumb that basic research costs, development costs and the costs of gearing up for production are in the approximate ratio of 1:10:100, the total funding for Eurogrid-related research must eventually be jacked up to $3 billion (see page 216).

Assuming that about half of this comes from the industrial firms engaged in the research, the total, Community-wide exchequer cost will need to be about $1.5 billion per annum, compared to the current value of about $150 billion per annum.

Various collaborative, long-term research projects are already under way in Europe, one example being a laboratory jointly financed by Bull, ICL and Siemens to undertake research in the field of advanced computer design. Several American companies with European research facilities (notably IBM) are also involved in trans-frontier, multi-organization ESPRIT projects.

Although these are encouraging signs, and ESPRIT is certainly of great significance in fostering a climate of multination co-operation, their importance should not be exaggerated. In the first place, it is charac-teristic, if understandable, that the area where trans-frontier high-tech partnership has first become evident is far removed from the hurly-burly of the marketplace – which is where it is really needed.

The second point, made with some force in Part One, is that neither the quality nor the quantity of basic research is seriously deficient in Europe at the present time. And thirdly, the spirit of co-operation is the very essence of basic research, where progress generally comes from creative resonance within a peer group, and rarely from an isolated laboratory.

Contracted development

Where difficulties really begin to appear is in applied research and devel-opment (AR & D). Several independent studies have shown that, in absolute terms, the scale of Europe's investment in AR & D in the IT sector is adequate when compared to that of Japan and the US. The problem arises because, development being uncomfortably close to the marketplace, there is little co-operation but much duplication of effort.

It goes without saying that either Europe must spend proportionately more on AR & D to compensate for these grossly inefficient, ill-afforded redundancies or, far more sensibly, the renaissance strategy must allow for the·provision of practical means for encouraging close AR & D relations between consenting corporations.

The starting point for the development aspects of the Plan Phèdre is the harmonization of the functional requirements for new, Eurogrid-related products. Ideally, these would be reasonably in advance of existing products, and the specifications would spell out the critical performance parameters and other features (including target production costs in many cases), but would not specify how the product should be made (e.g. by what technology). Such specifications would be drawn up by a development co-ordinating agency on which both the PTTs and the IT industry would be strongly represented.

This agency (or another one for that matter) would then issue contracts for development of the specified products. These would be awarded on a competitive basis, and confined to qualified companies or consortia with particular AR & D capabilities in Europe – of which more later.

The number of individual development projects would depend on a variety of factors such as the complexity of the product (e.g. very few contracts for the development of supercomputers or advanced microprocessors, several for high-definition video displays) and how many European suppliers would eventually be needed. There would always be a small degree of redundancy, however, in the sense that the number of developments commissioned would be such that success by at least one contractor would be virtually certain. The geographic distribution of the contracts would be on the basis of *juste retour*, as far as possible, although this would not preclude a disproportionate allocation to a country with disproportionate AR & D abilities in relevant technical disciplines.

The scheme would be open to participation by companies of any nationality provided they subscribed to certain conditions, as outlined below. The involvement of non-European organizations might be particularly welcome if they could contribute technical know-how which was lacking in European companies. In other cases where a technological deficiency was found to exist in Europe, the agency would liaise with particular Phèdre companies to negotiate technology transfer licences from transoceanic sources.

Many of the design specifications would arise naturally from the capabilities of the Eurogrid network and the uses to which it could be put. In this sense, the 'marketplace' would have a much enlarged influence (and rightly so) on the kind of products which were developed. Qualified companies would also be encouraged to submit unsolicited designs for official sanction and support, and they would be totally free, of course, to undertake private development work of their own and entirely at their own risk.

To ensure efficient operation of the designer-coupling effect, appropriate mechanisms would be created to stimulate frequent interactions between leading designers in 'developer' and 'user' organizations. And to avoid too parochial an approach, interaction would be encouraged between these groups and their counterparts in other geographical areas – probably using their overseas familial (i.e. parent or subsidiary) organizations.

As pointed out in Chapter 6, increasing technical sophistication implies escalating design costs, and fewer and fewer companies (especially the Europeans in their present weakened state) can afford the often horrendously high costs of development. To help redress the balance of advantage between European and non-European companies, therefore, something like 75 per cent of these costs would be at the public expense, through the medium of the development contracts.

Production warranted

In return for their 25 per cent ante, successful 'developer' companies or consortia would earn the right to participate, if they so wished, in the subsequent, potentially lucrative manufacture of the product (to meet the 'Eurogrid' demand plus the prospective export orders), to a minimum, specified level (see below). In addition, they would own part of the so-called 'intellectual property rights' (IPR) which would allow them to sell-on their design know-how and production rights to other 'qualified' companies.

On the other hand, the *quid pro quo* for the public underwriting of 75 per cent of the development costs would be a forward commitment by the company, whether successful in its development or not, to license the design and make available its associated manufacturing know-how to selected European-based producers at pre-ordained fees. In this way companies would be deterred from simply taking the money without really trying to push the development to a successful conclusion.

Other conditions imposed on companies wishing to join the scheme would be sweet and simple. Their country of ownership and control would be of no consequence, but they would have to possess R & D and production facilities, located in not less than two separate 'Theseus' countries, which were appropriate in size and technology to the product in question. This would sidestep any possible embarrassments – e.g. from 'foreign' acquisitions or divestments.

Any non-European company wishing to jump on the Eurogrid bandwagon would therefore be able to do so, but only if its European commitments were substantial enough to make it effectively part of the European IT industry, and if it was willing to disclose its development and production know-how to nominated partner companies. Fair to them; fair to the European taxpayers.

Designs which successfully met the performance and cost criteria would move into production by the award of manufacturing contracts of a size, and with a number of companies, appropriate to the expected size of the market. There would always be at least two, however, to ensure dual sourcing.

Each successful developer would be guaranteed a pre-specified price and minimum level of production over a pre-specified period of time, although these production warranties would not total more than about half of the expected market. Beyond that, there would be open competition between qualified suppliers, regardless of whether they were original developers or subsequent licensors.

Marketing mechanics

To avoid modem mountains and piles of processors, the agency responsible for placing the manufacturing contracts would have a statutory right to supply the first tranche of demand, consistent with its production guarantees, to either the private or public-sector market. These sales would be made from the supplies being received from the approved producers (there would be no other kind of producer!), and would be at prices set by comparison with similar products in the free-world market.

The customers would need to take a view of whether to buy early or to wait, just as they must presently judge when, in a period of continually tumbling prices, to buy a personal computer. For instance, after exhaustion of the initial 'official' stocks, prices might go down (i.e. more rapidly than usual in the electronics business) if qualified producers chose to ramp up production in anticipation of expanding, profitable sales. Prices might increase, however, if perceived lack of (production) profits caused supply to lag demand.

For the more expensive end-user equipments such as large office automation, factory automation or computer systems, the overall scheme might include a method for leasing to European customers at favourable rates. This sort of idea has already been used in Japan (for computers and industrial robots) and could offer the advantage of promoting European usage of the most advanced IT systems and thereby stimulating their production.

Finally, as with many other attempts to regulate orderly development of the market, there would inevitably be occasional glitches in the system (cf. OPEC, the International Tin Council and the Common Agricultural Policy). After all, keeping supply and demand more or less in balance in a sector as technically volatile as electronics is going to call for a lot of skill and a modicum of luck. This, however, should not be a serious worry with the overall scheme propounded, and any financial hiccups will have to be accepted as an integral part of the cost of the Plan Phèdre, which will be only a small portion of the overall investment in Project Theseus.

LA FAMILLE PHÈDRE

In search of a precedent

What is being proposed is without doubt complicated and controversial, but could it be otherwise? It is an attempt – essential to Europe's technology revival – to graft some of the branches of preferred procurement and central planning onto the sturdy tree of the free-market economy. Some might argue that this is impossible. But if one extreme is all-embracing state planning in the mould of the Communist Bloc, and the other is the ultimate collapse of the Western European economy, some middle way cannot but be appealing.

Central to the concern must be whether the plan will work in practice, to which the first, if facile, response must be that it will take lashings of skill, time and goodwill to put functioning flesh on the bare bones of the skeleton described in the previous section. But the intention has been merely to sketch out the main elements of the Plan Phèdre, in the clear knowledge that it leaves many questions unanswered. It would be a tremendous boost to confidence, however, if it could be shown that there exist feasibility proofs – other members of la famille Phèdre, so to speak – that have operated efficaciously. There are, and they have . . .

The defence sector is full of them, in fact, and this in itself sheds an interesting light on the politico-economic beliefs permeating Europe in the 1980s. Two clear perceptions of the public and politicians alike are firstly, that weapon systems in general are on a fast-rising escalator of technical sophistication and cost; and secondly, that the total sums of money required to develop and manufacture major new defence systems (such as an aircraft) are now too great to be borne without fiscal discomfort by any single, European nation.

Thus what has driven disparate European governments into one anothers' enveloping arms is the daunting expense of developing arms. Not, it should be noted, into the embrace of the US, generally because its defence and aerospace industry is so big and butch that it would dominate any putative partnership. Nor, obviously, into Japan's since it doesn't yet have a defence industry to speak of.

There is still much procurement of defence equipment from the US, of course, usually with an 'off-set' element. But so clearly is this particular need for European collaboration now recognized that the lonely politicians who still plead the cause of national programmes for developing big defence systems find an echo only from their counterpart minorities in other legislatures.

The foundation of military might is economic power, which is increasingly synonymous with technological strength. It is therefore to be hoped that the sort of informed pragmatism which has motivated trans-frontier collaboration in European defence technology will now come into play in forging similar linkages in the equally vital business of information technology.

Supersonic to subatomic

It comes as something of a pleasant surprise to realize that the full scope of multination European collaboration in the general field of high technology is really quite extensive, particularly in the public (or quasi-public) sector. Probably the first project of any real magnitude was Concorde. This can now be viewed as an exemplary manifestation of what is being preached throughout this treatise – namely, that technology push is futile in the absence of demand pull. Put succinctly, this gigantic technical achievement was negated by a tiny demand.

But the Concorde syndrome could still play an important role in muting the enthusiastic battle cries of those European high-tech generals who advocate one last, great technology push to breach the enemy's market strongholds.

Much European collaboration is evident in the field of high-energy physics. CERN (Conseil Européen pour la Recherche Nucléaire) has been operating for about a quarter-century to provide European nuclear physicists with common facilities comparable to those enjoyed by their American research colleagues. Under the auspices of Euratom, this collaborative effort was greatly enhanced when several European nations, facing insistent demands from their research establishments for a $1 billion particle accelerator, chose to join forces in the Joint European Torus (JET) project.

In the field of space there is an impressive array of European collaborative ventures. There are, for instance, three permanent European consortia in the area of rockets and missiles, where 'non-captive' export sales are claimed to have grown to more than half the total turnover. The most pertinent to Phèdre is the European Space Agency (ESA), which acts as a focus for the satellite and space programmes of European nations, because the business of ESA is regulated by the principle that countries receive contracts in proportion to their subscription to the ESA budget.

Although international collaboration within ESA has been effective at the research level, some countries have occasionally exercised their freedom to undertake commercial developments outside the ESA framework.

Individual European companies have also sometimes found it fruitful to co-operate with US firms on projects such as Intelsat and Arabsat.

Of some relevance to the Phèdre theme is that France, Germany and the UK all spend more on their own national space programmes than on their contributions to ESA, presumably because their commitment to ESA is qualified by their wish to foster purely national endeavours in space technology. The dispiriting result of this schizophrenia is that, even though Europe and individual countries are being strengthened in this area by a combination of multination, binational and national ventures, Europe as a whole still lags far behind the US. Only in the specific area of rocket technology does Europe – through the single-minded, long-term French commitment to the Ariane satellite launcher – have a comparable capability.

In the quasi-public sector, the biggest and most interesting example of European co-operation is the Airbus. This was originally promoted as a commercial venture by the companies involved, although predicated on government backing. Because the potential British contributor was refused official support, the initial partners were French, German and Spanish, although British Aerospace joined in 1979 without the safety net of public underwriting.

To no one's surprise, it has been a very expensive proposition, probably involving total risk capital of $3–4 billion to cover both development and production. Nevertheless, reports suggest that the project has been well managed, with only small disharmonies arising in the multi-layered, multilingual project committees. And, of great significance, the Airbus family is beginning to offer the prospect of eventual commercial returns.

Of greater importance is the undeniable fact that, but for the courage and commitment of the founder governments, Europe would now be bereft of a meaningful civil-aviation industry. By carefully assessing the demand and competitive factors, the governments and companies involved have kept Europe an important place in a key, high-technology industry, with incalculable spin-off benefits for sub-contractors, technological progress, trade balance and employment.

The Unidata saga

In the IT sector *per se*, there has only been one major attempt to forge a trans-frontier amalgamation of entire divisions of otherwise competing companies. This was Unidata, the Franco-German-Dutch computer company of the 1970s. It was such a high-profile failure that critics of

European IT collaboration invariably present it as evidence that such schemes simply will not work. It therefore warrants some attention here.

The story of Unidata is long and controversial, but it is possible to summarize the ingredients of special relevance to Project Theseus. In essence, Unidata was an alliance between CII (at that time the leading French contender in the computer business), Philips and Siemens aimed at rationalizing and co-ordinating product development, manufacture and marketing across the complete range of computer systems. The intention was to unify the company and integrate the staff as well as the product range. However, for reasons which are now obscure, agreements were difficult to secure at the working level and many problems tended to be referred upwards to the triumvirate of senior staff, drawn from the partner companies, whose job was to weld together the disparate parts and administer the integrated whole.

At some point in this far-sighted endeavour, the French authorities, it seems, got cold feet. In their determination to build a viable computer industry, they were torn between the European approach of Unidata and a national solution involving an alliance between the indigenous French computer companies and the American company Honeywell.

Those being the days (now far behind us, Gott si Dank) when French policy was overtly and excessively nationalistic, there was apparently great reluctance, at the highest levels, to commit French public funds to an industrial enterprise over which France would not have control. There was also a belief in some quarters that the Honeywell linkage would provide a good base range of equipment on which a new company, CII-Honeywell-Bull, could build. And some French politicians publicly voiced their doubts about the viability of the Unidata concept.

Whatever the precise nature of their misgivings, there is little doubt that the French government of the day decided to take the Honeywell path and in so doing caused the demise of Unidata, to which the other partners were willing to confirm their continuing commitment, but not merely on a binational basis.

It is ostensibly not a happy precedent for European commercial alliances in the electronics sector. On the other hand, things have changed fundamentally since those far-off days. In particular, despite a renewed burst of French technological chauvinism in the early 1980s, France now exudes a convincing dedication to European co-operation in most fields of high technology. It is arguable, therefore, that had Unidata been founded a decade later, it might now be regarded as a pathfinder for other trans-frontier IT linkages. In light of the special circumstances then prevailing, it certainly does nothing to invalidate the current, urgent need to put many more multination IT alliances into effect.

Tornado blows a way

The most convincing precedent for the Plan Phèdre is also the biggest
and the most recent. With a gestation period typical of major, new
defence systems, the Tornado aircraft was originally conceived in the
mid-1960s as a multi-role combat aircraft (MRCA) capable of eventually
replacing the Lockheed Starfighter F104. It has been in service since
about 1982 and by the time current orders for about 850 aircraft are all
fulfilled, in the mid-1990s, it will represent the backbone of NATO's
counter-attack abilities well into the next century.

Two particular aspects are of special relevance here: the cost of the
project, and the disconcerting maze of participants, of whom the three
constituent companies (Aeritalia of Italy, British Aerospace and Mes-
serschmidt Bolkow Blohm of the FRG) are the most important. With the
backing of their respective governments, these companies formed a joint
company, Panavia GmbH, which is the most reliable source of information
on the Tornado project.

On the question of costs, these have been huge but, within reason,
have maintained contact with the original budgets. The total bill to the
three European defence ministries for their final complement of 809
production aircraft (40 or so have been exported) will be approximately
$50 billion (1983 values). If the associated cost of simultaneously devel-
oping a new engine is excluded, then current estimates suggest that in
real terms (all others are unreal) the cost over-run was about 15 per cent
up to the start of full production, but only ten per cent if post-design
specification changes are eliminated. While all budget breaches are to be
deplored, Panavia and its main contractors have clearly done a far better
job in this respect than many earlier military development programmes
of lesser size and complexity, including several which were not burdened
with trans-frontier problems of liaison and administration.

Organizationally, Tornado (like Eurogrid) is mind-boggling. In the first
place, it is a hugely complicated technical system, both to develop and
manufacture. Secondly, its successful evolution and production has
involved three governments and three airforces, a joint policy agency and
a joint management agency, a prime contractor (Panavia), three main
contractors and over 200 individual sub-contract suppliers of components
and equipments located in at least four separate countries.

The sharing out of work has been in proportion to the percentage of
the 809 production aircraft each country buys. Work within each country
is paid for by its own main contractor so that no money crosses frontiers,

and each country manufactures a major portion of the total system and then assembles its own complete aircraft.

It might be imagined that all of this is massively bureaucratic and inefficient – but not so. The whole Panavia staff totalled only about 300 at its peak, with about 30–50 additional Tornado staff in each participating government. And as to its cost-effectiveness, British Aerospace has argued that, given the economies of scale commensurate with the UK's 220 aircraft, the three-nation programme represents a total cost to the defence ministry about 20 per cent lower than if the UK had gone it alone, and 17–25 per cent lower than purchasing an equivalent aircraft from the US.

In fact, so successful has the Tornado project been that, with a few refinements here and there, it is to serve as the model for the latest collosal project – the European fighter aircraft (EFA) – in which the original three Panavia nations will be joined by Spain and, probably, France.

Here, then, is the feasibility proof for Phèdre. Which is not to say that Project Theseus, embracing Eurogrid as its technical heart and Plan Phèdre as its circulatory system, is not more complicated yet. But the additional degree of complexity should be easily assimilated with the Tornado experience, inter alia, as a concrete reality on which to build the rules and procedures appropriate to the European IT renaissance.

THE RELIEF OF UNEMPLOYMENT

The pessimistic view

On present trends, we may remind ourselves, the US and Japan will both create more than 2 million new jobs directly in the IT sector by the end of the century, while Western Europe will *destroy* 200,000 (Table 5.5). Although the European psyche has been bombarded for years with despairing forecasts of the high-tech destruction of jobs in general, this is the first occasion, so far as is known, when the doom has spread to the IT sector itself, despite its acknowledged high-growth prospects.

All of this, moreover, is going on in a period when unemployment is the dominating political problem facing most European governments. The economic and social damage attributable, directly or indirectly, to long-term unemployment is incalculable, and most politicians know it. Yet few of them, alas, have even begun to understand that information technology lies at the core of the calamity in the sense that it can not only kill jobs (which *is* widely recognized), but can create them too (which is not).

Both of these aspects of the employment crisis justify some attention, therefore, particularly in light of the postulated Project Theseus. That is, will an accelerating increase in the *use* of IT, as advocated here, result in the collapse of employment in the office and the factory, as some have argued, or will it provide the key to greater efficiency, competitiveness, economic growth and employment?

And the second question, considering Project Theseus itself, is what would be its likely impact on European employment? Not simply whether it can reverse the present, distressing trends in IT employment in Europe, but by how much, and what might it do for the unemployment problem in general?

There is a third question which warrants discussion. In earlier chapters, it has been stressed that many parts of the industrialized world are suffering from a serious shortage of high-tech talent. If, as might be imagined, a European IT renaissance results in a considerable increase in IT job opportunities, will it be possible to fill them?

There are four critical resources required to solve the crisis of European advanced technology, the lack of any one of which would abort any renaissance plan. Put simplistically, the first is demand, the second is money and the third is technology, all of which have been dealt with – in outline, at least – in these proposals for Project Theseus. The fourth is skilled manpower. It is essential, therefore, to take a look at where the graduates and technicians will come from, and to assess what must be done to develop Europe's institutions of higher education in order to supply the kind and quantity of skills which will be needed. This aspect of the problem is discussed in the following section.

A century of office automation

Many prior studies of the impact of technology on employment have tended to concentrate on the manufacturing sector – mainly, it might be supposed, because the instant visibility of technology is probably highest in the production environment. For example, it is now common knowledge that the extensive use of ICs in electronic equipments (such as a television set) has reduced the number of individual components required, with a consequent reduction in assembly-worker time per unit of production. The application of robotics and computerized process-control techniques has also had a highly visible effect on manufacturing productivity. In fact, enough has probably already been said on this aspect of the problem for our present purposes.

It turns out, however, that the office environment has also had to assimilate a very long history of technological change, which has so far

Table 12.1 Technological landmarks for UK clerical workers (1840–1980)

Date	Development	Impact on clerical-worker productivity
1837	Telegraph	0
1840	Postage stamps	0
1863	Crude facsimile system	0
1873	Money orders	+
1874	Crude typewriter	0
1877	Commercial telephone	+
1881	Postal orders	+
1883	Parcel post	0
1885	Telephone switchboards	+
1889	Commercial dictaphone	+
1890	Practical typewriter	+
1891	PABX	+
c. 1900	Mechanical calculators	+
1919	Airmail (London/Paris)	0
1920	Electric typewriter	+
1920	Transatlantic airmail	0
c. 1920	Accounting machines	+
1926	Transatlantic telephony	0
c. 1947	Chemical copiers	0
1954	Plain-paper copiers	+
c. 1960	Business computers	+
1961	'Golf-ball' typewriters	0
1963	Satellite telephony	0
1964	Word processors	+
1968	Giro service	0
c. 1970	Electronic calculators	+
c. 1972	Communicating WPs	+
c. 1975	Personal computers, etc., etc.	+

attracted much less attention. Table 12.1 lists the principal innovations which have affected British clerical workers over the past 140 years or so, and the dates would be similar for most industrialized countries. Also shown is a rough assessment of whether each innovation enhanced the prevailing productivity of clerical workers.

The first significant invention was the telegraph system around 1837. This was obviously a major improvement in communications, allowing messages to be transmitted across the country very rapidly, and thus improving the efficiency of commercial, government and military activities. Nevertheless, it probably took about the same number of man-hours to prepare, despatch and receive the message so that, despite the increase in convenience brought about by this first step in the electrical/electronic transfer of information, the impact on office productivity was to all intents and purposes neutral.

The introduction of the first facsimile systems was of such limited application at that time that it also had a negligible influence on the office. More contentiously, perhaps, the introduction of the British postage stamp in 1840 again served to make communications more convenient, but almost certainly had little positive effect on office productivity.

The first innovation which could reasonably be presumed to have increased clerical-worker productivity was the introduction of money orders in 1873. This is based on the postulate that the labour involved in transferring funds by this new method was significantly less than that absorbed in physically packaging, transporting and unwrapping the relevant coins.

With this as a guide, it hardly seems necessary to go through the entire list of about 30 innovations – which tend to come thick and fast in the 1970s and are represented merely by the three quoted examples in that decade. Suffice it to say that there is overwhelming evidence that clerical-worker productivity has been repeatedly enhanced by a succession of innovations over a hundred years of more.

Here then, is a portion of the working population which, surely as much as any other, has had to ride wave after wave of technological change. According to the pessimists' viewpoint, the result should have been a marked reduction in the number of UK clerical workers, spanning the period from the quill pen to the automated office. The facts, as we shall see, are different.

It so happens that the British decennial census data have, since 1891, included clerical workers as one of the principal job categories. It is therefore possible to trace accurately the change in this statistic over the years 1891 – 1981, with only the inter-war year 1941 missing. The result is plotted in Figure 12.1, on which is superimposed the productivity-enhancing innovations from Table 12.1.

The growth trends are roughly exponential (i.e. a straight line when plotted on log-linear graph paper), with a particularly fast growth rate between 1911 and 1921 – presumably due to the rapid increase in telephone operators stimulated by the 1914–18 war. Extrapolating backwards

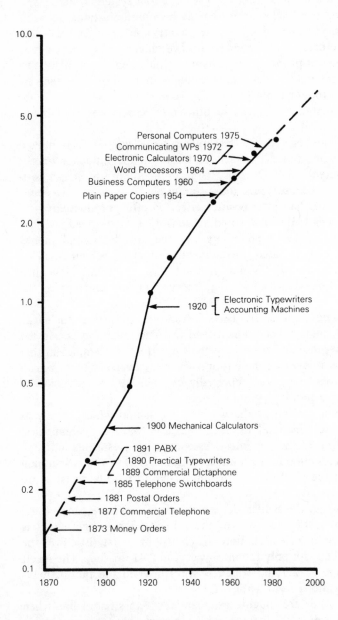

Figure 12.1. UK clerical workers (million).

to 1870 gives a UK clerical worker population at that time of roughly 140,000, which increased to about 4 million by 1981 and is projected to rise to *c*.6 million by 2000.

It is clear from this figure that, far from reducing the number of office workers, the productivity-enhancing inventions seem to have resulted in an increase, and this is not difficult to explain. As each innovation has made easier and cheaper the business of recording and conveying transactions, decisions, orders, lists, money, etc., the increased demand for these services has far outstripped the increase in productivity.

In short, instead of firing ten pushers of quill pens and hiring two typists, the typical early twentieth-century office manager found it necessary to hire a dozen typists, say, and a secretary, and some filing clerks, and a book-keeper and a couple of office juniors to fetch and carry. And all of this indirect cost burden was digestible because of the increased volume of business stimulated by the improved flow of information.

Thus the answer to the first question posed earlier seems to be that, at least in the office,[1] increased use of IT results in an *increase* in employment.

Job creation

To try to carry out an accurate forecast of the total number of jobs which would be created in Europe, if Project Thesus (or something like it) goes ahead, would obviously be immensely difficult. For a start, the market and production estimates have been very much macro-economic in nature, so any IT employment projections would necessarily be similarly approximate.

Even more difficult is the problem of estimating the downstream, or indirect, job creation. While it is quite certain (cf. Figure 12.1) that improved manufacturing and commercial efficiencies, through the intelligent use of IT, yield increased job opportunities, forecasting the particular make-up of the European economy in 2005 would be far too speculative for comfort. Moreover, estimates of the impact on indirect employment of job creation directly in IT have varied from 5-to-1 to 1-to-1. It must be said, however, that to assume five new employment posts created downstream for each direct IT job would be unduly optimistic in light of the publicly available evidence.

What we *can* do, nevertheless, taking a leaf out of the earlier methodology, is to assume as a first approximation that IT productivity in

---

[1] Similar analyses are not possible for the factory environment because of the great changes which have occurred over the years in the kinds of product manufactured in the UK.

2005 in a post-renaissance EEC would be comparable to that projected for Japan ($112,000, Table A.3) and the US ($101,000, Table A.5). Taking an average value of about $105,000, and EEC IT production of $550 billion (Figure 8.1), yields total sector employment in 2005 of about 5.2 million.

This is quite obviously a huge figure in comparison with the no-renaissance projection of 1.6 million (Table A.7). Nevertheless, even at that level the per-capita IT employment would be only 18 per thousand of population, compared to figures for Japan and the US (Appendix A) of 34 and 19, respectively.

The conclusion is inescapable. If the projected figures for the US and Japan are believable (and they are based, it should again be emphasized, solely on real, historical trends, and without the stimulus of some high-falutin' renaissance plan), then post-renaissance Europe must eventually achieve a comparable performance. On this basis, an increase of about 3.4 million IT jobs in the ten-nation EEC by 2005 is difficult to challenge.

Those are merely the direct jobs, of course, and exclude, as a particular example, possible increases in employment (due to Eurogrid) by the PTTs and the vendors of value-added-network (VAN) services. Despite that, on the conservative assumption that each new IT worker will create just one downstream job, on average, the total *additional* employment in the EEC would amount to about 7 million by 2005.

Understandably, the IT jobs created will be primarily for skilled and semi-skilled workers. But Europe would also benefit substantially from an uplift in the demand for construction workers needed to carry out the physical installation of Eurogrid. In 1983, the average productivity of construction workers in Europe was about $25,000 per worker. On the basis of about 140 million Eurogrid connections by 2005 (approximately 130 million domestic subscribers plus 10 million business establishments), at an average cost of $800 per connection (which will be lower, of course, in densely populated areas), the annual installation cost over a ten-year programme will be around $11.2 billion. Adding to this around $3 billion per annum for other construction costs associated with Eurogrid, and assuming an increased productivity figure of $30,000, the total number of construction workers employed on this infrastructure investment comes out at close to 0.5 million. Another substantial contribution to alleviating Europe's crushing unemployment burden.

Finally, the cost of creating these jobs can be estimated by comparing the total investment required to revitalize the IT industry ($300 billion, Chapter 8) with the total number of jobs created (*c*.7.5 million). It amounts to $40,000, or *c*.$88,000 (1983 values) if only direct IT jobs are included.

While not strictly comparable to the calculations of the costs of creating jobs through inward investment ($30,000–$60,000, Chapter 9), both can be only rough estimates and are comfortably close. The Theseus jobs, however, would largely be in companies controlled by Europeans, would cover the full range of IT activities, up to and including use of the most advanced technologies, and would be based on a sound European economy. In short, they would be permanent.

Project Theseus thus offers the prospect of creating many millions of new European jobs, at a heavy but bearable cost, and covering essentially all employment classifications. Given that it would also provide Europe with a brand new communications infrastructure, perfectly suited to the colossal information-processing needs of the twenty-first century, plus a wholly viable, world-scale IT industry, it may seem too good a bargain to miss.

SCARCE SKILLS

Defining demand

The roots of this brief analysis lie in the assumption that governments, the PTTs, the IT industry, its customers and the public in general really grasp the nettle, lovingly plant Project Theseus in fecund soil, fertilize it liberally and ward off marauding parasites with strong doses of insecticide.

In this event, total IT/electronics production in the EEC will increase from around $70 billion in 1985 (everything, as ever, in terms of 1983 dollar values) to c.$550 billion in 2005, representing a real growth rate (CAAGR) of approximately 10.8 per cent. Over the same period, as we have seen, IT productivity is expected to increase at a CAAGR of about 4.5 per cent – from $43,000 at the beginning to about $105,000 at the end of the 20-year renaissance period. Total IT employment will therefore increase from c.1.6 million (EEC) to c.5.2 million at a CAAGR of around six per cent.

The generic term for those who have reached a level of education equivalent to a first degree is third-level graduates. However, the British have an expression of more relevance to the IT industry; namely, qualified scientists and engineers (QSEs), and this is used liberally in what follows.

There is some uncertainty about the proportion of QSEs which the IT industry should ideally employ, but research suggests that an average of 40 per cent is not too wide of the mark. Moreover, there is no obvious reason to expect this to change significantly, the IT industry being heavily dependent on technical skills, by definition. Accordingly, present QSE employment in the European IT industry is about 720,000 and the revitalized industry of 2005 can expect to be employing (or needing) about 2.1 million IT-relevant QSEs.

Although precise figures are hard to come by, the best estimate is that the EEC is currently producing about 250,000 per annum science-related, third-level graduates. The bulk of these, however, cover a wide range of topics which are not of immediate relevance to the IT industry – such as the natural sciences, biology, mathematics and engineering in all its various guises. Perhaps about one-third (i.e. about 80,000) emerge with vocational knowledge of particular relevance to the electronics sector.

Despite much evidence that QSE demand exceeds supply in the IT sector, not all of these third-level graduates find their way into the industry. In fact, coupling this with the natural wastage which arises from emigration, retirement, drop-outs and the counter-attractions of other professions, gives the known result that, in Europe at least, the number of QSEs employed is fairly static. This implies a current 'wastage' rate in the European IT industry of about 80,000 in 720,000 or 11 per cent. Again, there is no good reason to suppose that this will change importantly in the future.

On this basis, IT-relevant QSE output in the EEC must rise, *cum* Theseus, from its present level of *c*.80,000 to about 360,000 in 2005. That is, of the 360,000 IT-relevant, third-level graduates who qualify in 2005, 235,000 (about 11 per cent of 2.1 million) will compensate for that year's total 'loss' from the sector as a whole, and 125,000 (six per cent of 2.1 million) will be available to further the growth of the European IT industry.

Supply scenario

In terms of the production of QSEs by the educational sector, this represents a CAAGR of 7.8 per cent. While this sort of growth rate is not enormous by the standards of the IT industry, it is bound to represent a serious challenge to the educationalists. Put more starkly, to serve the needs of revanchist, high-tech Europe, they will have to play a major part over the next 20 years in more than quadrupling the supply of IT-specific new graduates. Or, in different terms, by 2005 the output of QSEs appropriate to the needs of the IT industry will have to be about 50 per cent higher than the current output of *all* science-related graduates.

It is clearly pertinent to the prospects for Project Theseus to consider how this enormous demand might be met. One relatively easy measure could be to persuade a higher proportion of the 'non-IT' science graduates to make their career in electronics. This shift might be encouraged by the generally higher level of salaries in the IT sector, although the process could not be taken too far before other graduate-dependent sectors (many of which will also be stimulated, albeit indirectly, by the postulated European economic revival) began to feel the pinch. Further exacerbation of the salaries war for high-tech talent would obviously not be helpful to Europe's global competitiveness.

The only other route must be to expand the 'IT' graduate output itself, but this is easier said than done. In the first place, no significant increase in the flow of students into tertiary education can take place until there is a requisite increase in the number of second-level pupils studying pertinent subjects. This, in turn, requires the construction of new buildings and laboratories, and the recruitment and training of new teaching staff.

Also essential, quite obviously, will be a very substantial increase in the quality and quantity of lecturing staff in the universities and polytechnical colleges, with particular emphasis, it should be said, on vocational and applied science. And there, too, it will be necessary to provide much expanded and improved accommodation and teaching facilities.

For reasons such as these, the minimum elapsed time before a substantial increase in 'IT' graduates could be achieved is probably about eight years. This allows three years for the tertiary education itself, three years or so in which to effect a meaningful increase in the flow of qualified second-level students, and an additional two years in which to train additional second-level teachers, build facilities and create a climate of understanding in which more secondary pupils would be encouraged to select second-level topics of relevance to IT-related tertiary education. Even then, the overall system is likely to be far from what will ultimately be needed.

It is quite clear, therefore, that a major shortage of IT skills could emerge if Project Theseus goes ahead. Indeed, the whole renaissance strategy might founder on the lack of talent to put it into effect. On the overall renaissance timescale proposed, some amelioration of this problem could stem from the fact that the first five years must be spent largely on planning activities, prior to the critical decade (1990–2000) in which Eurogrid is installed and the European IT industry is built up to world-scale proportions.

The unavoidable conclusion is that a crash programme should be started, as rapidly as possible and on a pan-Community basis if possible, to take all of the actions and make all of the investments necessary to double the output of IT graduates by 1995 at the latest. Although there will still be talent shortages during the early renaissance years, the growth momentum thus instilled into the educational establishments, and the manifest European commitment to secondary and tertiary technical education, should result in achievement of the necessary balance of supply and demand by about the end of the century.

A count of costs

Of course, all of this cannot be accomplished on the cheap. It has proved to be exceedingly difficult to obtain reliable figures, from several different European countries, on the costs of producing QSEs. For example, there is sometimes no distinction drawn between capital costs and running expenses, the two being lumped together in the budgets for education. And very few countries make much attempt to calculate the particular costs of producing science/engineering graduates.

As a best current guess, we could assume a total exchequer cost per third-level, IT-relevant graduate of somewhere in the range $15,000–$25,000. Taking the average (and again assuming constant 1983 values), the total cost of producing the 360,000 IT-relevant QSEs in 2005 will be $7.2 billion, spread across the present ten EEC member states, or about $2 billion each for the bigger countries.

For comparison, the composite (big) European nation discussed in Chapter 8 had a 1983 GDP of $540 billion, of which 42 per cent was disbursed by the exchequer; and of that 12.9 per cent went on education. This works out as $29 billion. It can be concluded, therefore, that while the proposed crash programme of investment in IT-specific education would not in itself be cheap, it should be relatively easily contained within somewhat expanded and re-oriented educational budgets. In any event, these skills are an essential resource, as stated earlier, and the cost of ensuring that they are in adequate supply pales into insignificance in relation to the total required investment in Project Theseus.

FORTRESS EUROPA

In the preceding pages hints have been dropped from time to time that, during the renaissance era, it will be necessary to erect barriers to the importation of electronic goods into Europe. It will come as no surprise, therefore, that selective but effective control of high-tech imports is regarded as a crucial link in the Theseus chain.

The need for such a highly contentious constraint on international free trade can best be argued by contemplating what would happen without it. Project Theseus, it will be remembered, assumes no limitation on the freedom of the private buyer to purchase electronic equipment of his own choice, particularly when it functions on a purely stand-alone basis. If its use requires connection to the Eurogrid network then, as with all telecommunications terminals, it will obviously have to conform to the specified performance characteristics; and equipment purchased by and for the network authorities themselves will be subject to the kind of preferred procurement from indigenous suppliers which has operated in this business for generations.

In all other respects, the European IT market will be free and fully competitive, with the Phèdre marketing agency merely supplying the first tranche of demand (at free-world prices), after which the qualified suppliers will battle it out for private-sector orders.

But, as the plans for Eurogrid were being formulated, and inevitably publicized to some degree, the tremendous boost which it would give to IT demand would soon become clear to Europe's transoceanic competitors. Their formidable talents and energies would be focussed on capturing a large share of this market, as regularly happened, as we have seen, with successive waves of new IT products such as electronic watches and calculators, CB radio, VCRs, colour-television sets, computers, electronic instruments, word processors, ICs and the like.

In the meantime, even with public funds beginning to flow into the restructuring and expansion of the European IT industry, it would not yet be strong enough to compete head-to-head with foreign companies already functioning at much higher levels of AR & D, production and sales. The inescapable result would be that Project Theseus would be stillborn: its main objective, the revitalization of Europe's IT industry, would no longer be attainable.

Indeed, if Eurogrid still went ahead under these circumstances, and despite the $40 billion or so of direct business which they could expect in 2005 from the network authorities, the European IT companies would remain in the same position relative to foreign competition as they are today: too small to compete effectively, but too big not to be a source of grave concern to their shareholders and their governments.

Europe has no option, therefore. Import controls (*not* increased tariffs) will have to be imposed on a wide range of IT products during the whole of the renaissance period. While this is certain to incite much opprobrious comment from the leaders of those nations whose export ambitions will be most frustrated, the storm of protest will have to be weathered. The economic plight of an IT-deficient Europe may have to be invoked in excuse, perhaps combined with the mobilization of Europe's economic might in other areas.

And, after all, non-European companies will always be free to enjoy the commercial fruits of Eurogrid simply by planting large enough orchards of high technology in the newly fertile European soil, in accordance with the rules for participating in the Plan Phèdre.

But that is not the end of it, unfortunately. Another risk to be taken into consideration is that, following announcement of a commitment to Project Theseus, the European IT companies may find themselves the subject of unwanted attention from corporate raiders and other acquisitive bodies, particularly from the US. While any such advances would no doubt be rebuffed by the directors and senior managements of the hunted companies, it is difficult to have much faith in the willingness of European institutional investors to resist the temptations of what could be mouth-watering capital gains.

It might be argued that none of this would really matter, especially since the country of ownership is not being proposed as a qualification for joining Phèdre. But it would.

The ultimate goal of Project Theseus is to put Europe back on its feet, with a strong economy, full employment and control of, and competence at, the most advanced forms of information technology, to give it the capability of safely negotiating the stresses of the twenty-first century in the face of escalating competition from all corners of the world. The model must be an amalgam of Japan and the US, with regional pride and commitment allied to the unfettered working of the free-market economy and the creative investment in high technology of Europe's immense financial resources. This ideal, it seems clear, will be unattainable if significant portions of the future employment by, investment in and profit from these European enterprises are controlled by foreign investors whose commitment to a fully competitive Europe may not be unqualified.

So a number of unpopular actions will be necessary to build a protective wall around Europe as she girds her loins for rejoining the free and open high-tech markets at the end of the 20-year renaissance era. At that time, as in the legend, the termination of Phèdre's life will be timely, Europa will be restored to its rightful place in the sun, and Theseus can subside gently into a well-earned retirement.

Epilogue

EUROPE TODAY

Had this book been written two years earlier it would probably not have found a publisher. Even if it had, many readers would have poured scorn on both its diagnosis of Europe's high-tech maladies and the drastic treatment which it advocates to effect a cure.

This may still happen, of course, but I doubt it. A number of encouraging changes have become discernible in Europe since early 1984. For a start, there is now a much wider understanding among government officials and leaders of European electronics companies that the scale and scope of Europe's high-tech problem is becoming acutely worrying. What used to be regarded as a transient ailment, to be cured by a stiff dose of technological investment sugar-coated by government subsidies for R&D, is now more widely perceived to be a chronic and debilitating disease of dwarfism, for which the remedy may have to be drastic surgery followed by a long period of forced feeding and a cossetted convalescence. It will be clear that my thermometer gives a similar reading.

It also used to be a common view in such circles that commercial co-operation in the IT sector between companies in different member states was undesirable and irrelevant. Unions of the weak with the weak, it was argued, usually produce frail progeny. But today, albeit tentatively and selectively, some European IT companies can be observed seeking out sympatico partners in other corners of Europe rather than, as in the past, betting their future on transoceanic linkages.

Most important of all, the age of chauvinism is waning. Led by France, once the most selfishly nationalistic of all European administrations, governments are now groping for intra-European co-operative ventures in electronics in the hope of alleviating the manifest decline in their own national capabilities.

The recent French initiative on the Eureka project is a case in point. Stung into action by the American Strategic Defence Initiative (SDI), or Star Wars project, France (with substantial German support) has proposed a wide-ranging programme of European co-operative ventures in many segments of advanced technology. While some governments still view this suspiciously as a clever scheme for conferring European technological leadership on France at the expense of their own taxpayers, an improved climate of co-operation is nevertheless emerging.

That, of course, is all to the good, although Eureka does not really meet Europe's salient high-tech needs, at least according to my own beliefs. While its heart is in the right place, its eyes are still too keenly focussed on technology push when, according to my interpretation, the crying need is to develop demand pull to fill its empty stomach.

Summing up, the climate in Europe is gradually improving. Very slowly – two clouds out and one cloud in, so to speak – the first fitful rays of sunshine are beginning to filter through. So I am hopeful (always hopeful) that any breeze created by this book may help to sweep the skies clear and improve the prospects for a new dawn and a brilliant sunrise.

EUROPE POST-RENAISSANCE

The image I have tried to convey of the revitalized, technology-rich Europe of 2005 is one dominated by massive Euro-champions, creatively coupled together in design and development, competing vigorously in the unified, burgeoning European high-tech marketplace and battling ferociously for export sales. It is competitive, efficient and innovative, and is a powerful magnet for the technical talent pouring from its institutions of higher education.

By and large, that image is correct, since I am convinced that this is the only structure which will confer competitive capabilities on the European IT industry during its period of renaissance. But it shouldn't simply stay that way. The historical performance of national champions serving, in some measure, protected markets is not an encouraging precedent. They have an inherent tendency to become fat and lazy, fed on a rich diet of government funds and insulated from the cruelly competitive outside world by the infinite, and infinitely alluring, prospect of public sector sales.

My proposed scheme avoids this pitfall, I believe, by setting a rigid limit to the renaissance timescale. These companies will know, and so will the European official agencies who oversee their activities, that the gravy train has only a limited run. Beyond journey's end, they must be fully competitive in free-world markets or Europe must finally reconcile itself to being shunted off permanently onto a high-tech siding.

But that is by no means all. To ensure that the momentum imparted to the European IT industry is not dissipated by intra-European friction, or by lack of the lubrication of competition, it will be essential for post-renaissance Europe to construct mechanisms for the encouragement of smaller, thrusting enterprises capable of snapping uncomfortably at the heels of the top dogs.

In this realm, the Europe of the twenty-first century must take a leaf out of America's entrepreneurial, devil-take-the-hindmost industrial culture. We will need to encourage small start-ups by providing adequate venture capital. The financial institutions and the investing public will have to summon up the courage, and the faith, to anticipate (patiently) the financial rewards from speculative, high-tech inventions. And the taxation system will need to be adjusted to provide tangible incentives to bright, young, innovative risk-takers to quit the comfortable warmth of large-company security for the harsher, but more stimulating, cold air of high-tech do-it-yourself.

Even then, many qualitative criticisms of Europe's past performance in high technology have so far been glossed over in this overtly quantitative analysis. What faith can we have, in light of weaknesses already expounded, that Europe's managements and financial institutions will play their essential, creative, risk-taking roles in establishing a new, technology-based European economy? How can we be sure that large dollops of public money will do the trick, since there is convincing historical evidence that government money alone has so far had little positive impact? And with what degree of confidence can we assume that the consumers, workers and managers in the 'new Europe' of the twenty-first century will eagerly grasp the benefits of the information revolution and buy the bulk of the products pouring out of their revitalized IT design centres and factories?

There is no certain answer to any of these crucial questions, of course, but we can at least examine some of the evidence. First, there is the dispiriting record of lack of vision and risk aversion exhibited by many European high-tech managers over the last quarter-century. But it wasn't always so. As pointed out in Chapter 1, the nineteenth century was characterized by a European community of industrial entrepreneurs able and willing to face substantial financial risks for technical innovations in which they had faith. Not all of them succeeded, of course, but neither do all of the vaunted American high-tech entrepreneurs and venture capitalists.

It hardly seems credible that this strain of European venture talent has genetically disappeared in three or four generations, or that its twentieth-century exponents have all emigrated to the United States. In fact, the present economy of Northern Italy, kept buoyant by a profusion of small enterprises, and the flowering of venture capitalism and the Unlisted Securities Market in the UK, give the lie to such small-minded doubts. Moreover, the European financial institutions are still in the vanguard of innovation and the stimulation of businesses which they understand.

There are many clues, in truth, to suggest that the spirit of business enterprise is still alive in Europe. What has been missing, for reasons already described, is the evolution in business and financial circles of the kind of instinctive appreciation of information technology which has been such an important factor in the successes of American and Japanese electronics companies. In the climate of technological renaissance here propounded – with, initially, a major proportion of the risks underwritten by governments – it is not difficult to believe in a renewed flowering of the skills, insight and courage which endowed Europe with the fruits of the first industrial revolution.

On the question of the efficacy of public funding, it is possible to be unequivocally bullish. The problem with past government IT support programmes has been that they were generally too small and too focussed on technology push. But in the kind of scenario sketched out in Project Theseus, the funds will be very large and will be devoted mainly to stimulating demand (through Eurogrid) and meeting it (through Phèdre). Moreover, the finite duration of the renaissance period will provide a sharp spur to the European IT companies to achieve worldscale standards of competitiveness before the drawbridge of Fortress Europe is lowered to the clamouring hordes of non-European competitiors anxious to sell their wares in what, by then, will be a gigantic, open, high-tech marketplace.

Finally, there is the uncertainty about Europe's willingness to use the Eurogrid broadband network to its fullest extent, through the purchase of terminals and the utilization of the wide range of services which it will provide. Here, the first step is to remind ourselves that, even in the postulated ten-nation EEC market of $475 billion in 2005, IT consumption per capita will still be only slightly greater than that projected for Japan, and only about 55 per cent of that projected for the United States.

Optimism is reinforced by considering the history of the video cassette recorder (VCR) and personal computer (PC) in some parts of Europe. Penetration levels of both kinds of product in the UK, for example, have been somewhat higher than in the US. The explanation probably lies in the willingness of Europeans to invest in high-tech products when – but only when – the benefits are obvious. Thus, in the UK, where quite a high proportion of TV programmes are worth viewing, the VCR is used primarily as a time-shift machine, allowing the programme to be seen at a different, and more convenient, time than the original broadcast.

In the case of the PC, even if used predominantly as a computer toy or video game, it clearly has an educational and intellectually stimulating effect on the young. This desirable influence is as obvious in London as it is in Chicago and hence the penetration levels are roughly the same.

On the other hand, in more general terms there *is* an IT 'procurement gap', as the market figures have shown, which is larger (compared with the US) in ICs, office equipment and computers, and smallest in the relatively long-established segment of telecommunications. The reasons, however, are not difficult to discern. Prices in Europe are generally higher; exciting new products almost always appear first on the American market and tend to be a bit passé by the time they arrive in Europe; the products are more actively promoted in the US; and GDP per-capita and discretionary incomes are higher in the US, so both businesses and consumers can actually *afford* to spend more. Most important, however, is the fact that the technical 'climate' is currently less advanced in offices, factories and homes – implying that many potential users are less informed, less interested and less inclined to buy.

All of this will gradually change during the renaissance period, however. Avant garde IT products will become available in Europe and will be heavily promoted; per-capita and discretionary incomes will increase as employment and prosperity rise; a new generation of computer-compatible youngsters will grow to adulthood; and the technical climate will improve out of recognition. All of which, it may be remembered, rests on the secure foundation of the Eurogrid terminal demand forecasts described briefly in Chapter 11.

Returning from the general to the specific, heartening trends in this direction can already be seen, particularly in France. In preparation for the high-tech third millenium, the French government is even now investing heavily in awareness programmes to educate the public about the information revolution, supported by a growing number of practical demonstrations of the power of IT. Prominent among these is a project to supply a significant sample of French telephone users with a 'computerized' terminal, the Minitel, to provide an electronic substitute for the cumbersome, microscopically printed telephone directory.

And, on a Community scale, a major new programme of research and development on broadband networks (Research on Advanced Communications in Europe – RACE) has recently been initiated by the CEC, hopefully as the forerunner of Eurogrid.

Le soleil se léve sur l'Europe.

EUROPE AND ME

So, now that it is all finished, just what have I been trying to do, and why?

The short answer, of course, is to map out a way for Europe to extricate itself from domination by the high-tech industries of Japan and the US. Because – and let there be no equivocation about this – economic wealth in the industrialized countries increasingly depends on their ability to manufacture and apply the most advanced products of the information technology industry.

By surveying the different ways in which the electronics industries took off in the US, Japan and Europe, I have attempted to point up some of the key factors which determine success and failure in this complicated and volatile business. I have also tried to highlight a number of individual strands of analysis and perception to show how these must be woven together to form the tapestry of Europe's high-tech renaissance strategy – things such as venture capital, 'commercial' science, the management of change and the declining importance of defence electronics.

The real worry, of course, has been over the numbers. I knew at the start that these would turn out to be alarmingly large, and probably far beyond even the wildest guesses of the non-specialized observer of this sector. It was essential, therefore, to spell them out in some detail, and with much evidential support. Otherwise no one would ever believe the enormity of the crisis facing Europe and the costs of recovering our fair share of the world's IT business.

What to do about it is the key question, of course. I am certainly not alone in producing doom-laden forecasts about Europe's high-tech maladies; nor is mine by any means the only voice to sing the virtues of broadband networks. But what I have tried to do is show that Europe's salvation can only come through stimulated demand; that it is now useless to contemplate purely national programmes of high-tech recovery; and that Eurogrid, within the context of Project Theseus, can both provide that demand uplift *and* endow Europe with the sort of communications infrastructure which is essential to the economic survivors in the information society of the next century.

Quite clearly, the problem is huge, but the political will to act decisively and co-operatively should be a natural consequence of the recognition that there is no other way. The plan might be complicated, but so is the Tornado project, and *that* works. And as for the cost: is a dollar a week for every man, woman and child in the European Community too crushing a burden to provide their successor generations with a Europe which would enjoy restored economic health through the commercial conquest of technology?

As for my motives: I believe in Europe. It has much to offer in its cultural heritage, its basically civilized and good-natured attitudes to people and institutions, its new-found love of peace, and its potential for a rational, caring approach to the world's multifarious problems. I do not want to see that potential for good destroyed by its inability to earn a respected voice on world affairs through the undermining of its economic strength by its failure in high technology.

To refine the image, therefore, I foresee a high-tech Europe in the early decades of the next century consisting of a mass of competing companies of all sizes, with the good prospering at the expense of the not-so-good. I see the emergence of global business plans, placing as much emphasis on penetrating triad markets as on combating determined competition from low-cost NICs. I see a united Europe basking in the renewed glow of industrial competence and competitiveness, and able to afford once again the social conscience to alleviate the misery of the unfortunates, whether within its own borders or beyond its frontiers.

Appendix A
Derivation of data projections

The main objective of this appendix is to derive real growth rates of IT markets and production in each of the three main 'countries' – Japan, the US and Western Europe – and then to use these rates to extrapolate the projected figures out to the end of the postulated renaissance period in 2005.

The starting point is to obtain reliable historical data for total IT markets and production in current-value terms for each 'country'. These data are then corrected for past inflation rates in the 'local' currency, to give real 'national' growth rates. To make valid international comparisons, however, these 'local' values must be normalized to a single currency (i.e. the US dollar), and further corrections made for historical variations in exchange rates. This process thus yields real growth rates (for each country) which are directly comparable.

The projections are then expressed entirely in constant-value, single-currency terms, invoking the unlikely but unavoidable assumptions that inflation rates will be zero and that the other currencies will maintain their normalized values in relation to the dollar.

The analytical process begins, therefore, by taking actual data – in Japan, the US and Western Europe – for electronics production and markets. The longest recent span over which self-consistent data are available (for each 'country'), which are also mutually comparable, is 1977 – 1983.

The overall methodology can best be explained by means of an example – in this case, Japan. The inflation index in yen increased from 118 in 1977 to 150 in 1983, giving an average annual Japanese inflation rate over the six years of 4.1 per cent. Over the same period the yen appreciated against the US dollar by an annual average of 2.1 per cent (see Table A.1).

Table A.1   Corrections to growth rates for the Japanese IT markets

	1977	CAAGR	1983*	CAAGR	1985*	1995*	2000*	2005*
Inflation index	118		150					
Inflation rate		4.1%						
Exchange rate (Y = $1.00)	269		238					
Exchange-rate appreciation		2.1%						
Markets (Y bn)	3683		6775					
Apparent Growth (in Y values)		10.7%						
Real growth (in $ values)		8.6%						
Markets ($ bn)	13.7		28.5	8.6%	33.6	76.3	115	173

* Constant 1983 US dollar values.

Reliable market and production data are available from the Electronic Industries Association of Japan (EIAJ) in current values for the years covered.[1] In the case of markets, and in terms of EIAJ's definitions, the value increased from Y3683 billion in 1977 to Y6775 billion in 1983, giving an apparent growth (in yen) of 10.7 per cent per annum.

Now, however, comes a bit of algebra. To convert this *apparent* growth rate in the *local* currency, a_1, to a *real* growth rate, r_b, in the *base* currency (US dollars), we must use the formula:

$$r_b = \frac{(1 + a_l)(1 + e)}{(1 + i_l)} - 1,$$

where e is the average annual percentage *appreciation* of currency 1 against currency b, and i_1 is the annual average rate of inflation (in local currency), as measured by the Consumer Price Index (or equivalent).

Applying this formula, the real growth in the Japanese electronics market, as measured in terms of constant 1983 dollars, becomes 8.6 per cent per annum. This growth rate (assuming that it remains constant in the future) can then be applied (Table A.1) to the 1983 market of $28.5 billion to give a projected value in the year 2000 of $115 billion. (While other values – for 1985, 1995 and 2005 – are shown in this and subsequent

---

[1] *Electronic Industries in Japan*, 1984 Edition. Published by EIAJ.

Table A.2 IT production and market projections for Japan

	1977	CAAGR	1983*	CAAGR	1985*	1995*	2000*	2005*
Inflation index	118		150					
Inflation rate		4.1%						
Exchange rate (Y = $1.00)	269		238					
Exchange-rate appreciation		2.1%						
Markets (Y bn)	3683		6775					
Apparent growth (in Y values)		10.7%						
Real growth (in $ values)		8.6%						
Markets ($ bn)	13.7		28.5	8.6%	33.6	76.3	115	173
Production (Y bn)	6069		12685					
Apparent growth (in Y values)		13.1%						
Real growth (in $ values)		10.9%						
Production ($ bn)	22.6		53.3	10.9%	65.5	184	309	519
Trade balance ($bn)	8.9		24.8		31.9	108	194	346

* Constant 1983 US dollar values.

Tables, the analysis in this Appendix, as in Chapter 5, focusses primarily on the year 2000.)

Although this procedure may seem a little convoluted, it is the only way in which valid extrapolation, – and, more importantly, valid *comparisons* – can be made. For the purists, the derivation of the above formula is given in Appendix B.

With the same basic methodology applied over and over again, it is now possible to derive similar projections, all in terms of constant 1983 US dollar values, for markets and production in all three 'countries'.

Continuing with Japan, EIAJ's statistics show (Table A.2) that IT production has been growing historically at the apparent rate of 13.1 per cent (in yen), which converts to a real growth rate of 10.9 per cent per annum in constant dollar terms. Applying this rate to the 1983 production output of $53.3 billion extrapolates to a figure of $309 billion by the year 2000.

Taken in conjunction with the earlier market projection of $115 billion, the analysis thus indicates a trade balance of IT products increasing from about $25 billion in 1983 to $194 billion in 2000, which is wholly due, of course, to the fact that Japan's rate of IT production growth is projected to continue at a significantly higher rate than its IT market growth.

From the same EIAJ source, it is possible to obtain figures for IT employment in Japan in the two fiducial years of 1977 and 1983 (Table A.3), showing an increase from 650,000 to nearly one million.

A note of caution must be sounded, however. Detailed research has shown that IT employment numbers can be regarded as only an approximate guide, whatever the country or the year. It seems that a definition of IT employment has not yet been agreed internationally, in the absence of which each country tends to use its own. While the data are still comparable, year on year, for any one country, they may not be fully reliable for making country-by-country comparisons.

In any event, assuming that the EIAJ statistics for IT production and IT employment are mutually compatible, simple division yields an apparent, historical growth of productivity in Japan of 7.6 per cent per annum (Table A.3). This, corrected as before, translates into a real

Table A.3   IT employment, productivity and population data for Japan

	1977	CAAGR	1983*	CAAGR	1985*	1995*	2000*	2005*
Markets ($ bn)	13.7		28.5	8.6%	33.6	76.3	115	173
Production ($ bn)	22.6		53.3	10.9%	65.5	184	309	519
IT employment (million)	0.65		0.99		1.14	2.3	3.25	4.6
Productivity ($ k)	34.7		53.8					
Apparent growth		7.6%						
Real growth		3.4%						
Forecast productivity ($ k)				3.4%	57.5	80	95	112
Population (million)	115		120		121	127	131	135
IT employ-ment/population (×1000)	5.6		8.2		9.4	18.1	24.8	34
Per-capita expenditure on electronics ($)	119		237		280	600	880	1300

*Constant 1983 US dollar values.

growth rate of 3.4 per cent, which then projects to a productivity figure in 2000 of $95,000 per IT worker. And dividing that number into the projected production output of $309 billion, gives prospective Japanese total IT employment of 3.25 million in the year 2000 – i.e. 2.25 million more than in 1983 despite the assumed large increases in productivity.

Two other interesting statistics can be obtained. From the data for total population, IT employment and IT markets it is a simple matter to calculate, as shown in Table A.3, the trend in IT employment per head of population (projected to reach nearly 2.5 per cent by 2000) and the per-capita expenditure on IT (increasing from about $250 in 1983 to nearly $900 in 2000).

This latter figure, of course, is obtained from the total spend on electronics goods, including expenditure on items such as new tele-communications equipments, defence electronics, transportation electronics (e.g. new civil radar or blind-landing systems), instrumentation and factory automation, as well as the more evident electronic products in the home, the office and the automobile.

Turning to the US, all of the information on that country is derived from *The Electronics Market Data Book*, published by the Electronic Industries Association (EIA). Data for 1977 are from the 1980 edition, and for 1983 from the 1984 edition.

On the evidence of its performance between 1977 and 1983, America's IT markets are growing at a real rate of 7.1 per cent per annum, whereas its production is increasing at only 6.1 per cent per annum (Table A.4). The effect of this one per cent difference between the growth rates of markets and production is sufficient to amplify the US trade deficit in electronic goods from just less than $1 billion in 1983 to $68 billion in 2000.

The IT employment data (Table A.5) are also published by the EIA, and show an increase of about 450,000 over the six historical years. The resultant productivity figures, once the effects of inflation have been removed, are unimpressive. A real increase of only 0.7 per cent per annum would take the US from its excellent 1983 IT productivity of *c.*$86,000 to a competitive but uninspiring $97,000 in 2000.

Working this figure back into the projected 2000 production output of $396 billion, gives a postulated total IT employment by then of nearly 4.1 million, an increase of almost 2.5 million on 1983. Similarly, the per-capita IT employment in total will have increased from about 0.7 per cent in 1983 to *c.*1.5 per cent in 2000. By similar means, the per-capita spend on electronics in the US is projected to increase from about $625 in 1983 to over $1700 by 2000.

In order to give as representative a picture as possible, Western Europe

Table A.4   IT production and market projections for the US

	1977	CAAGR	1983*	CAAGR	1985*	1995*	2000*	2005*
Inflation index	113		185					
Inflation rate		8.56%						
Markets ($ bn– current values)	58.5		145					
Apparent growth		16.3%						
Real growth		7.1%						
Forecast markets ($ bn–1983 values)				7.1%	166	330	464	655
Production ($ bn– current values)	61.3		144					
Apparent growth		15.3%						
Real growth		6.1%						
Forecast production ($ bn–1983 values)				6.1%	162	294	396	530
Trade balance ($ bn)	2.8		(0.9)		(4)	(36)	(68)	(125)

* Constant 1983 US dollar values.

is here defined to include the ten countries which are, at the time of writing, full members of the EEC (Belgium, Denmark, France, Federal Republic of Germany, Greece, Republic of Ireland, Italy, Luxembourg, Netherlands and the UK), the two members-elect (Portugal and Spain), plus Austria, Finland, Norway, Sweden and Switzerland – a total of 17.

Whereas each of these countries produces its own IT statistics, the quality and scope tends to be variable. The most authoritative source of pan-European electronics data is the *Mackintosh Yearbook of West European Electronics Data*[2] (MYEE), which is currently in its twelvth year of publication and has made a great effort over the years to produce consistent data (i.e. anomalies in some countries have to be re-jigged to fit into the well-defined overall categories). The data for 1977 are from the 1980 edition, and for 1983 from the 1985 edition of MYEE.

From Table A.6 it can be seen that the real, historical growth rates have been merely 3.0 per cent and 1.3 per cent for markets and production,

[2] Publlished by Benn Electronics Publications Ltd.

Table A.5   IT employment, productivity and population data for the US

	1977	CAAGR	1983*	CAAGR	1985*	1995*	2000*	2005*
Markets ($ bn)	58.5		145	7.1%	166	330	464	655
Production ($ bn)	61.3		144	6.1%	162	294	396	530
IT employment (million)	1.213		1.664		1.85	3.13	4.08	5.25
Productivity ($ k)	50.56		86.4					
Apparent growth		9.3%						
Real growth		0.7%						
Forecast productivity ($ k)				0.7%	87.6	94	97	101
Population (million)	220		232		235	256	266	275
IT employ- ment/population (×1000)	5.5		7.2		7.9	12.2	15.3	19.1
Per-capita expenditure on electronics ($)	266		625		710	1290	1740	2400

* Constant 1983 US dollar values.

respectively. Extrapolating to the year 2000 suggests that by then European IT production will be only about two-thirds of its own market, resulting in a sector trade deficit of about $46 billion.

With the largest population (Table A.7), it is not surprising that Western Europe also has the highest current level of IT employment (1.85 million in 1983) in absolute terms. However, as a percentage of the total population it is already very low at c.0.53 per cent.

The calculated European IT productivity in 1983 is at the low level of $41,500 and has been increasing at an average real rate of 1.9 per cent. Extrapolating this to 2000 gives a projected productivity of $57,500.

At this level of 1.9 per cent, the real historical European rate of productivity increase falls almost midway between that of the US (0.7 per cent) and Japan (3.4 per cent). But because the rate of production increase, at 1.3 per cent, is lower than the increase in productivity (the only 'country' where this is so), the inevitable result is a projected *decrease* in European IT employment, to a level of about 1.65 million by 2000 (Table A.7).

The relatively modest real growth of markets (3.0 per cent per annum)

Table A.6   IT production and market projections for Western Europe

	1977	CAAGR	1983*	CAAGR	1985*	1995*	2000*	2005*
Inflation index	123		214					
Inflation rate		9.7%						
Exchange rate (ECUs=$1.00)	0.876		1.123					
Exchange-rate appreciation		−4.05%						
Markets (ECU bn)	36.1		96.0					
Apparent growth (in ECU values)		17.7%						
Real growth (in US $ values)		3.0%						
Markets ($ bn)	41.2		85.5	3.0%	90.7	122	141	164
Production (ECU bn)	35.8		86.1					
Apparent growth (in ECU values)		15.8%						
Real growth (in US $ values)		1.3%						
Production ($ bn)	40.8		76.7	1.3%	78.7	90	95	102
Trade balance ($ bn)	(0.4)		(8.8)		(12)	(32)	(46)	(62)

* Constant 1983 US dollar values.

also implies that the European per-capita expenditure on electronics is projected to grow slowly, from about $250 in 1983 to $380 in 2000.

Table A.7   IT employment, productivity and population data for Western Europe

	1977	CAAGR	1983*	CAAGR*	1985*	1995*	2000*	2005*
Markets ($ bn)	41.2		85.6	3.0%	90.7	122	141	164
Production ($ bn)	40.8		76.7	1.3%	78.7	90	95	102
IT employment (million)	1.92		1.85		1.83	1.73	1.65	1.62
Productivity ($ k)	21.3		41.5					
Apparent growth		11.8%						
Real growth		1.9%						
Forecast productivity ($ k)					43.1	52	57.5	63
Population (million)	341		351		355	365	370	375
IT employment/ population (× 1000)	5.6		5.3		5.2	4.7	4.5	4.3
Per-capita expenditure on electronics ($)	121		244		255	335	380	440

* Constant 1983 US dollar values.

Appendix B
A formula for correcting for historical inflation and exchange-rate variations

Most historical compound annual average growth rates (CAAGRs) are first calculated in *current-value terms* – i.e. taking no account of the apparent boost in growth rates caused by inflation – and in a single local currency – e.g. pounds sterling.

Because it is always impossible to forecast inflation over an extended period of time, to make meaningful extrapolations of historical growth trends it is necessary to work in *constant-value terms* – i.e. to correct for past known inflation rates and to convert all data to the values appropriate to the first year of the forecasting period.

Moreover, if it is necessary to make international comparisons of growth rates, then all data must be normalized to a single currency – the 1983 US dollar in this case. But that raises the additional complication that exchange rates vary – sometimes in a haphazard manner.

Accordingly, the following three-step procedure has been used in carrying out the analyses and projections outlined in Chapter 5 and detailed in Appendix A.

1. To correct for historical inflation, the formula used is:

   $$(1 + a_1) = (1 + r_1)(1 + i_1),$$

   where a_1 is the *apparent* CAAGR (in *local* currency), r_1 is the *real* CAAGR (in *local* currency), and i_1 is the annual average rate of *inflation* (in *local* currency), as measured by the Consumer Price Index or equivalent.

2. Having obtained r_1, corrections for historical changes in exchange rates are made by using:

$$(1 + r_b) = (1 + r_l) (1 + e),$$

where r_b is the real growth rate in the base currency (the US dollar in this case), and e is the average annual percentage *appreciation* of currency l against currency b.

3. To calculate the value of e, the appropriate formula is:

$$(b/l_n) = (b/l_o) (1 + e)^n,$$

where (b/l_n) is the ratio of the base currency (i.e. US dollar) to the local currency (e.g. ECUs) in year n. Thus,

$$1 + e = \sqrt[n]{(b/l_n)/(b/l_o)}.$$

(Note: e will be negative if the base currency is the US dollar and, as normal in recent years, the local currency has depreciated against the dollar.

Summarizing, unless all of the factors a_l, i_l and e are very small (e.g. less than 0.02) there is no *accurate* way of shortening the calculation of r_b from the equation which consolidates all of the above:

$$r_b = \frac{(1 + a_l) (1 + e)}{(1 + i_l)} - 1.$$

Appendix C

Derivation of the value for the maintain-parity coefficient, C_m

The maintain-parity coefficient, C_m, is used in Chapter 7 as part of the methodology for calculating the overall costs of a typical, non-viable European company advancing to the much higher level of sales of its typical, viable non-European competitors. It is defined to be the number of *additional* dollars of investment required to achieve each *additional* dollar of sales (long-term) while maintaining a reasonably constant share of free-world markets.

The basic methodology used to establish a value for C_m was to analyse the balance sheets and profit-and-loss accounts, over the most recent five years for which financial data were available, of about 50 companies in the IT sector in order to calculate the total increased investment and the overall growth in IT sales. In most cases, the five-year span lies in the 1978–83 time frame.

The calculation of investment was made by adding together shareholders' funds, long- and short-term loans and bank borrowings, and deducting therefrom any short-term investments and bank deposits. Thus the increase in investment represents the difference between the results of this calculation at the beginning and end of the five-year period considered and, hence, includes retained earnings. It similarly includes additional investment required to fund any trading losses over the period. Calculation of the increase in sales was a simple matter of subtracting the annual sales at the beginning of the period from the annual sales five years later.

Of the original 50 or so companies analysed, 20 were later eliminated. This was either because it emerged that their financial performance was not dominated by electronic products, or because they were judged not to be leading-edge competitors in their particular segment(s) of the IT sector. Consistent with the approach used throughout this book, companies predominantly in software were not included.

The investment:incremental-sales ratios for the remaining 30 companies are shown in Table C.1, on which several comments need to be

Table C.1   Five-year ratios of incremental investment to incremental sales for leading-edge IT companies

Company	Ratio	Company	Ratio
AMD	0.22	National Semiconductor	0.48
Amdahl	1.82	NCR	3.7
Burroughs	0.46	Nixdorf	0.22
Control Data	2.0	Philips	0.79
Data General	0.78	Plessey	0.96
Datapoint	0.67	Prime	0.30
Data Products	0.86	Racal	0.34
Digital Equipment	0.63	Raytheon	0.44
Ferranti	0.22	Sperry	0.75
Fluke	0.87	Tandem	0.79
Hewlett Packard	0.43	Tandy	0.58
IBM	0.68	Tektronix	0.75
Intel	1.03	Texas Instruments	0.24
Mitel	1.03	Wang	0.78
Mostek	0.70	Average ratio	0.80
Motorola	0.58		

made. In the first place, as is clear, no Japanese companies are included. This is either because of the obscurity of the financial data publicly available and/or because the IT activities were merely a minority part of a large industrial conglomerate.

Not many European companies could be examined either – usually for the same reasons as in Japan. In fact, only Ferranti, Nixdorf, Philips, Plessey and Racal finally survived the rather stringent selection criteria. In the case of Philips, this was because of its wide involvement in electronic products generally, and its significant US sales. The others were retained because they are mainly 'pure' electronics companies with not insignificant sales in the US.

Thus, of the 30 companies, 25 are American and all of these were judged to be leading-edge producers serving a leading-edge market.

The average ratio of the 30 companies is 0.80, although the range is extraordinarily wide (0.22 – 3.7). The reasons for some of the extreme values can readily be surmised, others not. For instance, the coefficient for NCR (3.7) may be exceptionally high because this company has recently been bearing the high cost of transforming itself from (mainly) electromechanical to (mainly) electronics technology. Similarly, two companies which have been striving to succeed in large mainframe computers, Amdahl and Control Data, are also anomalously high (1.82 and 2.0, respectively).

Companies prominent in the IC industry have coefficients covering the range 0.22 (AMD) to 1.03 (Intel), with TI at 0.24, National Semiconductors at 0.48 and Mostek (now a subsidiary of Thomson, France) at 0.7. Thus all except Intel were below average, although it is pertinent that, in general, data for these companies do not extend to 1983, which was a year of heavy investment in new IC facilities.

A low coefficient suggests, of course, that either a company is hyperefficient in using its capital, or that its sales growth is primarily based on product segments which do not entail leading-edge investment costs. It is noteworthy that the average ratio for the five European companies, at 0.51, is markedly lower than that for the US companies (0.865), although the reasons for this must remain a matter for conjecture.

The fact of the matter is that without access to highly detailed (and often highly confidential) financial information, this method of analysis is necessarily approximate. Many factors extraneous to the IT industry can influence the value of the coefficient for a particular company. Control Data, for example, currently gains significant revenues from its commercial credit financial services division; Philips, as another example, earns substantial revenues from its non-electronic consumer products (e.g. electric shavers) and lighting activities.

Nevertheless, allowing for the varying state and strategy of each company during the particular five-year period examined, and the fact that neither the sample size nor the financial 'weight' of the companies analysed is insubstantial, it does not seem unreasonable to treat the average value of the coefficient as representative of the IT industry as a whole.

In finally choosing a value for the coefficient, greatest weight must obviously be given to the US companies. Because of the approximate nature of this analysis, and because of the particular value of the US coefficient (0.865), a rounded value of unity has been used for C_m in the calculations of Chapter 7.

Appendix D

Derivation of the value for the quantum-leap coefficient, C_q

Similar to Appendix C, the quantum-leap coefficient, C_q, is an integral part of the Chapter-7 methodology for calculating the overall cost of relatively small, non-viable European companies expanding to a level of sales representing the economies of scale enjoyed by their leading, viable non-European competitors. In particular, it is defined to be the ratio of the *additional* dollars of investment required to achieve a major, more-or-less instantaneous *increase* in segment sales. It is the ratio, in short, of incremental investment to incremental sales involving an abrupt increase in market share.

In principle, this coefficient could be calculated by examining the case histories of companies which have gone through the process of 'greenfield' investment. Unfortunately, none of those examined was deemed of much relevance to the particular case of the IT industry. Moreover, without access to very detailed financial information on companies which have secured such quantum sales increases by bringing greenfield facilities on stream, it is simply not possible to judge the particular sales which have resulted from a specific new investment.

Instead of concentrating on greenfield investments, therefore, the analyst is driven to the other principal method by which an instantaneous increase in market share can be achieved - namely, by acquisition.

On reflection it becomes clear that this approach has considerable relevance to the present analysis. The main reason is that purchasing a leading-edge IT company does result in an immediate increase in market share – and, in most instances, in the acquisition of avant-garde technology. In addition, the location of the acquired capability is not, in the first instance, a primary factor since, properly managed, it should be entirely possible to transfer the technology back to the location of the acquiring corporation (i.e. Europe) without necessarily losing market share in the country in which the acquired company resides.

Accordingly, the present calculation of the 'quantum-leap' cost coefficient relies completely on financial data relating to acquisitions. And, relevant to the main theme, the acquisitions studied are confined solely to buying facilities and market share in the leading-edge American IT markets.

Table D.1 is a list of 19 such acquisitions which took place between about 1978 and 1983, in which the cost of acquisition (C) is compared with the sales (S) of the acquired company at the time of acquisition in order to calculate the cost-to-sales ratio (C/S).

Not surprisingly, a cursory glance at Table D.1 reveals that the price paid, compared to the acquired sales, varies significantly over the sample analysed. The reason why this is not surprising is that the motives of the acquiring company will obviously have varied from case to case and may, in each case, embrace a mixture of strategic objectives.

Since the object of this analysis is to determine the cost of acquiring a *leading-edge, viable* IT capability, a number of well-known acquisitions have been omitted where these conditions manifestly are not met. For example, Burroughs acquired Memorex when the latter was close to bankruptcy, and AB Dick was not a leading-edge IT company when acquired by GEC.

Another point is that, although various partial acquisitions are included in Table D.1, 'venture' investments have been eliminated from consideration since these are usually in companies which have not yet exhibited long-term viability. Olivetti's numerous equity investments in fairly small US electronics companies have not been included, therefore. On the other hand, a few full-scale acquisitions of smaller companies have been included where the perceived motivation of the acquirer was specifically to obtain access to leading-edge products.

The average cost:sales ratio of the 19 acquisitions which have survived this sort of filtering process is 1.93. But, as in the derivation of C_m, there is enough uncertainty in this analysis, despite its innate credibility, that the value of C_q used in the segment analyses of Chapter 7 has been rounded off to a figure of 2.0. For other reasons, quoted in the main text, this sort of value is regarded as wholly believable.

Table D.1 Acquisition costs of buying market shares

Company name	Company acquired	Sales at time of acquistion (S)	% acquired	Cost of acquisition (C)	Ratio (C/S)
Allied	Bunker Ramo	$468 m	100	$358 m	0.76
	Bendix	c.$4 bn	100	$1.9 bn	0.48
	Eltra	c.$1 bn	100	$589 m	0.59
Computervision	Cambridge Interactive Systems	c.$5 m	100	$ 30 m	6.0
GE	Intersil	$140 m	100	$235 m	1.68
Gould	AMI	$141 m	100	$200 m	1.42
Harris	Lanier	$303 m	100	$415 m	1.37
IBM	Intel	$900 m	12	$250 m	2.31
	Rohm	$381 m	15	$229 m	4.01
Motorola	Four Phase	$113.8 m	100	$250 m	2.20
	Codex	$17.9 m	100	$89 m	4.97
Plessey	Stromberg Carlson	c.$154 m	100	$58 m	0.38
Racal	Decca	$426 m	100	$247 m	0.58
Signal	Ampex	$469 m	100	$560 m	1.19
Schlumberger	Fairchild	$550.4 m	100	$363 m	0.66
United Technologies	Mostek	$134 m	91	$314 m	2.57
Xerox	Daconics	$1.6 m	100	$4.5 m	2.81
	Versatec	$12.2 m	100	$19 m	1.56
	Shugart	$35 m	100	$41 m	1.17

Average 1.93

Appendix E
Market data for the six key product segments

In Appendix A, correction factors have been applied to convert apparent growth rates of IT markets and production, expressed in local currencies, into real growth rates in terms of a normalized currency. In other words, these calculations allow any rates of change, given in current-value local terms, to be corrected for historical local inflation and then expressed in constant-value 1983 US dollars.

In this appendix, the same general method is used to translate the historical growth of markets in the six key product segments into real growth rates and, as before, to use these to make projections of segment markets to the year 2005. These market values are then used in the calculations of the costs of achieving long-term viable levels of product sales (Chapter 7).

The procedure, in summary, is as follows. First, it is necessary to find the most reliable historical market data – in Japan, the US and Western Europe – for each key segment. These figures must cover as recent and as long a time period as possible consistent with a reasonable degree of compatibility of segment definitions (i.e. what products each segment covers) at the beginning and end of the period. The timescale used is 1977–83, as in Appendix A.

In the second step, the 'raw' market data are corrected for domestic inflation rates and converted into 1983 US dollar values in the usual way. Finally, the market values for individual 'countries' are aggregated, from which real growth rates, and the projected market values in 2005, can easily be calculated.

The data sources used are essentially the same as in Appendix A; namely, the Electronics Industry Association of Japan (EIAJ), the Electronics Industry Association (EIA) in the US, and the *Mackintosh Yearbook of West European Electronics Data* (MYEE), covering the same 17 countries as before. In the case, however, of the office-equipment segment in the US, the EIA statistics do not provide a separate breakdown, so the data used are from the magazine *Electronics International*.

Table E.1 gives the market figures, in 1983 dollar values, for all three 'countries' and all six product segments, at the beginning and end of the historical period analysed (i.e. 1977 and 1983). Clearly, the data for 1983 are 'actuals' whereas those for 1977 have already been converted as described above.

First, an interesting, if parenthetical observation. If the 1983 national totals (i.e. for all segments) are compared with the total IT market data for 1983 given in Table 5.2, it becomes clear that, in all three 'countries', the six segments represent roughly the same proportion of the total – i.e. about two-thirds. (The precise figures are: Japan, 72 per cent; US, 65 per cent; and Europe, 70 per cent.) This is encouraging in two ways. The similarity of these percentages increases confidence in the comparability of the data for different 'countries', despite the diverse original sources. And it also shows that the six product segments are not only salient for the reasons given in Chapter 5, but that they also, collectively, represent a significant majority of business in the IT sector as a whole, thus reinforcing their status as key segments.

A second comment on Table E.1 is that it is clear from a glance that most of the growth rates in Europe are substantially less than in Japan and the US. This, of course, is not surprising and is merely another way of looking at the trends illustrated in Figure 5.1.

It has an important implication for this analysis, however. The whole object of this exercise is to calculate the costs of a company achieving, and sustaining, a fully viable level of segment sales. But this calculation would give misleading results if based on growth rates which were lower than the *viable* producers would expect to achieve. In other words, market growth, and the concomitant rising level of company sales required to maintain competitive economies of scale, will be set by the leaders not the laggards.

For this reason, the 'viable' segment market growth rates have been based on the US and Japan only. Table E.2 thus shows the combined US/Japanese markets in the six segments, in 1977 and 1983, and the resultant compound annual average growth rates (CAAGRs). The projected total markets in the three 'countries', in 1985, 1995 and 2005, are obtained by applying these growth rates to the totals for 1983 from Table E.1 (i.e. assuming, now, that the European market does actually grow at the same rate as its intercontinental competitors), and are shown in Table E.3.

Two brief comments are in order. First, it cannot be assumed that the

Table E.1 Historical market data for the six key product segments

Country or region		Computers	Consumer electronics	Industrial automation	Integrated circuits	Office equipment	Telecommunications	Totals
Japan	1977	3.5	3.9	1.5	1.1	0.36	1.8	12.2
	1983	6.0	4.8	2.6	3.7	0.52	3.0	20.6
US	1977	19.2	13.4	8.2	4.4	4.8	11.3	61.2
	1983	37.9	14.6	10.9	7.9	10.9	11.5	93.7
Western Europe	1977	11.6	14.0	7.5	2.1	1.7	13.0	49.9
	1983	19.2	12.1	9.4	2.2	4.4	12.2	59.5
Total	1977	34.3	31.3	17.2	7.6	6.9	26.1	123
	1983	63.1	31.5	22.9	13.7	15.8	26.7	174

All figures in 1983 US dollars (billions).

Table E.2   Derivation of segment market growth rates

Countries	Product segments						
	Computers	Consumer electronics	Industrial automation	Integrated circuits	Office equipment	Telecommunications	Totals
Japan plus US 1977	22.7	17.3	9.7	5.5	5.2	13.1	73.5
1983	43.9	19.4	13.5	11.6	11.4	14.5	114
Growth rates	11.6%	2.0%	5.7%	13.3%	14.1%	1.8%	7.7%

Market figures in 1983 US dollars (billions).

Table E.3   Projected markets for the six key product segments

Country or region	Product segments						
	Computers	Consumer electronics	Industrial automation	Integrated circuits	Office equipment	Telecommunications	Totals
Japan plus US plus Europe 1983	63.1	31.5	22.9	13.7	15.8	26.7	174
1985	80	32.8	25.6	17.6	20.6	27.6	204
1995	235	40	45	61	77	33	490
2000	410	44	60	115	150	36	815
2005	700	49	78	215	290	40	1370

All figures in 1983 US dollars (billions).

segment growth rates of Table E.2 are as reliable as the overall sector rates of Table 5.3. For one thing, whereas the sector as a whole has a reasonable degree of intrinsic momentum, as discussed in Chapter 5, individual segments are more subject to particular influences. For example, in 1984/5 the worldwide IC industry suffered from a severe recession resulting in a total market significantly less than the figure of *c.*$18 billion given in Table E.3. Nevertheless, there is no reason to believe that the long-term growth rate of about 13 per cent will not be resumed once this latest cyclical downturn has run its course.

Another doubtful figure is the low (1.8 per cent) growth rate for telecommunications. While this is certainly a valid historical rate, it does not take full account of the major changeover from analogue to digital systems which is now under way. Nor does it allow for the convergence of this segment with office equipment, which probably implies that the actual future growth rates for these two segments will lie somewhere between the two extremes of Table E.2.

A last point about the market data is that even small changes in the growth rates would obviously introduce an increasing error in the projections the more remote the year. As in all of these analyses, therefore, the figures for 2005 are the least credible.

All this being said, however, it is worthwhile stressing again the relative credibility of the overall sector growth rates and market projections. For the IT industry as a whole, of course, changes in the future growth rates of individual segments will tend to cancel out, as with the convergence phenomenon just discussed. Moreover, the total renaissance costs are based on aggregating the costs of achieving viability sales levels in all of the six segments so that, again, a comforting process of averaging is built in.

Finally, a brief explanatory note. The fact that data in these three tables are given in many cases to the third significant digit should obviously not be construed as in any way reflecting the accuracy of the figures. It is merely that presenting all data in this way minimizes rounding errors.

Appendix F
Economic aspects of Eurogrid

The main purpose of this appendix is to provide a summary of the analyses of traffic demand, tariffs, network costs and revenues, together with equipment (mainly terminal) demand, which would result from the installation of Eurogrid. Although the timescale of the analysis has been shifted to make it coincident with the postulated IT renaissance window (1985–2005), the original research was carried out for the Commission of the European Communities, to whom due acknowledgment and thanks have already been expressed.

The computer model

At the heart of the analysis is a network forecasting model which takes as its primary inputs:

I-1 The rate and order at which subscribers are connected to the network.

I-2 The rate at which subscribers take up the network services, in accordance with three distinct take-up scenarios – pessimistic, baseline and optimistic.

I-3 The demand for Eurogrid services in terms of traffic and terminals in the final year of the forecast period, for each of the take-up scenarios.

I-4 The terminal prices and costs of network components as a function of network size, usage and technology.

The primary output data provided by the models are:

O-1 Market forecasts for IT products for each of the 16 generic types of network service.

O-2 Traffic forecasts for each of the network services.

O-3 Implementation costs for the network by component parts.

In the original work, the analysis was further complicated by considering four separate network options: the so-called full Eurogrid (i.e. all domestic and business establishments connected to the network by 2005); business-only Eurogrid (i.e. network connections restricted to the ten million or so business establishments within the Community, the bulk of which are in high-density city areas); full ISDN (i.e. all subscribers connected to the new Integrated Services Digital Network by 2005, but limited in the main to 64 kbits/s network speeds); and business-only ISDN. However, because the analysis proved that the other options would not provide sufficient stimulus to the European IT industry, this appendix concentrates solely on the full Eurogrid.

Similarly, although the three distinct scenarios (pessimistic, baseline and optimistic) were applied to those parameters which are most difficult to forecast accurately, only the most realistic baseline case is considered in this appendix.

While it would be inappropriate to go through all the details here, for general interest a schematic of the Network Forecasting Model is shown in Figure F.1, on which the following brief comments can be made.

1. The population and establishment statistics (Input 1) were obtained mainly from official publications, plus a detailed breakdown of the establishments according to size, density (people/km^2) and 12 specific types of establishment users (e.g. local government, health, travel, etc.), plus domestic users.
2. The typical network connection rate was assumed to be ten per cent of all the relevant establishments each year for ten years.
3. Combining these yielded the rates of network implementation.
4. A range of assumed final rates (i.e. in 2005) of terminal demand was obtained from a highly detailed research programme concentrating on the applications, costs and benefits of the services for which the terminals would be required, plus an assessment of terminal usage rates in each of the 13 categories of users.
5. The demand curves (see Figure F.2) were built up from detailed consideration of the effect of economic influences, labour attitudes, user attitudes and the speed of product standardization, also taking into account real-life experience with the build-up of new communications services such as International Direct Dialling.
6. Combining 3, 4 and 5 yielded the build-up of network usage, as depicted schematically in Figure F.2.
7. The network usage calculation could then be used, in conjunction with detailed demand estimates for each of the 16 types of service,

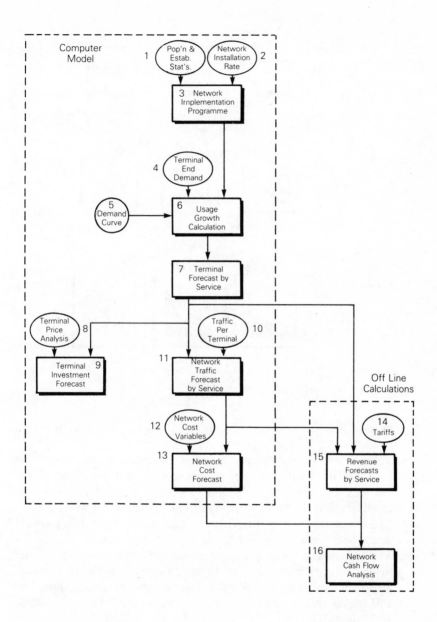

Figure F.1. Network forecasting model.

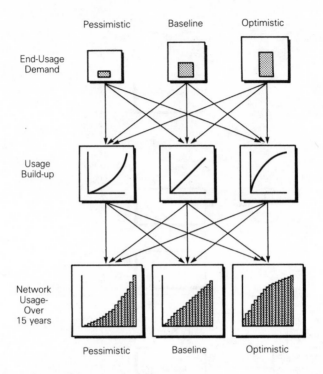

Figure F.2. Network usage calculation.

to produce the forecasts of terminal markets (in units) by main product category and type of service (Output 1).

8. The prices of the multiplicity of terminals were estimated by allowing for a continued fall in the cost of components, cost reductions resulting from economies of scale and technological development of the terminals during the forecast period, all of which led to . . .

9. The forecasts of terminal markets, by multiplying individual terminal prices and demand (in units).

10. The forecasts of traffic per terminal for each type of service offered by the network were based on detailed estimates of the demand for broadband services, by taking account of specific applications, the anticipated amount of network usage and the establishment statistics, and this yielded . . .

11. The forecasts of network traffic by type of service, as measured, for example, in Gigabit/s, or still-image 'pages' per day, or 8 Mbit/s channel-hours per day (Output 2).

Table F.1 Example tariffs used for revenue calculations

Service	Traffic tariffs ($/hour or $/1000 pages)	
	Today	Baseline
Voice, one-way switched	NA	0.75
Voice, two-way switched	3.00*	1.5
Audio, one-way switched	NA	0.75
Audio, two-way switched	NA	4.5
Video, one-way switched	NA	0.75
Video, two-way switched	NA	50.0
Still-image, standard	41.6	1.22
Still-image, high quality	NA	8.7
Still-image, publishing quality	NA	57.0
Text and data, slow speed	2.17	0.16
Text and data, fast	NA	0.08

* Average of short, medium and long distance tariffs in European countries.

12. Network cost variables were assumed to depend primarily on a combination of the number of network subscribers and the amount of traffic they generated of each type, and were assessed by segregating out 16 specific cost ingredients.
13. This, taken together with the network traffic forecasts, yielded the forecasts of network costs.
14. The tariff assumptions were based on zero charge for network connections, and a range of possible tariffs which are shown in Table F.1 where they are compared, where possible, with present-day average tariffs for equivalent services. It can be seen that even the baseline projected tariffs have been set at values substantially below today's, reflecting the improved efficiencies and costs which Eurogrid should bring.
15. The net revenue forecasts by service are the sum of the assumed (small) standing charges per establishment and the multiple of the traffic and tariff forecasts for each service.
16. The analysis of return on investment, etc., stems naturally from the forecasts of network costs and network revenues.

It should be stressed that the main advantages which accrued from using the computer model were the arithmetic reliability of the results – produced in considerable detail – plus the ability to run sensitivity analyses based on changes of the input data (e.g. user demand, growth rates). By this means, the credibility of particular forecasts could be tested by combining a variety of input data and demand growth rates.

The basis for all of these calculations is a schedule for the implementation of Eurogrid which is realizable and in tune with the overall renaissance window previously discussed. Planning, it is assumed, would take up the first five years (1985–90), network installation would cover ten years (1990–2000) and network revenues would increase gradually (as would the network itself and its population of subscribers) from 1990 up to and beyond 2005.

Forecasts of traffic demand

From these foundation assumptions, it is a straightforward matter to compute the value of various parameters associated with the full operation of Eurogrid.

Taking traffic as the first case, the baseline assumption yields total traffic at the subscriber connections for a full, pan-EEC Eurogrid as nearly 400,000 Gigabits/s[1] by the year 2005. This, however, is a bit of an over-simplification. Although about 80% of this traffic represents the broadcast audio and video services, these are non-switched and have only a modest effect on network loading as a whole. The more important switched services are calculated to represent a traffic level of about 80,000 Gbit/s by 2005.

This total switched traffic can also be broken down into the 16 basic Eurogrid services (see pages 206–211) and into the 12 business- (plus domestic-) user categories already mentioned, for each of which a range of tariff assumptions can be examined by means of the computer model. For example, the price-sensitivity curves for two-way switched video will clearly be very different for business users (video conferencing and videophone) as compared with domestic users (mainly videophone).

The total Community PTT revenues which will result from this traffic have been calculated to lie in the range $350–400 billion[2] in 2005, depending on the particular tariffs and traffic patterns then pertaining. Taking the mid-range value of $375 billion, in association with a starting point of $41 billion in 1983, would represent a real CAAGR of just over ten per cent, which seems reasonable in light of the historical segment growth

---

[1] Traffic is originally expressed as hours/day (for voice, audio and video services) and pages/day (for still-image and text-and-data services), of which the common feature is the number of bits of information conveyed per second.

[2] As elsewhere in this book, all values are expressed in terms of 1983 US dollars.

rates of Table E.2. Allowing for a 'cable-TV' component of $100, say, the purely telecom per-capita, per-annum expenditure in 2005 would be about $1150, of which the bulk, naturally, would be business-related.

By way of comparison, if the total US per-capita expenditure on telecommunications continues to grow at five per cent per annum in real terms, even in the absence of an American equivalent of Eurogrid, it will reach a value of $c.$1000 by 2005. Thus, the transatlantic telecoms gap (Table 10.1) will have been closed. Europe, at long last, will have become information rich.

The terminal market

The all-important market for terminals in Europe will be enormously stimulated by Eurogrid, needless to say. It will consist of two main parts. First will be the direct market associated with the products which are required to work with, and are a direct consequence of, the network. In the domestic sector, these will primarily be the interface and channel-selection modules which enable existing TV receivers to be used – although, in the fullness of time, these will certainly be built in. Examples of other direct-market products in the domestic sector include voice recorders and telephones, high-definition TV sets and the videophone – which will become increasingly pervasive in 2005.

In the business sector, the direct market will be associated with the very extensive range of broadband (high-speed) terminals which will be developed especially to obtain maximum cost-effective use of the new network. These will include intelligent broadband terminals of a wide variety, high-fidelity telephones, videophone equipment, image scanners, transmission and reproduction equipment and very fast text-and-data terminals. There will also be a direct market for the interface and control modules required to enable existing terminals to be used with the broadband network.

The indirect market will be for products which, while having a stand-alone capability, may still need to be connected to Eurogrid, or will achieve enhanced usefulness thereby. In the domestic sector, examples include standard TV monitors and VCRs, the demand for which would be stimulated by access to a multi-channel cable system for information and entertainment; audio equipment for high-quality reproduction; and 'home' computers and word-processing systems.

In the business sector, the indirect market boost would be associated mainly with central dictation and on-site messaging equipment; on-site telephone systems, intercoms and stored-voice databases; local area networks; equipment for document and image storage; office products (such as copiers) which may be connected to the network via a suitable interface unit but which have a stand-alone function; and self-contained business computers which will sometimes need to communicate with their distant counterparts through the Eurogrid network.

The extensive analysis which has been carried out to forecast terminal demand levels has taken due account of the predicted traffic and tariffs, and of anticipated reductions in terminal prices stemming from both technological and economy-of-scale improvements.

As has been explained, the direct terminal demand is one of the results obtained from the computer model (item 9 above) once the other parameters (traffic, tariffs, etc.) have been established by means of the research programme and iterative runs of the computer model. The result is a predicted direct market in 2005 of *c.*$130 billion, covering a very extensive range of different equipments.

The research also predicted that, in the case of the full Eurogrid network, the indirect market would be some 20 per cent higher – i.e. *c.*$155 billion. Thus the total EEC 'terminal' demand associated with Eurogrid is forecast to be *c.*$285 billion by 2005. However, it needs to be recognized that whereas the direct market represents a wholly new boost to the IT market, some part of the indirect market will necessarily represent a substitution for markets which would have existed in any event (i.e. without Eurogrid).

Financial implications for the PTTs

The programme of research and analysis already referred to was directed in part at assessing the probable financial implications of the various network options on the Community PTTs. This was for the very obvious reason that Eurogrid would be a non-starter as Europe's 'Apollo' project for IT renaissance if it was not also capable of providing a satisfactory return to the network operators.

The calculations are, of course, very complicated and were necessarily simplified in the cited research. Indeed, if the Eurogrid concept is accepted in principle as a viable contender (the only contender!) for the role of European IT demand stimulator, then the PTTs which planned to join the Eurogrid club would undoubtedly carry out fresh research and financial analyses to their usual high standards.

Nevertheless, the essence of this present analysis is that the full Eurogrid would be a very profitable exercise for the PTTs in the long run. The total installation costs can be estimated with a reasonable degree of confidence and come out cumulatively as about $400 billion over the years 1990–2005, of which construction costs alone are more than 50 per cent – i.e. greater than \$200 billion. (This is a figure of relevance to the discussion of Eurogrid's employment implications in Chapter 12.)

While this may seem a large sum of money, it is in fact only about 50 per cent higher than the present aggregate annual investments of the European PTTs, and this rate is bound to increase with the unstoppable growth of digitalization.

PTT Eurogrid revenues, on the other hand, could vary enormously. The projected tariffs used here (Table F.1) are substantially lower than those now pertaining but still suggest total EEC-wide Eurogrid revenues in 2005 of about \$350–400 billion. However, particularly in the business sector, most of the new broadband services will not be unduly price-sensitive. In short, the policy will probably be to lower tariffs progressively in order to stimulate usage of the network while ensuring the PTTs an acceptable return on investment.

None of this analysis, it should be said, has been conducted without recognizing the adverse effect which Eurogrid would have on the PTT's existing networks. Clearly, as the new network grows, the rate of usage and revenues generated in the existing networks will decline. In some cases (especially ISDN), this will involve heavy costs of accelerated depreciation.

Just for the record, the original research, using a variety of tariff assumptions but the standard baseline-demand scenario, showed internal rates of return to the PTTs covering the range 25–40 per cent (with a fixed depreciation period of ten years) and pay-back periods of six to 11 years. These imply acceptable rates of profitability, and suggest that Eurogrid would still be a viable investment proposition at even lower tariff levels. This is because, in the period analysed, the tariff structure has only a marginal effect on the internal rate of return, etc., because the investment rate is high but the traffic carried by the network is low during the first five years.

Total IT Demand Stimulus

From the earlier part of this appendix it has been stated that the total EEC terminal demand, direct and indirect, associated with the full Community-wide implementation of Eurogrid should reach a level of about \$285 billion by 2005. While the accuracy of this figure could obviously be challenged on a number of grounds, it does represent the best existing estimate; moreover, on neither per-capita nor percentage-of-GDP grounds does it seem unreasonable in comparison with what is expected to be the IT market by then in both Japan and the US.

There is, however, another component of IT investment which will stem from the Eurogrid network itself. Of the *c*.$400 billion cumulative cost of installing Eurogrid, about $150 billion will be on IT products directly. Although this will peak about the middle of the installation period, a continuing annual investment programme on network extensions and improvements will be necessary – as has been the case for decades with the ancient Strowger and Crossbar electro-mechanical systems. On the assumption that the IT portion of this will represent at least ten per cent of Eurogrid revenues, this would amount to about $40 billion in 2005.

In summary, then, total IT demand stemming from the full-blooded installation of Eurogrid in all of the ten present full-member states of the European Community should amount to approximately $325 billion in the year 2005. This can now be compared with the postulated need to channel $375 billion of EEC-based demand (Figure 8.1) to EEC-owned IT companies in 2005 in order to ensure their long-term viability.

Index

Very many companies and organizations are mentioned in this book, but they have not been included in the Index if they merely appear in some form of list. Also, topics clearly identified in the Contents and Lists of Figures and Tables have been indexed in exceptional cases only.